COME, FOLLOW ME

2024 BOOK OF MORMON WORKBOOK FOR TEENS AND ADULTS

HONOR T. WRIGHT

ColorMeChristian.org
FREE! Download this workbook and much more!

ISBN-979-8872099062

Published by ColorMeChristian
ColorMeChristian.org

January 1–7
Introductory Pages of the Book of Mormon
Another Testament of Jesus Christ

Missing Vowels Word Search

Instructions: Find the hidden words. The words have been placed horizontally, vertically, diagonally, forwards, or backwards, and the vowels have been removed. When you locate a word, draw an ellipse around it and fill the vowels in. The first word, **translated**, has been done for you.

The Testimony of Three Witnesses

Be it **known** unto all **nations**, **kindreds**, **tongues**, and **people**, unto whom this **work** shall **come**: That we, through the **grace** of God the Father, and our Lord Jesus **Christ**, have **seen** the **plates** which contain this **record**, which is a record of the people of **Nephi**, and also of the **Lamanites**, their brethren, and also of the people of **Jared**, who came from the **tower** of which hath been spoken. And we also know that they have been **translated** by the gift and power of God, for his **voice** hath **declared** it unto us;

```
T T F R R Q R K Z R Z D S C L
  L N M H   S   C     D   H T
C     D X S R N R M N Q T R S
  G P N V D   D M   S W
R H H     G K R T Z W S L S D
G     L J   R   D   K   P T Q
S C     J Y   D T B   Z T Y
  M B M G W X S H D W   R K V
D  (T E L S N A R T) H N V   G
G X   N   H   D   R   L C   D
    N   K N   W N T M M N C
  B G T   F   T   Q C     J
      M P     P L   C   V B
F C   S   D N Y C S   M   C B
R L S W P S L L R D R   C   R
```

Knight Moves - Find a Word

Instructions: Start with the capital letter in the puzzle. To get to the next letter, jump two squares in any direction except diagonally, and then one square in a different direction. Your path will look like a capital L. To show you how it works, I've included numbers on this first puzzle to show you how to solve it. Only one route through the puzzle will make a word. Write the letters of the word you discover in the blanks below as you jump through the squares:

___ ___ ___ ___ ___ ___ ___ ___
1   2   3   4   5   6   7   8

Now can you find this word in the following scripture?

Introduction to the Book of Mormon

s	K	o
4	1	6
n		y
7		3
e	t	e
2	5	8

Hidden Picture: Can you find the 5 Book of Mormons hidden in the picture below? It will be tricky; the Books of Mormon may be smaller, on its side, or even upside down! Then, see if you can find one copy of the animals as well.

Introductory Pages of the Book of Mormon

Another Testament of Jesus Christ

Instructions: Fit the bold words from the scripture below into the encircled squares. Words will read forward, backward, up, down, and diagonally and will normally cross other words. Start with the hints provided.

The Testimony of the Prophet Joseph Smith

While I was thus in the act of **calling** upon God, I discovered a **light** appearing in my room, which continued to increase until the room was lighter than at **noonday**, when immediately a **personage** appeared at my **bedside**, standing in the **air**, for his feet did not touch the floor....He called me by **name**, and said unto me that he was a **messenger** sent from the **presence** of God to me, and that his name was **Moroni**; that **God** had a **work** for me to do; and that my **name** should be had for **good** and **evil** among all **nations**, **kindreds**, and **tongues**, or that it should be both good and evil spoken of among all **people**.

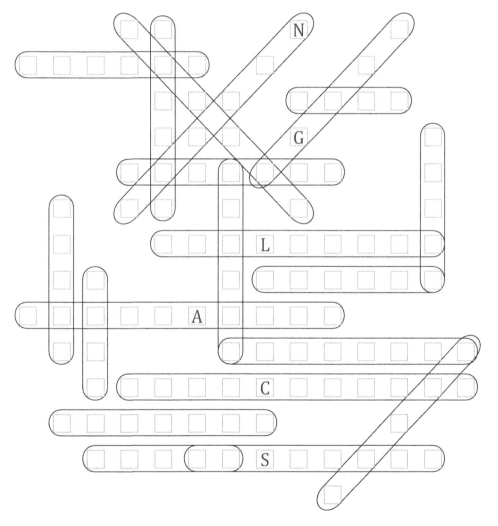

nothing	power	threatened	destruction	soften	hearts
swallowed	depths	repented	loosed	compass	prayed
winds	cease	calm	guide	sailed	again
promised	land				

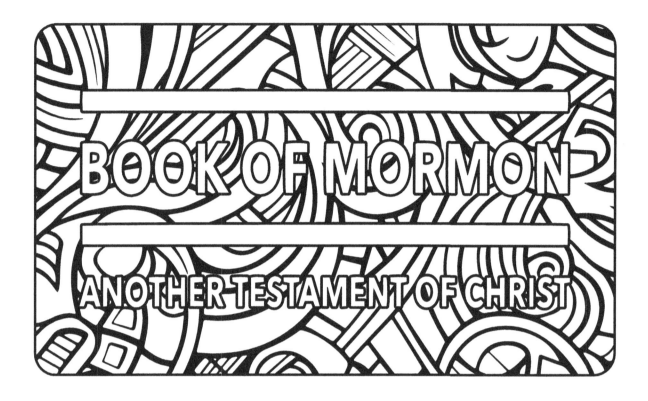

I can be a **witness** of the Book of Mormon.

January 1–7

Introductory Pages of the Book of Mormon

Another Testament of Jesus Christ

Come, Follow Me Manual, 2024

Start

End

Introductory Pages of the Book of Mormon

Another Testament of Jesus Christ

Secret Code

Instructions: The secret message is written in symbols. In the code key you can find what each symbol means. Write the letter above the symbol and you can read the secret message.

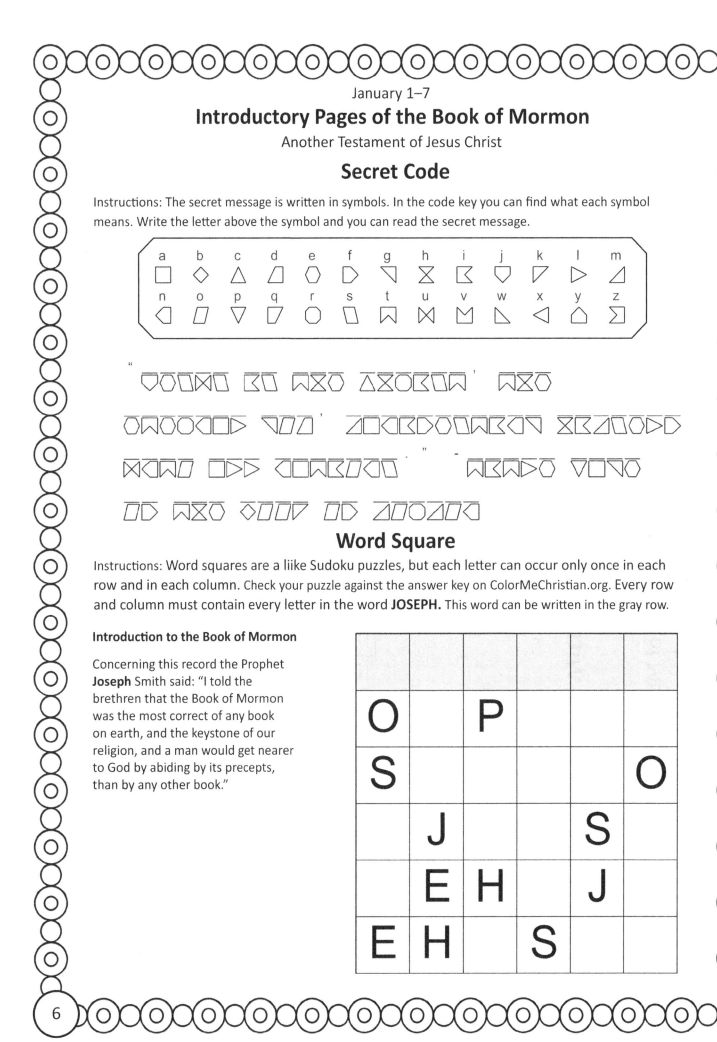

Word Square

Instructions: Word squares are a liike Sudoku puzzles, but each letter can occur only once in each row and in each column. Check your puzzle against the answer key on ColorMeChristian.org. Every row and column must contain every letter in the word **JOSEPH.** This word can be written in the gray row.

Introduction to the Book of Mormon

Concerning this record the Prophet **Joseph** Smith said: "I told the brethren that the Book of Mormon was the most correct of any book on earth, and the keystone of our religion, and a man would get nearer to God by abiding by its precepts, than by any other book."

O		P			
S					O
	J			S	
	E	H		J	
E	H		S		

January 8–14

1 Nephi 1–5

"I Will Go and Do"

Word Search

Instructions: Find the bold words from the scripture in the word search puzzle. Each word could be hidden forwards, backwards, up, down, or diagonally.

1 Nephi 5:21

And we had **obtained** the **records** which the **Lord** had **commanded** us, and **searched** them and **found** that they were **desirable**; **yea**, even of **great worth** unto us, **insomuch** that we could **preserve** the **commandments** of the Lord unto our **children**.

```
R O W J S L P U U T H G X B E
F W Y H L T H L A E T D P J L
M E R C O Z E E V I E H K C B
I T E U R G R L U D A C C N A
X V R M D G J V N W U P G C R
D N U O F S E A R C H E D D I
H R H S B E M J E A C M K E S
Y L T N A M V V S P H L S N E
R H R I O M L C Q R I C M I D
Y Q O C N I D I B E L S B A H
U E W R R Z X H U S D N R T E
B W A Z S D R O C E R W Q B K
E D I T R F A Z S R E S R O R
I B W T Z O A B T V N S U Z S
X C O M M A N D M E N T S K M
```

Fallen Phrase

Instructions:The letters in each column have fallen from the grid. Put them back correctly to rebuild the phrase. Cross out each letter in the jumble below once you place it in the grid. Pay attention because the letters in each column are scrambled. Start with simple 1 or 2 letter words and use the process of elimination. The 3 arrows below give you a start. To check your answer, read

1 Nephi 4:6

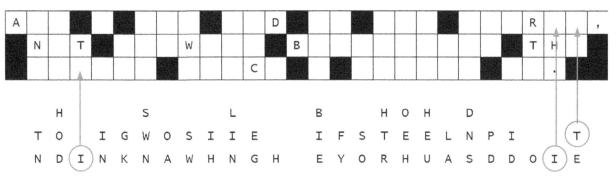

Nephi and the Brass Plates

Help Nephi retrieve the Brass plates

1 Nephi 1–5

"I Will Go and Do"

Handwriting Practice

Practice your handwriting by tracing the sentence below. Then use the blank lines to write the sentence on your own.

God will help me keep His commandments.

Cryptogram

Instructions: Each letter on the top stands for a letter in the alphabet. Solve the encrypted phrase by matching each letter on top to a letter in the alphabet on the bottom. Use the key to help you remember what the letters stand for so you can crack the code.

M	E	G	S	Z	H	U	J	A	T	K	C	Q	V	L	F	B	R	I	P	D	O	N	Y	W	X
A	B	C	D	E	F	G	H	I	J	K	L	M	N	O	P	Q	R	S	T	U	V	W	X	Y	Z

I W U S J L I A B J V T I D D J F I J J F B O V R U

D T I K B G W J V A B , D I X S W C : Q O B D D B U

I R J J F V G , W B T F S , Q B L I G D B V P J F X

P I S J F , P V R J F V G F I D J D V G C F J A B

U S O S C B W J O X , Y S J F O V Y O S W B D D V P

F B I R J . 1 W B T F S 2 : 19

Mystery Picture Graph

Instructions: Find the mystery picture below by plotting and connecting the points of each line on the coordinate graph. Connect all the points in Line 1, stop, pick up your pencil, and then connect all the points in Line 2, and so on for the rest of the lines. The dots for the first 3 (X,Y) coordinate pairs on Line 1 have been placed for you.

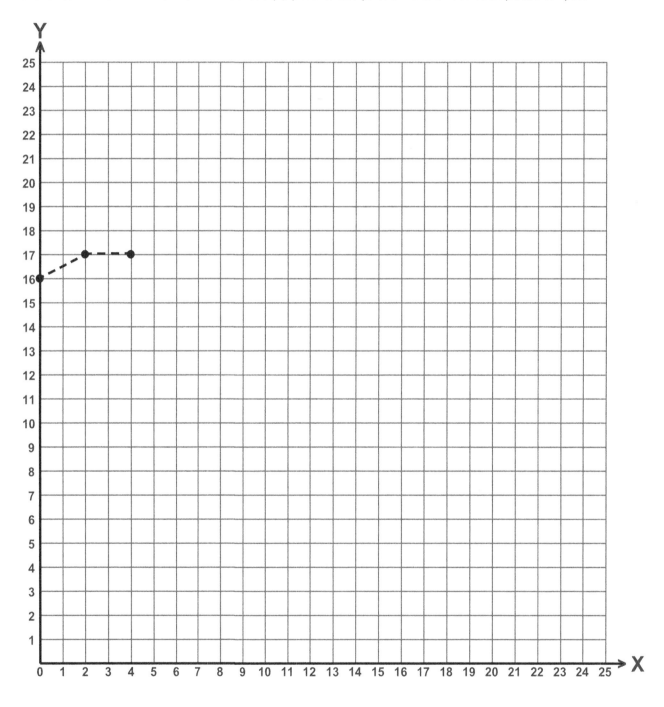

Line 1	(0, 16)	(2, 17)	(4, 17)	(5, 19)	(7, 17)	(7, 13)	(8, 13)	(13, 17)	(15, 17)	(17, 15)	(19, 17)	(21, 17)
(24, 13)	(20, 2)	(19, 1)	(17, 1)	(17, 2)	(19, 2)	(19, 9)	(13, 9)	(12, 2)	(12, 1)	(10, 1)	(10, 2)	(11, 2)
(11, 8)	(9, 9)	(7, 9)	(5, 11)	(5, 14)	(4, 15)	(3, 14)	(2, 14)	(0, 15)	(0, 16)	**Line 2**	(24, 13)	(24, 9)
(25, 8)	(24, 13)											

1 Nephi 1–5

"I Will Go and Do"

Instructions: Solve this word sudoku puzzle the same way that you'd solve a numeric sudoku. Each of the bold words in the scripture below is found once in every row, column and 3×3 box.

1 Nephi 2:16

And it came to pass that I, Nephi, being exceedingly **young**, nevertheless being large in **stature**, and also having great desires to know of the **mysteries** of **God**, wherefore, I did cry unto the Lord; and behold he did **visit** me, and did **soften** my **heart** that I did **believe** all the words which had been spoken by my father; wherefore, I did not **rebel** against him like unto my brothers.

		visit	believe	stature	mysteries			
stature		heart				visit	mysteries	God
	soften	mysteries			heart		stature	
		believe	soften			rebel	God	heart
	stature		heart		God	believe		
	heart	rebel		believe			young	
believe					soften		heart	young
		stature	visit				soften	rebel
		soften			young	mysteries	believe	

1 Nephi 1–5
"I Will Go and Do"

Unscrambler

Instructions: Unscramble the words below; look at the bold words in the scripture for a hint.

1 Nephi 3:4,6-7

Wherefore, the Lord hath commanded me that thou and thy brothers should go unto the house of **Laban**, and seek the **records**, and bring them down hither into the **wilderness**. Therefore go, my son, and thou shalt be **favored** of the Lord, because thou hast not murmured. And it came to pass that I, Nephi, said unto my father: I will go and do the things which the **Lord** hath commanded, for I know that the Lord giveth no **commandments** unto the **children** of **men**, save he shall **prepare** a **way** for them that they may **accomplish** the **thing** which he commandeth them.

recsrdo _____

cdhrilen _____

erearpp _____

swelndresi _____

awy _____

tnghi _____

rdol _____

nme _____

ablna _____

olacpmshci _____

raofedv _____

samnmtndecom _____

GO AND DO, I WILL, WHAT THE LORD COMMANDS. FOR KNOW I, I DO, THAT THE LORD GIVETH NO COMMANDMENTS UNTO THE CHILDREN OF MEN SAVE PREPARE A WAY HE SHALL FOR THEM TO ACCOMPLISH THE THING HE THEM COMMANDETH.

I'M GLAD YOU HAD THE FORESIGHT TO BRING THE DAGOBAH EDITION OF THE BOOK OF MORMON.

I FIGURED HE'D LIKE THIS SCRIPTURE.

mormoncartoonist.com

© Arie Van De Graaff

1 Nephi 6–10

"Come and Partake of the Fruit"

Instructions: Fill in the blank puzzle grid using the word bank with the bold words from the scripture below. Place the words in the correct place on the grid.

1 Nephi 12:16–18

And the angel spake unto me, saying: Behold the fountain of **filthy water** which thy father saw; yea, even the river of which he spake; and the depths thereof are the **depths** of **hell**. And the **mists** of **darkness** are the **temptations** of the **devil**, which **blindeth** the **eyes**, and **hardeneth** the **hearts** of the children of men, and leadeth them away into broad roads, that they **perish** and are **lost**. And the large and spacious **building**, which thy father saw, is vain **imaginations** and the **pride** of the children of men. And a great and a **terrible** gulf **divideth** them; yea, even the word of the **justice** of the Eternal God, and the **Messiah** who is the Lamb of God, of whom the Holy Ghost beareth record, from the beginning of the world until this time, and from this time henceforth and forever.

4 Letters	devil	7 Letters	terrible	12 Letters
lost	mists	Messiah	divideth	imaginations
hell		justice		
eyes	6 Letters		9 Letters	
	filthy	8 Letters	hardeneth	
5 Letters	hearts	building		
pride	perish	darkness	11 Letters	
water	depths	blindeth	temptations	

Holding fast to the word of God
leads me to Him
and helps me feel His love.

January 15–21
1 Nephi 6–10
"Come and Partake of the Fruit"

Word Angles

Instructions: Find the bold words from the scripture. Each word path may run north, east, south, or west, may make one right-angled turn, and may cross another word path. A few words may make no right angle turn at all.

1 Nephi 11:21–22

And the **angel** said unto me: **Behold** the **Lamb** of God, yea, even the Son of the **Eternal Father**! Knowest thou the meaning of the **tree** which thy father saw? And I **answered** him, saying: Yea, it is the **love** of God, which **sheddeth** itself **abroad** in the **hearts** of the **children** of men; wherefore, it is the most **desirable** above all **things**.

```
G R H L L L R J D E B A S J G Y
O C N G A N B C X E R T E F O X
K H W X M F Z E D D E T H F W P
O I M V B C R H T G Y E T Y Y J
O L W I N P M S U H F L I B M T
O D A U M X B V V U B B R M S L
O R U V E W S N A D E A E G G E
N E I O R O J Q N K H R I S E D
P J F L E J H I D S O L A B R M
W W D N D U E E W U L D E X O A
L B E S T R A V F O F M F G A C
H N K F T H I N K M B J A D D K
E V O L B E J G R H J C T H E R
R O J S O T M S Q K D L E G N A
I A P D T E Y G F J P J S H J S
V L A M Y R N A L C J X L C X Q
```

Translation Station

Instructions: Translate the sign language letters below into English to discover the hidden message. Write the alphabet letter beneath each hand sign. Use the key at the back of the book to help you.

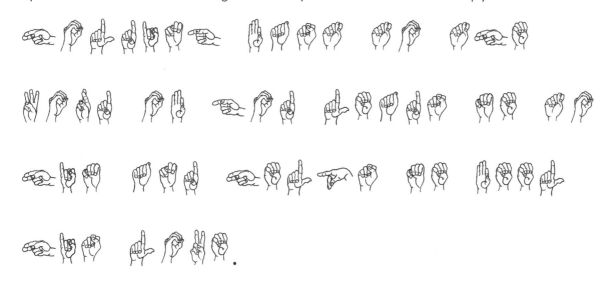

1 Nephi 6–10

"Come and Partake of the Fruit"

Reverse Word Search

Instructions: Instead of looking for words in a grid, place the bold words in the scripture in the empty word search puzzle. The words may be forwards, backwards, up, down, or diagonally The start letter of the words have been placed in the grid to get you started. The first word, **FIERY** has been done for you.

1 Nephi 15:23–24

And they said unto me: What meaneth the **rod** of **iron** which our father saw, that **led** to the **tree**? And I said unto them that it was the **word** of **God**; and whoso would **hearken** unto the word of God, and would **hold fast** unto it, they would **never perish**; neither could the **temptations** and the **fiery darts** of the **adversary overpower** them unto **blindness**, to lead them **away** to **destruction**.

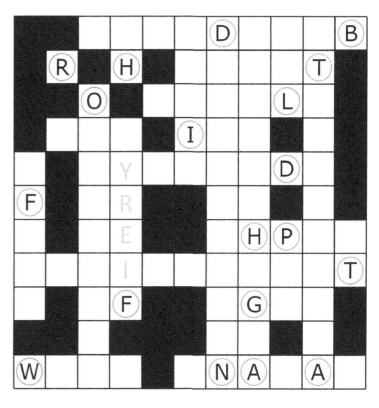

Book of Mormon Puzzler

By Ari Van De Graaff

Find the blocks of Book of Mormon symbols that match the numbered blocks below. Right the letters in the numbered spaced to find the name of the vision that Nephi and Lehi saw. The first set of blocks matches the set of blocks surrounding the T in the first column, third row below.

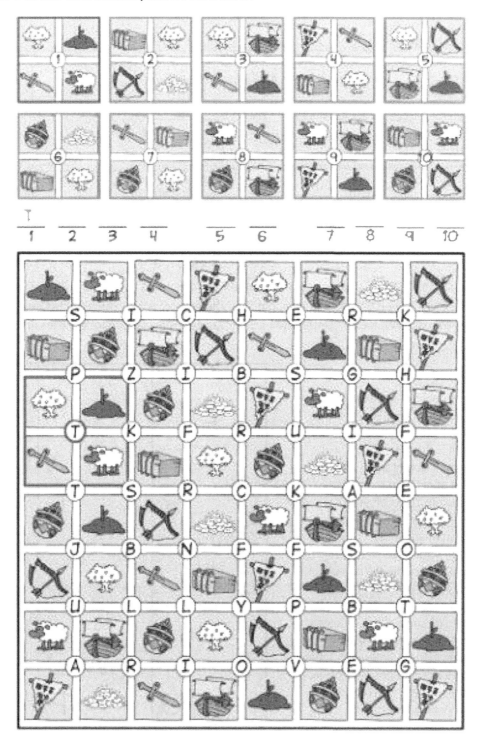

1 Nephi 6–10
"Come and Partake of the Fruit"

Fill in the Blank
1 Nephi 11:1

For it came to pass after I had _____ to _____ the things that my

_____ had seen, and _____ that the Lord was able to make them known

unto me, as I sat _____ in mine _____ I was _____ away in

the _____ of the Lord, yea, into an exceedingly high _____, which I never

had before _____, and upon which I _____ had before set my

_____.

foot	mountain	seen	believing	Spirit	never
know	father	pondering	desired	caught	heart

Letter Sudoku

Instructions: Solve the letter sudoku puzzle the same way you'd solve a numeric sudoku. Check your puzzle against the answer key on ColorMeChristian.org. Every column, row, and group of nine must contain every letter in the words **POWER GIFT.** Letters are used only once; cross out duplicate letters in the word(s) before you begin.

1 Nephi 10:17–19

I, Nephi, was desirous also that I might see, and hear, and know of these things, by the **power** of the Holy Ghost, which is the **gift** of God unto all those who diligently seek him, as well in times of old as in the time that he should manifest himself unto the children of men. For he is the same yesterday, today, and forever; and the way is prepared for all men from the foundation of the world, if it so be that they repent and come unto him. For he that diligently seeketh shall find; and the mysteries of God shall be unfolded unto them, by the power of the Holy Ghost, as well in these times as in times of old, and as well in times of old as in times to come; wherefore, the course of the Lord is one eternal round.

I E				W G
T		W	O E	
O	R	F		I
F W	I		G	O
E G				
G		W	O	
T	W O	P G	F
O		P		

1 Nephi 11–15

"Armed with Righteousness and with the Power of God"

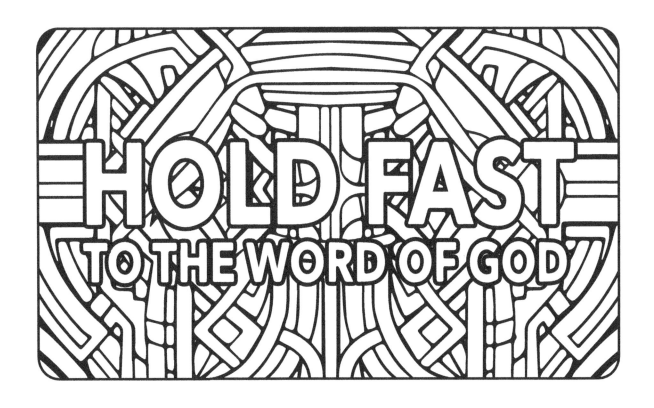

Word Star

Instructions: Start with the capital letter in the puzzle. Then choose one of the two lines to the next letter. Only one route through the word star will make a word. Write the letters of the word you discover in the blanks below as you travel through the star:

_ _ _ _ _ _ _ _

Now can you find this word in the following scripture?

1 Nephi 13:40

1 Nephi 11–15

"Armed with Righteousness and with the Power of God"

Wacky Word Trails

Instructions: Start with the circled letter, use the clues to find and mark the trail of letters of all the connected bolded words from the scripture through the maze to the last letter. The path can wander up, down, left, and right at any point, even in the middle of the word.

1 Nephi 11:22–23

And I **answered** him, saying: Yea, it is the **love** of **God**, which **sheddeth** itself **abroad** in the **hearts** of the **children** of **men**; wherefore, it is the **most desirable above all things**. And he **spake** unto me, saying: Yea, and the most **joyous** to the **soul**.

```
P  H  G  J  M  D  M  S  O  U  N  G  N  X  R
H  M  A  E  V  J  X  L  T  L  R  T  U  S  C
B  Z  C  H  Q  M  Q  L  H  I  N  G  S  S  P
F  S  B  C  T  S  B  A  O  E  V  O  L  F  Z
Z  Y  U  E  W  D  A  D  N  A  E  S  I  S  P
C  C  V  A  V  R  O  W  S  D  D  A  R  P  D
H  M  B  F  X  B  A  E  R  E  L  B  U  W  E
B  C  U  Z  B  C  N  E  H  S  E  R  W  D  O
U  S  E  H  C  H  E  D  D  E  T  H  H  E  V
F  Y  O  U  S  I  R  E  X  W  O  P  T  A  E
W  O (J) L  Z  L  D  L  F  Z  J  I  F  R  T
D  T  S  C  C  D  R  M  K  E  K  A  O  B  S
G  S  L  B  X  Z  A  N  R  M  W  P  V  A  G
B  Z  X  H  P  I  X  E  S  O  X  S  E  D  O
O  B  R  M  W  T  G  M  T  O  P  K  O  T  C
```

Word Bricks

Instructions: A sentence is written on the wall. But brick layers built the wall in the wrong order. Your job is to put the bricks in the right order. Hint: **1 Nephi 11:27**

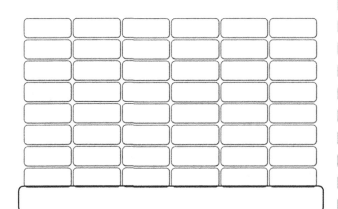

And	amb	of		the	L
God	we	nt	and	th	for
ba	pti	was	and	. . .	zed
G ho	the	st	l y		H o
e	d com	own	out	o	f
an	d a	e	ven	hea	bid
u po	i n	the		n	h im
f	a		for	do	ve. m o

1 Nephi 11–15
"Armed with Righteousness and with the Power of God"

Handwriting Practice

Practice your handwriting by tracing the sentence below. Then use the blank lines to write the sentence on your own.

The Book of Mormon teaches precious truths.

PRIOR TO ITS FALL, THE GREAT AND SPACIOUS BUILDING FIRST HAD TO DEAL WITH A BUILDING INSPECTOR.

1 Nephi 11–15

"Armed with Righteousness and with the Power of God"

Instructions: Connect all of the letters in the phrase bolded below. Don't be tricked by letters that take you into a dead end! There is only one path through the maze.

____ __ ___ ___, ___ ____ ___; '___ _____, ___ _____, ___ ____.
___ ____ ___ __ ___ ____ __ ___; '_____ _____ _____ __ _____.

(Hymn No. 274)

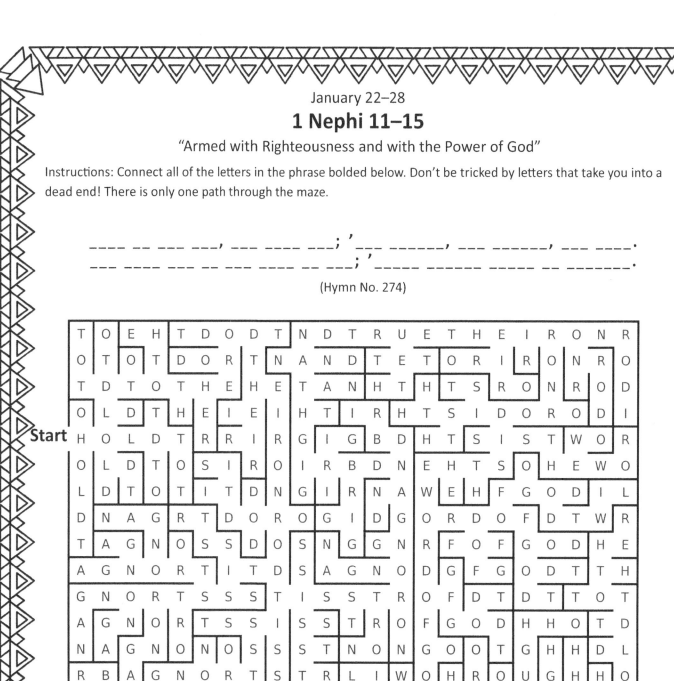

1 Nephi 11–15

"Armed with Righteousness and with the Power of God"

Instructions: Using the Across and Down clues, write the correct words in the numbered grid below. Hint: all of the words in the crossword come from the scripture below.

1 Nephi 15:23–25

ACROSS

2. eternal gospel principles that are necessary for our exaltation when given by God or the prophets
5. a synonym for spirit; as a spirit child of Heavenly Father you existed as a spirit before this life on earth.
7. spur on or encourage
11. forceful exertion
13. like or suggestive of a flame
14. have ownership of
15. pass from physical life
16. a tiny missile with a pointy end that can be a weapon or part of a game
18. a unit of language that native speakers can identify
19. careful attention
20. an event that completely ruins something

DOWN

1. an inherent cognitive or perceptual power of the mind
3. a plant having a permanently woody main stem or trunk, ordinarily growing to a considerable height, and usually developing branches at some distance from the ground
4. unable to see
6. someone who offers opposition
8. defeat by superior force
9. recall knowledge; have a recollection
10. listen and do
12. a long thin item to guide you when you hold onto it
17. the one Supreme Being, the creator and ruler of the universe

1 Nephi 11–15

"Armed with Righteousness and with the Power of God"

Translation Station

Instructions: Translate the Morse code below into English to discover the hidden message. Write the alphabet letter beneath each Morse Code letter. Each letter, number, and punctuation is separated by a slash: /. Use the key at the back of the book to help you.

· · · · / · / · — / · · · — / · / — · / · — · · / — · — — /

· · — · / · — / — / · · · · / · / · — · / · · · / · / — · / — /

· — — — / · / · · · / · · — / · · · / — · — · / · · · · / · — · / · · / · · · / — /

— · · · / · / — · — · / · — / · · — / · · · / · / · · · · / · /

· — · · / — — — / · · · — / · / · · · / — — / · / · — · · — · —

Word Square

Instructions: Word squares are a liike Sudoku puzzles, but each letter can occur only once in each row and in each column. Check your puzzle against the answer key on ColorMeChristian.org. Every row and column must contain every letter in the word **POWER.** This word can be written in the gray row.

1 Nephi 11:31

And he spake unto me again, saying: Look! And I looked, and I beheld the Lamb of God going forth among the children of men. And I beheld multitudes of people who were sick, and who were afflicted with all manner of diseases, and with devils and unclean spirits; and the angel spake and showed all these things unto me. And they were healed by the **power** of the Lamb of God; and the devils and the unclean spirits were cast out.

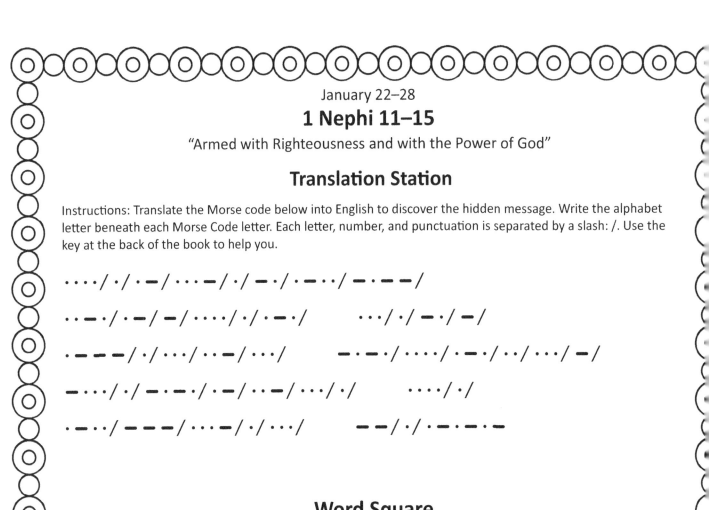

		O	P	W
	P	E		
O			W	
	R			P

1 Nephi 16–22

"I Will Prepare the Way before You"

Missing Vowels Word Search

Instructions: Find the hidden words. The words have been placed horizontally, vertically, diagonally, forwards, or backwards, and the vowels have been removed. When you locate a word, draw an ellipse around it and fill the vowels in.

Alma 37:40-41

And it did work for them **according** to their **faith** in **God**; therefore, if they had faith to **believe** that God could cause that those **spindles** should **point** the **way** they should go, behold, it was **done**; therefore they had this **miracle**, and also many other miracles wrought by the **power** of God, day by day. Nevertheless, because those miracles were worked by **small means** it did show unto them **marvelous works**. They were **slothful**, and **forgot** to **exercise** their faith and **diligence** and then those marvelous works **ceased**, and they did not

```
C C   R D   N G   J B T G
T C V Y B Q T Z X X C   D
B J   S L D G   F   G W S D B
D W R H   M   D X R M K   H G
P   N T   B N   C H T L F D
L   B   X Q F     T Q D   V
G M   R V   L   S   N V S
  Z K   V J R P S     C   S
L Y L   F H T   L S F N P   K
C C   W H W W Z S P   S L R
    M S T   T   M Z G G
R   D     S R B   D   B W
  S G   Q Y F L L   L X B B
M   L W Q N   B L G     T
H D B K F X S C B X S D T H
```

Secret Code

Instructions: The secret message is written in symbols. In the code key you can find what each symbol means. Write the letter above the symbol and you can read the secret message.

Hidden Picture: Can you find the 5 liahonas hidden in the picture below? It will be tricky; the liahonas may be smaller, on its side, or even upside down! Then, see if you can find one copy of the animals as well.

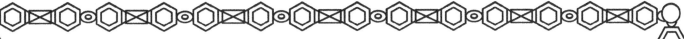

1 Nephi 16–22

"I Will Prepare the Way before You"

Instructions: Fit the bold words from the scripture below into the encircled squares. Words will read forward, backward, up, down, and diagonally and will normally cross other words. Start with the hints provided.

1 Nephi 18:20-22

And there was **nothing** save it were the **power** of God, which **threatened** them with **destruction**, could **soften** their **hearts**; wherefore, when they saw that they were about to be **swallowed** up in the **depths** of the sea they **repented** of the thing which they had done, insomuch that they **loosed** me. And it came to pass after they had loosed me, behold, I took the **compass**, and it did work whither I desired it. And it came to pass that I **prayed** unto the Lord; and after I had prayed the **winds** did **cease**, and the storm did cease, and there was a great **calm**. And it came to pass that I, Nephi, did **guide** the ship, that we **sailed** **again** towards the **promised land**.

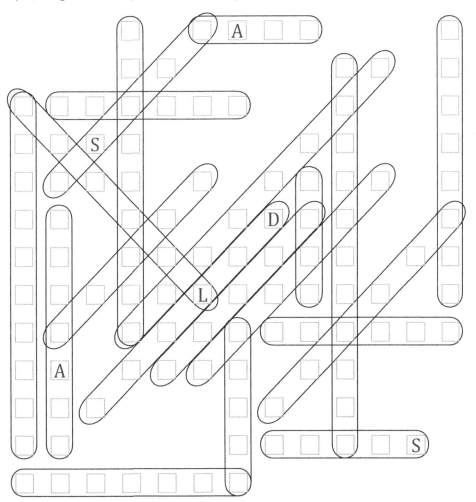

nothing	power	threatened	destruction	soften	hearts
swallowed	depths	repented	loosed	compass	prayed
winds	cease	calm	guide	sailed	again
promised	land				

1 Nephi 16–22

"I Will Prepare the Way before You"

Instructions: Solve this word sudoku puzzle the same way that you'd solve a numeric sudoku. Each of the bold words in the scripture below is found once in every row, column and 3×3 box.

1 Nephi 18:3

And I, Nephi, did **go** into the **mount** oft, and I did **pray oft unto** the **Lord**; wherefore the Lord **showed** unto me **great things**.

				go		unto		oft
	go	unto				pray		mount
oft		pray		unto				go
	things				great	mount		unto
	unto		mount		go		great	
mount			oft			things	go	
			showed		things	go		great
	great					oft	mount	showed
go	mount				oft			things

January 29–February 4
1 Nephi 16–22
"I Will Prepare the Way before You"

I can be a good **example** to my family.

Come, Follow Me Manual, 2024

Start

End

1 Nephi 16–22

"I Will Prepare the Way before You"

Unscrambler

Instructions: Unscramble the words below; look at the bold words in the scripture for a hint.

1 Nephi 16:28-29

And it came to pass that I, Nephi, beheld the **pointers** which were in the ball, that they did work according to the **faith** and **diligence** and **heed** which we did give unto them. And there was also **written** upon them a new writing, which was **plain** to be read, which did give us **understanding** concerning the **ways** of the Lord; and it was written and **changed** from time to time, according to the faith and diligence which we gave unto it. And thus we see that by **small** means the Lord can bring about **great things**.

syaw _____   deeh _____

htiaf _____   sretniop _____

llams _____   ecnegilid _____

nialp _____   gnidnatsrednu _____

degnahc _____   nettirw _____

taerg _____   sgniht _____

I'M FOLLOWING THE BRETHREN ON FACEBOOK, I'VE RETWEETED NEW ERA ARTICLES ON TWITTER, NOW I JUST NEED TO FIGURE OUT WHICH SOCIAL MEDIA PLATFORM I NEED TO "LIKEN THE SCRIPTURES."

mormoncartoonist.com

© Arie Van De Graaff

2 Nephi 1–2

"Free to Choose Liberty and Eternal Life, through the Great Mediator"

Instructions: Fill in the blank puzzle grid using the word bank with the bold words from the scripture below. Place the words in the correct place on the grid.

2 Nephi 2:27

Wherefore, men are **free** according to the **flesh**; and all **things** are **given** them which are **expedient** unto man. And they are free to **choose liberty** and **eternal life**, through the **great Mediator** of all men, or to choose **captivity** and **death**, **according** to the captivity and power of the **devil**; for he seeketh that all **men** might be **miserable** like unto **himself**.

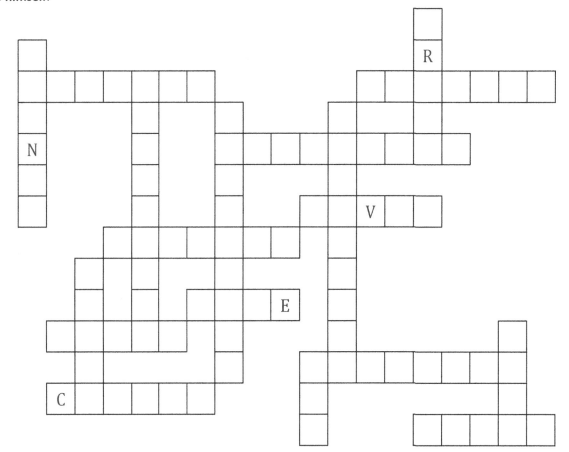

3 Letters	5 Letters	6 Letters	eternal	expedient
men	devil	things		captivity
	great	choose	8 Letters	miserable
4 Letters	death		Mediator	
life	given	7 Letters		
free	flesh	liberty	9 Letters	
		himself	according	

Graft Back In The Branch

Bring the cut off branch to the tree to be grafted back in. When we keep the commandments of God, we are blessed. When we don't keep them, we are cut off from God's presence.

2 Nephi 1–2

"Free to Choose Liberty and Eternal Life, through the Great Mediator"

Word Search

Instructions: Find the bold words from the scripture in the word search puzzle. Each word could be hidden forwards, backwards, up, down, or diagonally.

2 Nephi 2:11, 16

For it must needs be, that there is an **opposition** in all things. If not so, my firstborn in the wilderness, **righteousness** could not be brought to pass, neither **wickedness**, neither **holiness** nor **misery**, neither **good** nor **bad**. Wherefore, all things must needs be a **compound** in **one**; wherefore, if it should be one body it must needs remain as dead, having no **life** neither **death**, nor **corruption** nor **incorruption**, **happiness** nor **misery**, neither **sense** nor **insensibility**. Wherefore, the Lord God **gave** unto man that he should **act** for **himself**. Wherefore, man could not act for himself save it should be that he was **enticed** by the one or the other.

```
Y O M I S E R Y I L M C D T S
T W P J T B P C I G E H E F S
I B U P C W J F A I Y O A I E
L I F A O A E V Y G N L T D N
I F N O M S E S R I D I H U S
B P Y C P Q I P E K E N I J U
I H H N O Z L T S F C E M C O
S A I F U R D U I S I S T Z E
N P M T N H R F M O T S U S T
E P S F D U I U F P N Q N B H
S I E G O O D R P V E E A B G
N N L T S U M G O T S D M J I
I E F C O R R U P T I O N N R
A S V A Y X Z N X B J O N E I
M S W I C K E D N E S S N U S
```

Knight Moves - Find a Word

Instructions: Start with the capital letter in the puzzle. To get to the next letter, jump two squares in any direction except diagonally, and then one square in a different direction. Your path will look like a capital L. To show you how it works, Only one route through the puzzle will make a word. Write the letters of the word you discover in the blanks below as you jump through the squares:

__ __ __ __ __ __ __ __
 1 2 3 4 5 6 7 8

Now can you find this word in the following scripture?

2 Nephi 1:20

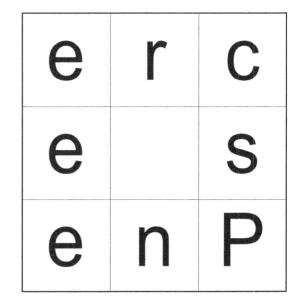

Mystery Picture Graph

Instructions: Find the mystery picture below by plotting and connecting the points of each line on the coordinate graph. Connect all the points in Line 1, stop, pick up your pencil, and then connect all the points in Line 2, and so on for the rest of the lines. The dot for the first (X,Y) coordinate pair on Line 1 has been placed for you.

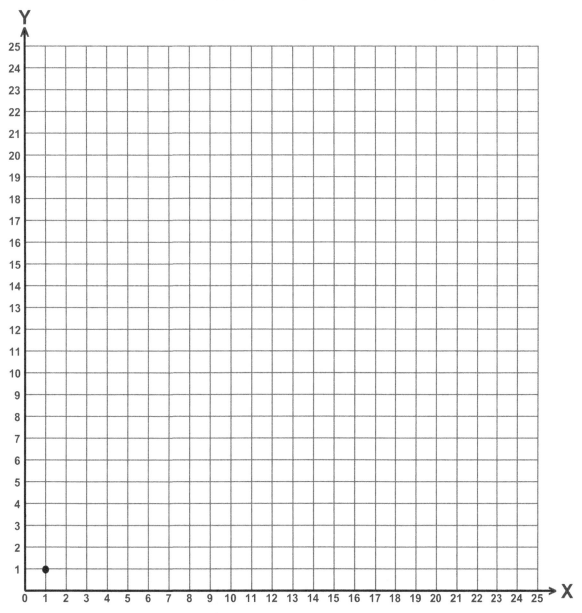

Line 1	(1, 1)	(23, 1)	(23, 5)	(1, 5)	(1, 2)	Line 2	(1, 25)	(1, 21)	(23, 21)	(23, 25)	(1, 25)	Line 3
(1, 21)	(1, 5)	(2, 5)	(2, 21)	Line 4	(8, 21)	(8, 5)	**(9, 5)**	(9, 21)	Line 5	(15, 21)	(15, 5)	(16, 5)
(16, 21)	Line 6	(22, 21)	(22, 5)	(23, 5)	(23, 21)	Line 7	(8, 20)	(6, 20)	(6, 14)	(8, 15)	(7, 13)	(7, 10)
(8, 9)	(6, 5)	Line 8	(10, 8)	(15, 8)	Line 9	(11, 12)	(12, 11)	(13, 12)	(12, 12)	Line 10	(10, 16)	(10, 15)
(11, 15)	(11, 16)	(10, 16)	Line 11	(14, 16)	(13, 16)	(13, 15)	(14, 15)	(14, 16)	Line 12	(11, 20)	(10, 20)	(14, 20)
Line 13	(14, 20)	(15, 20)	Line 14	(16, 20)	(18, 20)	(18, 14)	(16, 15)	(17, 13)	(17, 10)	(16, 9)	(18, 5)	Line 15
(9, 20)	(10, 20)	Line 16	(11, 12)	(12, 12)	Line 17	(9, 8)	(10, 8)	Line 18	(10, 9)	(11, 10)	(13, 10)	(14, 9)
Line 19	(6, 14)	(8, 20)	Line 20	(16, 20)	(18, 14)							

2 Nephi 1–2

"Free to Choose Liberty and Eternal Life, through the Great Mediator"

Letter Sudoku

Instructions: Solve the letter sudoku puzzle the same way you'd solve a numeric sudoku. Check your puzzle against the answer key on ColorMeChristian.org. Every column, row, and group of nine must contain every letter in the word **OBSCURITY.** Letters are used only once;

2 Nephi 1:13, 15, 23

O that ye would awake; awake from a deep sleep, yea, even from the sleep of hell, and shake off the awful chains by which ye are bound, which are the chains which bind the children of men, that they are carried away captive down to the eternal gulf of misery and woe. But behold, the Lord hath redeemed my soul from hell; I have beheld his glory, and I am encircled about eternally in the arms of his love. Awake, my sons; put on the armor of righteousness. Shake off the chains with which ye are bound, and come forth out of **obscurity**, and arise from the dust.

T	U				Y	C		
C	I	Y		B		R		
	C	T				S		
		O			U	B		
								I
	O	U						
S			Y	B	O			
	R		O	T	U	B		

2 Nephi 3–5
"We Lived after the Manner of Happiness"

Cryptogram

Instructions: Each letter on the top stands for a letter in the alphabet. Solve the encrypted phrase by matching each letter on top to a letter in the alphabet on the bottom. Use the key to help you remember what the letters stand for so you can crack the code.

D	E	S	F	Z	K	I	Q	Y	W	U	G	V	P	N	A	M	R	H	J	T	X	B	L	O	C
A	B	C	D	E	F	G	H	I	J	K	L	M	N	O	P	Q	R	S	T	U	V	W	X	Y	Z

" P X J P I C   W B   J Y R U S I   U Y   P U U B O A   U S B

U B Q N X B .   G   Z P X X   G U   W B G O L

R B Z Y Q Q B O A B A   U Y   U S B   X Y R A .   J S B U S B R

I Y K   S P M B   P Z Z B C C   U Y   P   U B Q N X B   Y R

O Y U ,   W B G O L   J Y R U S I   Y D   P   Z K R R B O U

U B Q N X B   R B Z Y Q Q B O A   F B B N C   I Y K

D G R Q X I   D Y Z K C B A   Y O   U S B   U S G O L C

U S P U   Q P U U B R ,   U S B   Z Y M B O P O U   N P U S . "

B X A B R   R B O X K O A ,   U S B   U S G O L C   Y D   Q I   C Y K X .

February 12–18
2 Nephi 3–5
"We Lived after the Manner of Happiness"

Word Angles

Instructions: Find the bold words from the scripture. Each word path may run north, east, south, or west, may make one right-angled turn, and may cross another word path. A few words may make no right angle turn at all.

2 Nephi 5:16

And I, **Nephi**, did **build** a **temple**; and I did **construct** it after the **manner** of the temple of **Solomon save** it were not built of so many **precious** things; for they were not to be **found** upon the **land**, wherefore, it could not be built **like unto** Solomon's temple. But the manner of the **construction** was like unto the temple of Solomon; and the **workmanship** thereof was **exceedingly fine**.

```
F N E R V U V L R Q W N R G N J
R N W X K S T N C N O T N Y B I
Y A L E O M G S H E Y K U N E L
B M P D N U I O C P H I G V X U
J L M Q D O D L O M O N O C O R
V W E W L F X F X G U M X X E J
P P T G I S I X Q N U E W Y L G
V S S B U M P R E C I K E K S N
L Y P L B N Q Y O V O O E V A I
C K M A N S H I P Q U J D Y T D
O R C K U W J K K E S F N F Y E
N O O D A S Z B I M F T A L J E
S W N H M L G U L D N T C J J C
T V S F I N E Y E U Y C I X Q X
R A T R U C T T E G Z L L J O E
U C T I O N O M J B F I W M N Q
```

Word Star

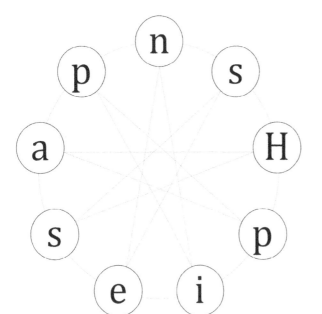

Instructions: Start with the capital letter in the puzzle. Then choose one of the two lines to the next letter. Only one route through the word star will make a word. Write the letters of the word you discover in the blanks below as you travel through the star:

— — — — — — — — —

Now can you find this word in the following scripture?

2 Nephi 5:27

2 Nephi 3–5
"We Lived after the Manner of Happiness"

Handwriting Practice

Practice your handwriting by tracing the sentence below. Then use the blank lines to write the sentence on your own.

Joseph Smith was a prophet.

Joseph Smith was a prophet.

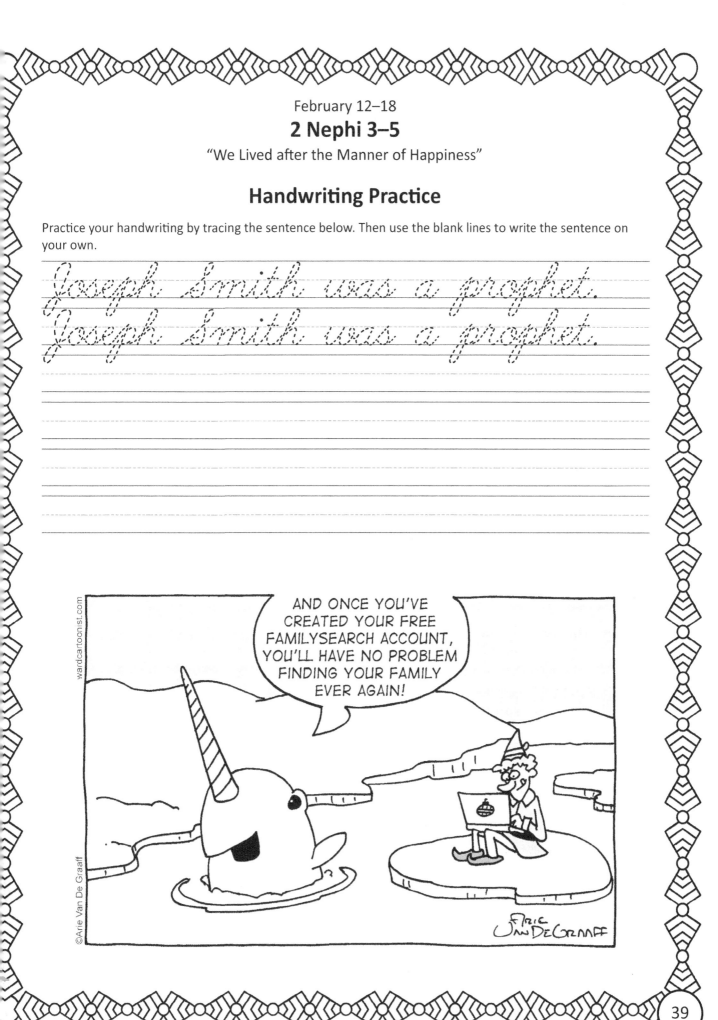

AND ONCE YOU'VE CREATED YOUR FREE FAMILYSEARCH ACCOUNT, YOU'LL HAVE NO PROBLEM FINDING YOUR FAMILY EVER AGAIN!

wardcartoonist.com

©Arie Van De Graaff

February 12–18
2 Nephi 3–5
"We Lived after the Manner of Happiness"

Instructions: Using the Across and Down clues, write the correct words in the numbered grid below. Hint: all of the words in the crossword come from the scripture below.

2 Nephi 4:15–16, 20–25, 34–35

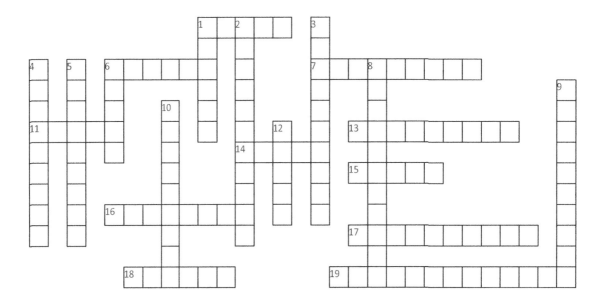

ACROSS

1. A shiny, yellowish metal often used for making musical instruments and decorative items.
6. To go up or climb, often to a higher place.
7. Doing something generously or in abundance.
11. The flat, movable parts of a bird, insect, or aircraft that allow it to fly.
13. To keep something in its original state or condition.
14. To believe in and rely on someone or something.
15. To increase or grow, like the moon becoming larger.
16. When you carve or cut a design or words into a surface.
17. To provide help, support, or care to someone.
18. To have seen or observed something.
19. Acting in a morally right and just way.

DOWN

1. Past tense of "bid," which means to command, invite, or request.
2. Difficulties, troubles, or problems that cause suffering.
3. A feeling of great happiness or joy.
4. Information, facts, and understanding gained through learning and experience.
5. Large, tall landforms with peaks and slopes, often covered in rocks and snow.
6. Not right or correct, indicating something is wrong.
8. Something that lasts forever or for a very long time.
9. A wild and natural area without many people, often with forests or mountains.
10. To think deeply or carefully about something.
12. To shake or tremble, often due to an earthquake.

The **temple** is the house of the Lord.

Come, Follow Me Manual, 2024

Start

End

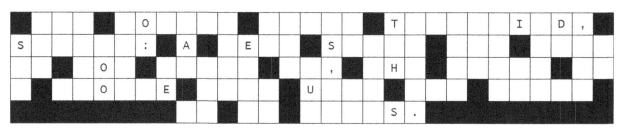

2 Nephi 3–5

"We Lived after the Manner of Happiness"

Fallen Phrase

Instructions: The letters in each column have fallen from the grid. Put them back correctly to rebuild the phrase. Cross out each letter in the jumble below once you place it in the grid. Pay attention because the letters in each column are scrambled. Start with simple 1 or 2 letter words and use the process of elimination. To check your answer, read **2 Nephi 3:6**

Word Square

Instructions: Word squares are a liike Sudoku puzzles, but each letter can occur only once in each row and in each column. Check your puzzle against the answer key on ColorMeChristian.org. Every row and column must contain every letter in the word **FAMILY.** This word can be written in the gray row.

2 Nephi 5:6

Wherefore, it came to pass that I, Nephi, did take my family, and also Zoram and his **family**, and Sam, mine elder brother and his family, and Jacob and Joseph, my younger brethren, and also my sisters, and all those who would go with me. And all those who would go with me were those who believed in the warnings and the revelations of God; wherefore, they did hearken unto my words.

2 Nephi 6–10
"O How Great the Plan of Our God"

Reverse Word Search

Instructions: Instead of looking for words in a grid, place the bold words in the scripture in the empty word search puzzle. The words may be forwards, backwards, up, down, or diagonally The start letter of the words have been placed in the grid to get you started.

2 Nephi 9:21–22

And he **cometh** into the world that he may **save** all men if they will **hearken** unto his **voice**; for behold, he **suffereth** the **pains** of all men, yea, the pains of **every living creature**, both **men**, **women**, and **children**, who belong to the **family** of **Adam**. And he suffereth this that the **resurrection** might pass upon all men, that all might **stand before** him at the **great** and **judgment day**.

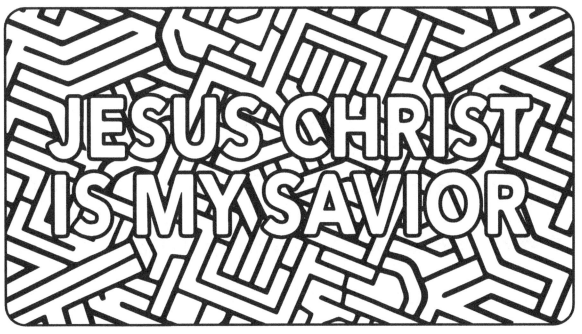

2 Nephi 6–10

"O How Great the Plan of Our God"

Wacky Word Trails

Instructions: Start with the circled letter, use the clues to find and mark the trail of letters of all the connected bolded words from the scripture through the maze to the last letter. The path can wander up, down, left, and right at any point, even in the middle of the word.

2 Nephi 9:28–29

O that **cunning plan** of the **evil one**! O the **vainness**, and the **frailties**, and the foolishness of men! When they are **learned** they think they are **wise**, and they **hearken not** unto the **counsel** of **God**, for they set it aside, supposing they **know** of **themselves**, wherefore, their **wisdom** is **foolishness** and it **profiteth** them **not**. And they shall **perish**. But to be learned is **good** if they hearken unto the counsels of God.

```
X  K  N  F  Q  U  P  E  N  G  E  D  Z  T  V
C  Y  S  G  C  Z  R  K  P  O  V  H  E  L  P
R  S  Q  V  T  Y  A  K  E  O  K  G  S  N  E
J  O (F) N  C  E  E  E  R  D  C  U  N  U  R
B  O  L  E  M  B  H  T  X  Z  X  G  N  O  I
S  S  I  D  N  T  N  O  M  Q  L  E  I  C  S
N  H  E  S  V  O  N  N  R  A  F  R  N  G  H
E  W  J  X  W  E  D  E  L  E  A  S  S  I  W
S  S  I  E  J  I  Z  U  N  N  O  A  U  S  D
R  F  T  S  V  A  I  L  A  C  U  J  E  N  O
A  I  L  S  V  K  N  P  V  L  D  P  W  O  M
L  Y  N  Y  C  E  N  S  E  E  S  M  O  V  E
F  V  H  P  S  S  Y  N  U  S  H  E  N  I  H
Q  W  X  R  G  E  E  T  I  S  T  D  K  L  X
K  D  T  O  F  I  T  H  W  E  G  O  Y  C  K
```

Translation Station

Instructions: Translate the sign language letters below into English to discover the hidden message. Write the alphabet letter beneath each hand sign. Use the key at the back of the book to help you.

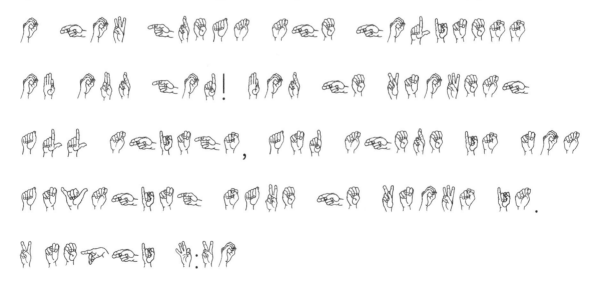

February 19–25

2 Nephi 6–10

"O How Great the Plan of Our God"

Instructions: Connect all of the letters in the phrase bolded below. Don't be tricked by letters that take you into a dead end! There is only one path through the maze.

___ __ __________ ___ ___ ____ ____ ____ ______, ___ __
________ __ ___ ____, ______ _______ _____ __ ___ ____ ___ __
______, __ ____ ______ __ _____ __ ___ _______ __ ___.

2 Nephi 9:23

Finish

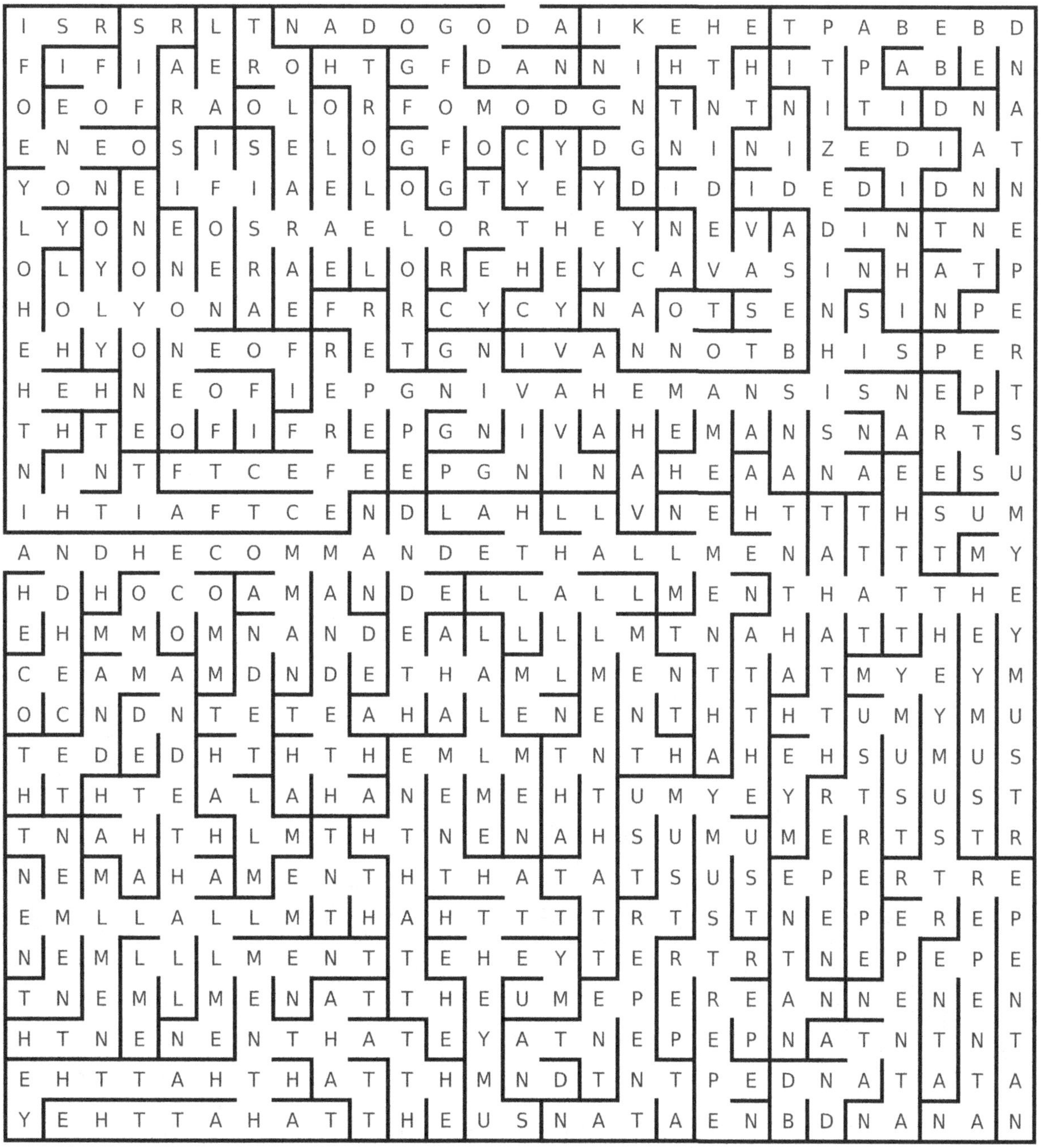

Start

Hidden Picture: We need Jesus Christ to help us return to Heavenly Father after Adam and Eve fell and had to leave the Garden of Eden. Can you find the 3 pictures each of Adam and Eve below? It will be tricky; the pictures may be smaller, on its side, or even upside down! Then, see if you can find 1 picture of the animals as well.

2 Nephi 6–10

"O How Great the Plan of Our God"

Instructions: Solve this word sudoku puzzle the same way that you'd solve a numeric sudoku. Each of the bold words in the scripture below is found once in every row, column and 3×3 box.

2 Nephi 9:49

Behold, my soul abhorreth sin, and my **heart delighteth** in **righteousness**; and I **will praise** the **holy name** of **my God**.

	heart	holy				righteousness		my
God		righteousness	holy	praise				
	will					praise	holy	God
	holy		God			will	my	
righteousness	God				heart			delighteth
	my	delighteth	praise		holy			
holy	name				praise		God	
delighteth				my		name		holy
			delighteth				my	heart	praise

2 Nephi 6–10

"O How Great the Plan of Our God"

Fill in the Blank

2 Nephi 9:10

O how _____ the _____ of our _____, who _____ a way for our _____ from the _____ of this awful _____; yea, that monster, _____ and _____, which I _____ the death of the _____, and also the death of the _____.

spirit	monster	prepareth	great	call	goodness
escape	death	God	body	hell	grasp

WELL, I CAN'T FIND ANY REFERENCE OF IT IN THE ADAM AND EVE STORY EITHER. I GUESS THERE REALLY IS NO SUCH THING AS A FORBIDDEN VEGETABLE.

warccartoonist.com

©Arie Van De Graaff

February 26–March 3

2 Nephi 11–19

"His Name Shall Be Called … The Prince of Peace"

Missing Vowels Word Search

Instructions: Find the hidden words. The words have been placed horizontally, vertically, diagonally, forwards, or backwards, and the vowels have been removed. When you locate a word, draw an ellipse around it and fill the vowels in.

2 Nephi 12:2–3

And it shall come to pass in the **last days**, when the **mountain** of the Lord's **house** shall be **established** in the **top** of the mountains, and shall be **exalted** above the **hills**, and all **nations** shall **flow** unto it. And many people shall go and say, **Come** ye, and let us go up to the mountain of the **Lord**, to the **house** of the **God** of **Jacob**; and he will **teach** us of his **ways**, and we will **walk** in his **paths**; for out of **Zion** shall go forth the **law**, and the **word** of the Lord from **Jerusalem**.

```
L F N D X    F T J W J N
S C S Y   D B F   R     P   T
T K   X   L L C     L R     X
  J M F       T T H     Q V L
B L K K W B F   L     L S W S H
L R Q D L S Y   W L Q     H H C
  Z   M H   X C L L B L   T K
S G D G   G W H P S D     K
H L F P W   L   S T   M S P K
    Z   X   N   X   L T   D M
D R R D F Q P T H     S   H C
  D J L Y   Q D   K Y X C   P
T G J X K   W   Z     V M R L
N   Z S N     T   N   H   Q
D Y   Q H   W   R   C Z Z   G
```

Word Bricks

Instructions: A sentence is written on the wall. But brick layers built the wall in the wrong order. Your job is to put the bricks in the right order. Hint: **2 Nephi 17:14**

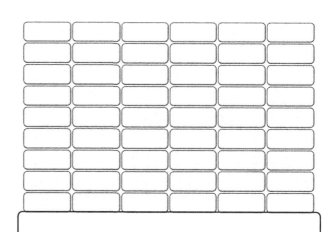

```
he         , t o r e r e f The
i m s   s h L o r a l l e l f d  h
i g n a  s   -  e  y g i v o u
 v i ,  a r g i o l d B e h n
l l        c o n c e i s h a v e ,
 b e a r  a       s h a l l a n d
n d  ,  a s h a l l        s o n
c a l    n a m i s  l   h e
e l .    I m m        a n u
```

Finding Jesus

Jesus Christ is my Savior - help guide the children through the maze to Jesus.

February 26–March 3

2 Nephi 11–19

"His Name Shall Be Called … The Prince of Peace"

Instructions: Fit the bold words from the scripture below into the encircled squares. Words will read forward, backward, up, down, and diagonally and will normally cross other words. Start with the hints provided.

2 Nephi 19:6

For **unto** us a **child** is **born**, unto us a **son** is **given**; and the **government** shall be **upon** his **shoulder**; and his **name** shall be **called**, **Wonderful**, **Counselor**, The **Mighty God**, The **Everlasting Father**, The **Prince** of **Peace**.

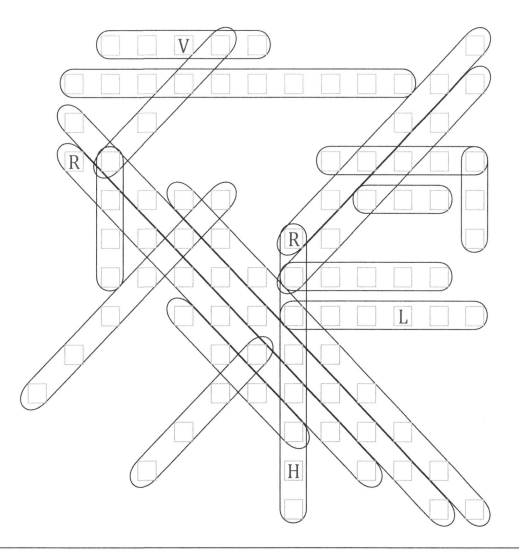

unto	child	born	son	given
government	upon	shoulder	name	called
Wonderful	Counselor	Mighty	God	Everlasting
Father	Prince	Peace		

Hidden Picture

By Arie Van De Graaff

Bailey and Ty are looking for their grandparents so they can go through the open house at the temple together. Can you help them out? Grandpa has a mustache and Grandma is wearing glasses and gold earrings. Can you also find the hidden objects?

2 Nephi 11–19

"His Name Shall Be Called … The Prince of Peace"

Handwriting Practice

Practice your handwriting by tracing the sentence below. Then use the blank lines to write the sentence on your own.

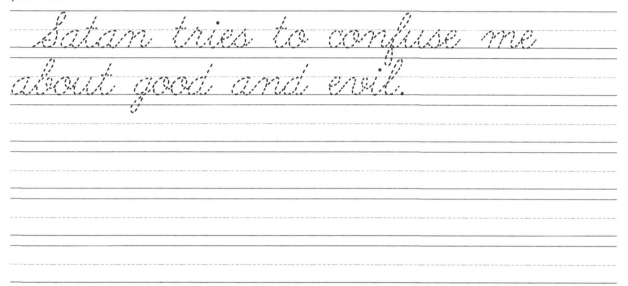

Satan tries to confuse me about good and evil.

2 Nephi 11–19

"His Name Shall Be Called … The Prince of Peace"

Secret Code

Instructions: The secret message is written in symbols. In the code key you can find what each symbol means. Write the letter above the symbol and you can read the secret message.

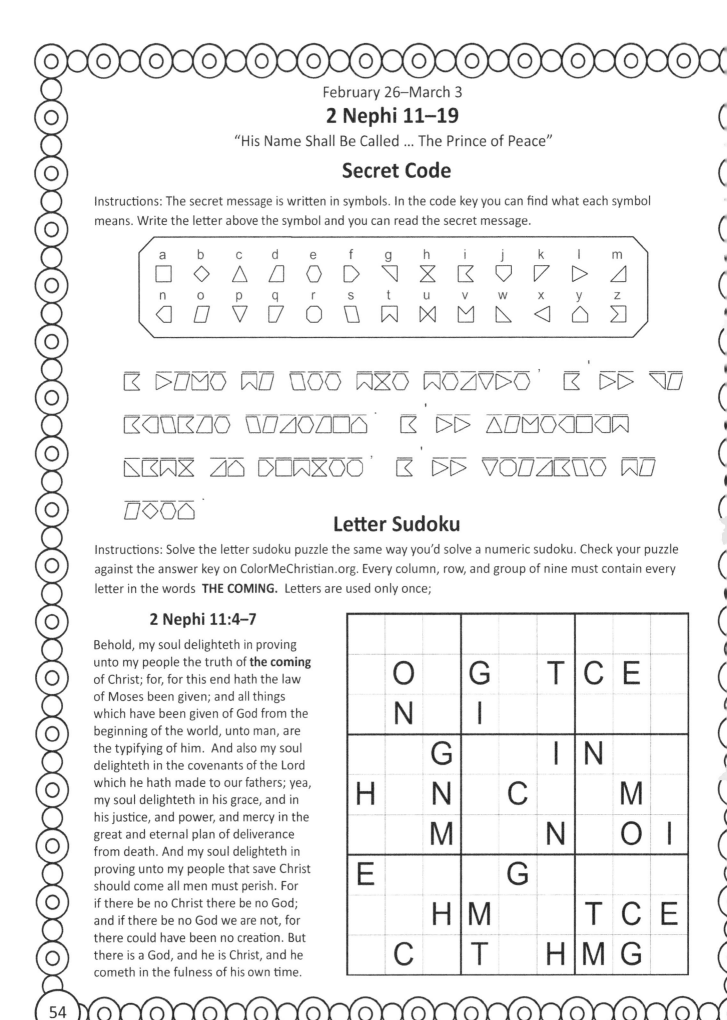

Letter Sudoku

Instructions: Solve the letter sudoku puzzle the same way you'd solve a numeric sudoku. Check your puzzle against the answer key on ColorMeChristian.org. Every column, row, and group of nine must contain every letter in the words **THE COMING.** Letters are used only once;

2 Nephi 11:4–7

Behold, my soul delighteth in proving unto my people the truth of **the coming** of Christ; for, for this end hath the law of Moses been given; and all things which have been given of God from the beginning of the world, unto man, are the typifying of him. And also my soul delighteth in the covenants of the Lord which he hath made to our fathers; yea, my soul delighteth in his grace, and in his justice, and power, and mercy in the great and eternal plan of deliverance from death. And my soul delighteth in proving unto my people that save Christ should come all men must perish. For if there be no Christ there be no God; and if there be no God we are not, for there could have been no creation. But there is a God, and he is Christ, and he cometh in the fulness of his own time.

SWORDS INTO PLOWSHARES, HUH? WHAT DO YOU SUPPOSE WOULD BE A GOOD USE FOR UNBREAKABLE, RETRACTABLE ADAMANTIUM CLAWS IN THE MILLENNIUM?

mormoncartoonist.com

© Arie Van De Graaff

Mystery Picture Graph

Instructions: Find the mystery picture below by plotting and connecting the points of each line on the coordinate graph. Connect all the points in Line 1, stop, pick up your pencil, and then connect all the points in Line 2, and so on for the rest of the lines. The dot for the first (X,Y) coordinate pair on Line 1 has been placed for you.

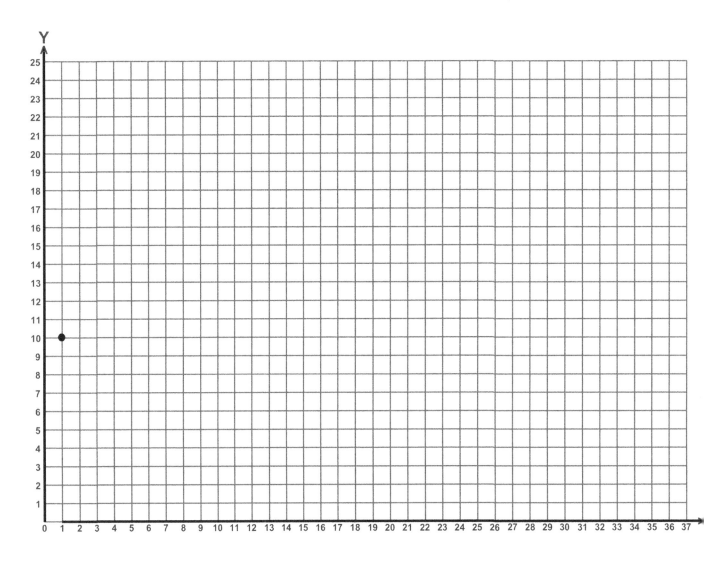

Line 1	(1, 10)	(10, 1)	(18, 10)	(14, 22)	(10, 21)	(6, 22)	(1, 10)	Line 2	(4, 17)	(3, 18)	(5, 20)	Line 3
(15, 20)	(17, 18)	(16, 17)	Line 4	(5, 14)	(7, 19)	(10, 18)	(13, 19)	(15, 14)	(13, 11)	(13, 10)	(12, 8)	(12, 7)
(10, 6)	(8, 7)	(8, 8)	(7, 10)	(7, 11)	(5, 14)	Line 5	(8, 8)	(12, 8)	Line 6	(10, 8)	(10, 9)	(11, 10)
(9, 10)	(10, 9)	Line 7	(7, 11)	(9, 13)	(8, 15)	(7, 15)	(7, 14)	(8, 14)	Line 8	(13, 11)	(11, 13)	(12, 15)
(13, 15)	(13, 14)	(12, 14)	Line 9	(22, 13)	(23, 8)	(24, 6)	(26, 5)	(28, 5)	(30, 6)	(31, 8)	(32, 13)	(34, 14)
(34, 15)	(37, 15)	(33, 18)	(32, 19)	(32, 20)	(31, 20)	(31, 21)	(29, 21)	(29, 22)	(26, 22)	(26, 21)	(24, 21)	(24, 20)
(23, 20)	(23, 19)	(18, 15)	(21, 15)	(21, 14)	(22, 13)	Line 10	(23, 14)	(24, 13)	(25, 14)	Line 11	(29, 14)	(30, 13)
(31, 14)	Line 12	(25, 7)	(26, 6)	(28, 6)	(29, 7)	Line 13	(27, 6)	(27, 8)	(28, 9)	(26, 9)	(27, 8)	

56

2 Nephi 20–25

"We Rejoice in Christ"

Word Search

Instructions: Find the bold words from the scripture in the word search puzzle. Each word could be hidden forwards, backwards, up, down, or diagonally.

4 Nephi 1:15–18

And it came to pass that there was no contention in the land, because of the **love** of God which did **dwell** in the **hearts** of the **people**. And there were no **envyings**, nor **strifes**, nor **tumults**, nor whoredoms, nor **lyings**, nor **murders**, nor any manner of lasciviousness; and surely there could not be a **happier** people among all the people who had been created by the hand of God. There were no robbers, nor murderers, neither were there Lamanites, nor any manner of -ites; but they were in **one**, the **children** of **Christ**, and **heirs** to the **kingdom** of **God**. And how **blessed** were they! For the Lord did bless them in all their doings; yea, even they were blessed and **prospered** until an hundred and ten years had passed away; and the first **generation** from Christ had passed away, and there was no **contention** in all the land.

```
W H B H X C O N T E N T I O N
P F E L S C H I L D R E N R F
R D X I E I W G L E Z N C E L
O I D N R S F E L J W O P I Z
S S D Y P S S N E E M S R P Y
P G K W D A C E W L O T Z P H
E N Z O Y H S R D P D L T A C
R I G P O R E A F O G U Q H I
E Y H T E J N T Q E N M I N S
D L O D J S V I W P I U L C T
Y Q R W T E Y O Z P K T H A R
G U S R B I I N U E S R C M I
M A A J K P N U Q Z I Q V F F
F E B Q X H G Q F S N L O V E
H I J C D U S N T P I M P A S
```

Translation Station

Instructions: Translate the Morse code below into English to discover the hidden message. Write the alphabet letter beneath each Morse Code letter. Each letter, number, and punctuation is separated by a slash: /. Use the key at the back of the book to help you.

··/ —····/·/·—··/··/·/····—/·/ ··/—·/ —·—/····/·—/··/···/—/—··—·—·

···/———/ —·—/———/——/· ·——/····/·—/— ——/·—/—···—/——···—

·——/··/—/····/ ····/··——/ ··/ ' ·——/·—·/ ···/—·—/—·/—··/

··/—·/ —/····/·—/ ——/·—·/·/·—/— —··/·—·—/—·/

·——/····/·/—·/ ———/—·/ —/····/··/·/ ·/·—·/·—/—/····/ ····/·/

—·—/———/——/·/···/ ·—/———/·—·/·/—·/ —/———/ ·—·/··/·—···/·

·—/——/———/—·/—·/ —·/····/·/ ···/———/—·/···/ ———/···—/

——/·/—·/·—··—·

2 Nephi 20–25

"We Rejoice in Christ"

Instructions: Fill in the blank puzzle grid using the word bank with the bold words from the scripture below. Place the words in the correct place on the grid.

2 Nephi 21:6–9

The wolf also shall dwell with the **lamb**, and the **leopard** shall lie down with the **kid**, and the **calf** and the young **lion** and fatling **together**; and a little **child** shall **lead** them. And the **cow** and the **bear** shall **feed**; their young ones shall lie down together; and the lion shall eat **straw** like the **ox**. And the sucking child shall play on the hole of the **asp**, and the weaned child shall put his **hand** on the **cockatrice's** den. They shall not **hurt** nor **destroy** in all my **holy mountain**, for the **earth** shall be **full** of the **knowledge** of the **Lord**, as the **waters** cover the **sea**.

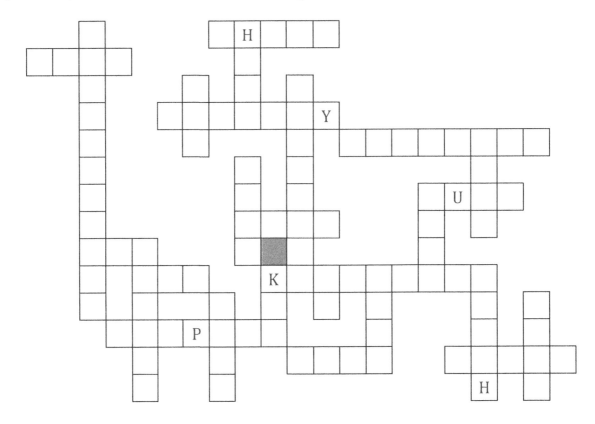

2 Letters	4 Letters	full	6 Letters	together
ox	lead	lion	waters	
	hurt	holy		9 Letters
3 Letters	calf		7 Letters	knowledge
sea	Lord	5 Letters	destroy	
kid	hand	child	leopard	11 Letters
cow	lamb	earth		cockatrice's
asp	bear	straw	8 Letters	
	feed		mountain	

March 4–10
2 Nephi 20–25
"We Rejoice in Christ"

The Lord is **gathering** His people.

Come, Follow Me Manual, 2024

Start

End

2 Nephi 20–25

"We Rejoice in Christ"

Unscrambler

Instructions: Unscramble the words below; look at the bold words in the scripture for a hint.

2 Nephi 21:11–12

And it shall come to pass in that day that the **Lord** shall set his **hand** again the **second** time to **recover** the **remnant** of his **people** which shall be **left**, from Assyria, and from Egypt, and from Pathros, and from Cush, and from Elam, and from Shinar, and from Hamath, and from the islands of the sea. And he shall set up an **ensign** for the **nations**, and shall assemble the outcasts of Israel, and gather together the **dispersed** of **Judah** from the four **corners** of the earth.

antremn _____

ahjud _____

ftle _____

plepeo _____

eddispers _____

dhan _____

nsnatio _____

rrecove _____

ondsec _____

rdlo _____

erscorn _____

gnensi _____

Word Square

Instructions: Word squares are a liike Sudoku puzzles, but each letter can occur only once in each row and in each column. Check your puzzle against the answer key on ColorMeChristian.org. Every row and column must contain every letter in the word **PREACH.** This word can be written in the gray row.

2 Nephi 25:26

And we talk of Christ, we rejoice in Christ, we **preach** of Christ, we prophesy of Christ, and we write according to our prophecies, that our children may know to what source they may look for a remission of their sins.

		E			A
	A			H	E
E				P	
	P		R	E	
H		R	C		

2 Nephi 26–30

"A Marvelous Work and a Wonder"

For behold, thus saith the Lord God: I will give unto the children of men line upon line, precept upon precept, here a little and there a little; and blessed are those who hearken unto my precepts, and lend an ear unto my counsel, for they shall learn wisdom; for unto him that receiveth I will give more; and from them that shall say, We have enough, from them shall be taken away even that which they have.

2 Nephi 28:30

2 Nephi 26–30

"A Marvelous Work and a Wonder"

Word Angles

Instructions: Find the bold words from the scripture. Each word path may run north, east, south, or west, may make one right-angled turn, and may cross another word path. A few words may make no right angle turn at all.

2 Nephi 29:7–8

Know ye not that there are **more nations** than **one**? Know ye not that I, the Lord your God, have **created all men**, and that I **remember** those who are upon the isles of the sea; and that I **rule** in the **heavens** above and in the **earth beneath**; and I bring forth my word unto the children of men, yea, even upon all the nations of the earth? Wherefore **murmur** ye, because that ye shall **receive** more of my word? Know ye not that the **testimony** of **two nations** is a **witness** unto you that I am God, that I remember one nation like unto another? Wherefore, I speak the **same words** unto one nation like unto another. And when the two nations shall run **together** the testimony of the two nations shall run together also.

```
H N S N E V A X H F R E H T G Y
M E O V Z A E B G H Z O T E U N
I T S E T S H A L W R M R G R W
M N E M R Z E C P T E E A O L D
O O C Z N L E V I E C F H T M O
N K D E T A Z B E N E A T P U U
Y V Z T O E D S A C F P V C R U
F L T O Y R K T K G Q O R U M W
D F A L A C B I I D R W Q M S O
H R M L V W S D W L E T B M N R
E R O O E V H Z E H M A L Z O D
L O S A M V K O J Q E N A T I S
J T N E S S D Q S U M B E R C Z
J I U C K O A N O I T A N L C Y
R W X S U V F S V U E I W D E Y
M H H N B U T V J S L U R L W Y
```

Knight Moves - Find a Word

Instructions: Start with the capital letter in the puzzle. To get to the next letter, jump two squares in any direction except diagonally, and then one square in a different direction. Your path will look like a capital L. To show you how it works, Only one route through the puzzle will make a word. Write the letters of the word you discover in the blanks below as you jump through the squares:

___ ___ ___ ___ ___ ___ ___ ___
 1   2   3   4   5   6   7   8

Now can you find this word in the following scripture?

2 Nephi 30:3–6

n	l	s
s		g
B	i	e

March 11–17
2 Nephi 26–30
"A Marvelous Work and a Wonder"

Instructions: Connect all of the letters in the phrase bolded below. Don't be tricked by letters that take you into a dead end! There is only one path through the maze.

___ ___ _____ _____ ____ __ _____ ___ __ ___ ____ ____ __
__ _____ ____ ___ ___ _____ __ ___, ___ _____ ____ ___
____, _____ __ _ _____ __ ___ ____ __ _____.

2 Nephi 28:2

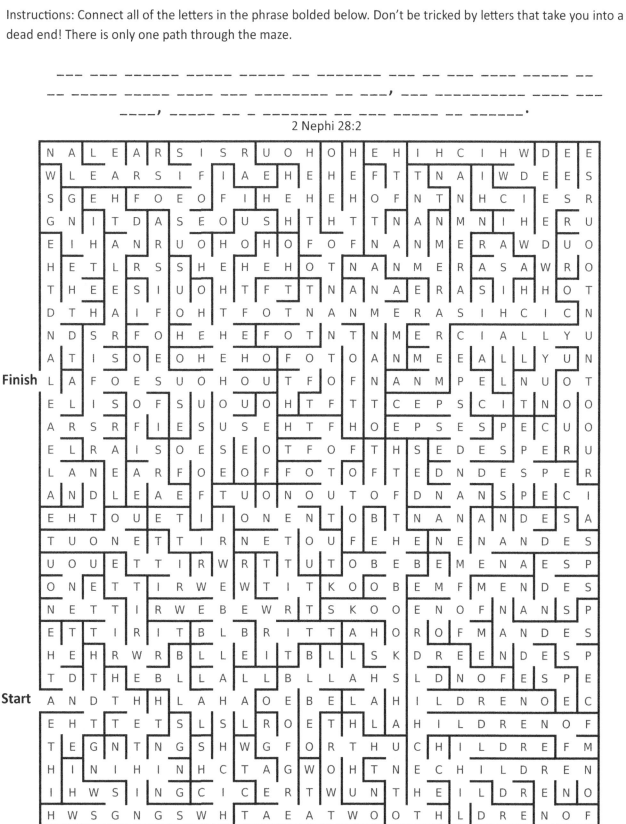

Finish

Start

2 Nephi 26–30
"A Marvelous Work and a Wonder"

LOOKS LIKE WE CAN POSTPONE ANY PLANS FOR THE END OF THE WORLD. NEPHI SAYS THAT IN THE LAST DAYS THE WORDS OF ISAIAH WILL BE UNDERSTOOD.

Cryptogram

Instructions: Each letter on the top stands for a letter in the alphabet. Solve the encrypted phrase by matching each letter on top to a letter in the alphabet on the bottom. Use the key to help you remember what the letters stand for so you can crack the code.

S	U	K	E	B	D	N	T	M	C	L	H	V	Q	J	Z	F	W	Y	X	A	O	R	P	G	I
A	B	C	D	E	F	G	H	I	J	K	L	M	N	O	P	Q	R	S	T	U	V	W	X	Y	Z

Z RZKK YZMD BGHV HLD JLZKFWDG VQ

IDG KZGD BXVG KZGD, XWDJDXH BXVG

XWDJDXH, LDWD U KZHHKD UGF HLDWD

U KZHHKD; UGF EKDAADF UWD HLVAD

RLV LDUWCDG BGHV IS XWDJDXHA,

UGF KDGF UG DUW BGHV IS JVBGADK,

QVW HLDS ALUKK KDUWG RZAFVI; QVW

BGHV LZI HLUH WDJDZMDHL Z RZKK

YZMD IVWD; 2 GDXLZ 28:30

2 Nephi 26–30

"A Marvelous Work and a Wonder"

Instructions: Solve this word sudoku puzzle the same way that you'd solve a numeric sudoku. Each of the bold words in the scripture below is found once in every row, column and 3×3 box.

2 Nephi 26:24

And there are also **secret combinations**, even as in times of old, according to the combinations of the devil, for he is the **founder** of all these things; yea, the founder of murder, and works of darkness; yea, and he **leadeth** them by the neck with a **flaxen** cord, until he **bindeth** them with his **strong cords forever**.

		strong	cords	bindeth		flaxen	secret	
	flaxen	cords	founder	strong			bindeth	combinations
	bindeth	forever			secret		cords	strong
founder	combinations		leadeth	bindeth	strong	flaxen		
strong				flaxen	secret	leadeth	founder	
	secret	strong		founder	combinations	forever	bindeth	
bindeth	secret			forever		cords	strong	
	flaxen		founder	cords	bindeth	combinations	secret	
cords	leadeth	bindeth		strong			flaxen	

2 Nephi 26–30

"A Marvelous Work and a Wonder"

Fallen Phrase

Instructions: The letters in each column have fallen from the grid. Put them back correctly to rebuild the phrase. Cross out each letter in the jumble below once you place it in the grid. Pay attention because the letters in each column are scrambled. Start with simple 1 or 2 letter words and use the process of elimination. To check your answer, read **2 Nephi 26:28**

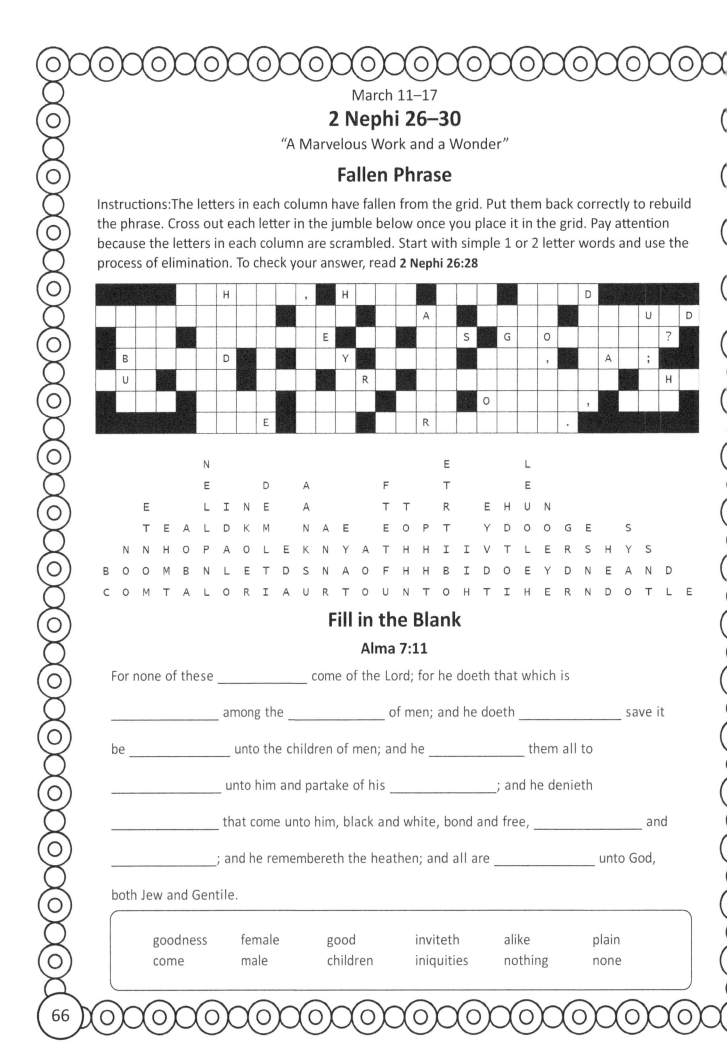

Fill in the Blank

Alma 7:11

For none of these _____ come of the Lord; for he doeth that which is

_____ among the _____ of men; and he doeth _____ save it

be _____ unto the children of men; and he _____ them all to

_____ unto him and partake of his _____; and he denieth

_____ that come unto him, black and white, bond and free, _____ and

_____; and he remembereth the heathen; and all are _____ unto God,

both Jew and Gentile.

goodness	female	good	inviteth	alike	plain
come	male	children	iniquities	nothing	none

March 18–24
2 Nephi 31–33
"This Is the Way"

Wacky Word Trails

Instructions: Start with the circled letter, use the clues to find and mark the trail of letters of all the connected bolded words from the scripture through the maze to the last letter. The path can wander up, down, left, and right at any point, even in the middle of the word.

2 Nephi 31:4-5

Wherefore, I would that ye should **remember** that I have **spoken** unto you **concerning** that **prophet** which the Lord **showed** unto me, that should **baptize** the **Lamb** of **God**, which should take **away** the **sins** of the **world**. And now, if the Lamb of God, he being **holy**, should have **need** to be baptized by **water**, to **fulfil** all **righteousness**, O then, how much **more** need have **we**, being **unholy**, to be baptized, yea, even by water!

```
B E U O E C X Z I Y L O H N U
G M S M T R Q E T N B F U I L
V G N V H G I L P E E G L F R
I V E H O S R A A B D N I N N
A F S S L E R M B U A R N T C
E A Y U Y B M E R K O E C T J
P Q V J W V E M Q I C V N O C
R U Q Z P D U N K D T O G A Y
D I (S) V C M O X G N C D A W W
G O H A M M W R X R D L Y I Z
L W E E L U A W E P Q R O W A
E W D K R A A S E U F T S S P
G O E S U T O Q H R H E I N S
G D W B L H U J K Y P O R P N
B T A T E R M O R E S P O K E
```

Word Star

Instructions: Start with the capital letter in the puzzle. Then choose one of the two lines to the next letter. Only one route through the word star will make a word. Write the letters of the word you discover in the blanks below as you travel through the star:

_ _ _ _ _ _ _ _ _ _ _ _ _

Now can you find this word in the following scripture?

2 Nephi 5:27

Returning to Heavenly Father

Jesus Christ teaches us how to return to Heavenly Father.Help these children reach Jesus at the end of the maze so Jesus can help them return to Heavenly Father.

2 Nephi 31–33
"This Is the Way"

Handwriting Practice

Practice your handwriting by tracing the sentence below. Then use the blank lines to write the sentence on your own.

I can feast upon the words of Christ.

Translation Station

Instructions: Translate the sign language letters below into English to discover the hidden message. Write the alphabet letter beneath each hand sign. Use the key at the back of the book to help you.

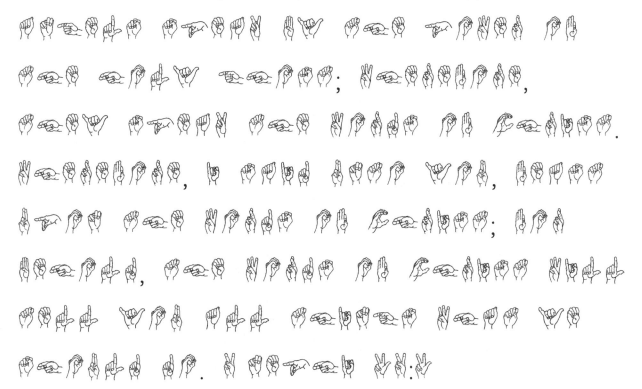

Hidden Picture: Heavenly Father wants us to pray always. Can you find 6 pictures of this praying man below? It will be tricky; the picturemay be smaller, on its side, or even upside down! Then, see if you can find 1 picture of the animals as well.

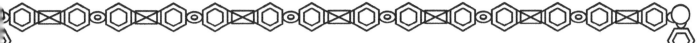

2 Nephi 31–33

"This Is the Way"

Instructions: Using the Across and Down clues, write the correct words in the numbered grid below. Hint: all of the words in the crossword come from the scripture below.

2 Nephi 32:8–9

ACROSS

1. listen and then act
4. to fold your arms, bow your head, and speak to your Heavenly Father
5. Holy Ghost
8. reflect deeply on a subject
9. get something done
10. to lose consciousness temporarily
14. the Supreme Being in whom we believe and whom we worship. Father of our spirits.
15. morally bad or wrong
16. feel intense sorrow, especially due to a loss
17. impart skills or knowledge to
18. Savior
19. To dedicate, to make holy, or to become righteous.

DOWN

2. morally bad or wrong
3. get something done
4. become aware of through the senses
6. reflect deeply on a subject
7. something that aids or promotes well-being
11. the Supreme Being in whom we believe and whom we worship. Father of our spirits.
12. Savior
13. at all times; all the time and on every occasion

2 Nephi 31–33

"This Is the Way"

Letter Sudoku

Instructions: Solve the letter sudoku puzzle the same way you'd solve a numeric sudoku. Check your puzzle against the answer key on ColorMeChristian.org. Every column, row, and group of nine must contain every letter in the words **ASK IF DONE.** Letters are used only once;

2 Nephi 31:19–20

And now, my beloved brethren, after ye have gotten into this strait and narrow path, I would **ask if** all is **done**? Behold, I say unto you, Nay; for ye have not come thus far save it were by the word of Christ with unshaken faith in him, relying wholly upon the merits of him who is mighty to save. Wherefore, ye must press forward with a steadfastness in Christ, having a perfect brightness of hope, and a love of God and of all men. Wherefore, if ye shall press forward, feasting upon the word of Christ, and endure to the end, behold, thus saith the Father: Ye shall have eternal life.

E				O				F
		K	A		D	S	I	
	A	E	D		I			S
D					N			
			S					
	I	F						
O	K	E	D	S				
A	S		O					

Easter

"He Shall Rise … with Healing in His Wings"

Missing Vowels Word Search

Instructions: Find the hidden words. The words have been placed horizontally, vertically, diagonally, forwards, or backwards, and the vowels have been removed. When you locate a word, draw an ellipse around it and fill the vowels in.

Alma 7:12

And he will **take** upon him **death**, that he may **loose** the **bands** of death which **bind** his **people**; and he will take upon him their **infirmities**, that his **bowels** may be **filled** with **mercy**, according to the **flesh**, that he may **know** according to the flesh how to **succor** his **people according** to their **infirmities**.

```
C Q S G C D   J B P     P L
Q J D   N M R   R Q B S   H N
      N P Y   N P R Q L K P R Q
N     X N D D P H C   Q L G N
F N B   N F   R M   T   S X
      Z R B K W     S D N   F S
R W K N Y M   R   C   Z T M L
M H     B   N Y Y X C W H B
    C T   V S K Z J Z     S S W
T Y N     M   R C Y F     F
    T H T   X P V     C   T L B
    K   T B D T N L C L   H   K
S N   B C   F L   R X     S K
R F N     F   R B F L   W H H
L J C T D D   L P     P F H
```

Easter

"He Shall Rise … with Healing in His Wings"

Secret Code

Instructions: The secret message is written in symbols. In the code key you can find what each symbol means. Write the letter above the symbol and you can read the secret message.

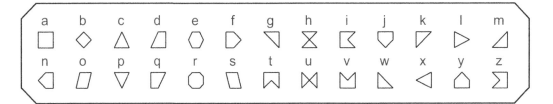

a	b	c	d	e	f	g	h	i	j	k	l	m
□	◇	△	◺	⬠	⬠	◺	✕	⊏	⋎	▽	▷	◿

n	o	p	q	r	s	t	u	v	w	x	y	z
◁	⧄	▽	▽	⬡	⊓	⊔	⋈	⋈	⋊	◁	△	⋝

(secret message written in symbols)

3   17:21

AUGGH!

WHAT IS IS? ARE YOU ALL RIGHT?

I'M GOING BALD! WHAT HAPPENED TO ALL THOSE BLESSINGS OF NOT LOSING A HAIR ON YOUR HEAD?

I DON'T THINK THOSE COUNT UNTIL AFTER THE RESURRECTION.

mormoncartoonist.com

©Arie Van De Graaff

Mystery Picture Graph

Instructions: Find the mystery picture below by plotting and connecting the points of each line on the coordinate graph. Connect all the points in Line 1, stop, pick up your pencil, and then connect all the points in Line 2, and so on for the rest of the lines. The dot for the first (X,Y) coordinate pair on Line 1 has been placed for you.

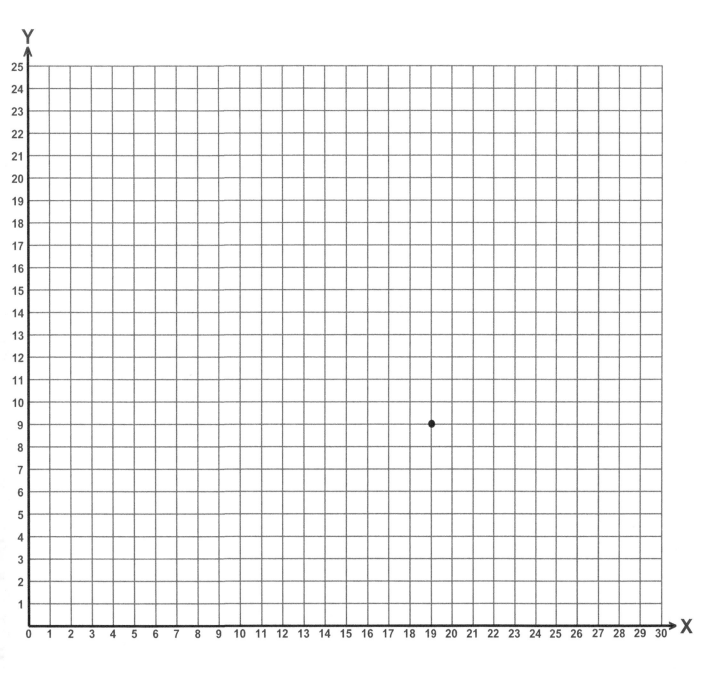

Line 1	(19, 9)	(21, 11)	(26, 11)	(28, 9)	(29, 7)	(29, 4)	(28, 2)	(26, 0)	(21, 0)	(19, 2)	(18, 4)	(18, 7)
(19, 9)	Line 2	(24, 11)	(21, 13)	(18, 14)	(14, 14)	(10, 13)	(8, 12)	(6, 10)	(4, 9)	(3, 5)	(2, 3)	(0, 2)
(0, 1)	(20, 1)	Line 3	(12, 1)	(12, 9)	(16, 9)	(16, 1)	Line 4	(0, 1)	(0, 2)			

Easter

"He Shall Rise ... with Healing in His Wings"

Instructions: Fit the bold words from the scripture below into the encircled squares. Words will read forward, backward, up, down, and diagonally and will normally cross other words. Start with the hints provided.

Enos 1:4–8

And my soul **hungered**; and I **kneeled** down before my Maker, and I cried unto him in mighty **prayer** and **supplication** for mine own soul; and all the day long did I cry unto him; yea, and when the night came I did still **raise** my voice high that it reached the heavens. And there came a voice unto me, saying: Enos, thy **sins** are **forgiven** thee, and thou shalt be **blessed**. And I, Enos, knew that God could not lie; wherefore, my **guilt** was **swept away**. And I said: Lord, how is it done? And he said unto me: **Because** of thy **faith** in **Christ**, whom thou hast **never** before **heard** nor **seen**. And many years pass away before he shall **manifest** himself in the **flesh**; wherefore, go to, thy **faith** hath made thee whole.

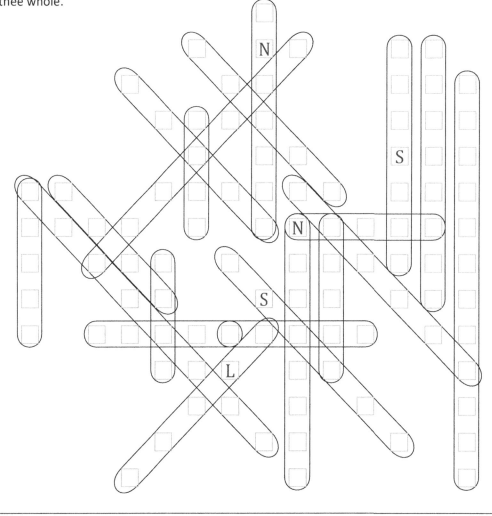

hungered	kneeled	prayer	supplication	raise
sins	forgiven	blessed	guilt	swept
away	Because	faith	Christ	never
heard	seen	manifest	flesh	faith

March 25–31

Easter

"He Shall Rise ... with Healing in His Wings"

Jesus Christ can cleanse me and help me change.

Come, Follow Me Manual, 2024

Start

End

Easter

"He Shall Rise … with Healing in His Wings"

Fill in the Blank

Alma 7:11

And he shall go _____, suffering _____ and _____ and

_____ of every _____; and this that the _____ might be

_____ which saith he will take upon him the _____ and the

_____ of his _____.

afflictions	forth	people	pains	temptations	sicknesses
word	fulfilled	pains	kind		

Word Square

Instructions: Word squares are a liike Sudoku puzzles, but each letter can occur only once in each row and in each column. Check your puzzle against the answer key on ColorMeChristian.org. Every row and column must contain every letter in the word **WASHED.** This word can be written in the gray row.

Alma 13:11–12

Therefore they were called after this holy order, and were sanctified, and their garments were **washed** white through the blood of the Lamb.

	S		D	A	W
		D	A	W	
			W	S	H
A	D				
S				E	

Jacob 1–4

Be Reconciled unto God through the Atonement of Christ

Wherefore, we search the prophets, and we have many revelations and the spirit of prophecy; and having all these witnesses we obtain a hope, and our faith becometh unshaken, insomuch that we truly can command in the name of Jesus and the very trees obey us, or the mountains, or the waves of the sea.

Jacob 4:6

Jacob 1–4

Be Reconciled unto God through the Atonement of Christ

Word Search

Instructions: Find the bold words from the scripture in the word search puzzle. Each word could be hidden forwards, backwards, up, down, or diagonally.

Jacob 2:17–19

Think of your **brethren** like unto yourselves, and be **familiar** with all and free with your **substance**, that they may be **rich** like unto you. But **before** ye **seek** for riches, seek ye for the **kingdom** of **God**. And after ye have obtained a **hope** in **Christ** ye shall obtain riches, if ye seek them; and ye will seek them for the **intent** to do **good**—to clothe the **naked**, and to feed the **hungry**, and to liberate the **captive**, and administer relief to the **sick** and the **afflicted**.

```
A E C N A T S B U S S Y N A H
V D J R E R H O M Q D O G S P
R C O J X R C I N T E N T L P
H H T O N H H R B G K S I C K
J A C C G M S T A E A A J G Y
N J W A H E E V E I N Z G J R
K Q K E P N E C Y R L E L C G
I P D Q G T K G T O B I P I N
N K H H M A I R I C H M M O U
G B E F O R E V S F L P Z A H
D A U G T H B J E W W W T H F
O B R K P X A F F L I C T E D
M S Z T S I R H C G P I Z T N
S T J D S Z B M Y K I I J J E
X W R M R A F V Q X U M L J K
```

Word Bricks

Instructions: A sentence is written on the wall. But brick layers built the wall in the wrong order. Your job is to put the bricks in the right order. Hint: **Jacob 2:17**

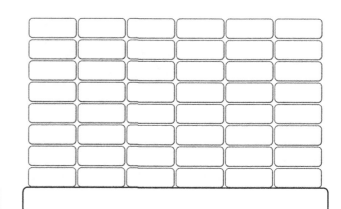

Faith: Growing A Mighty Tree

Fatih takes time to grow, just like this seedling will with time grow into a mighty tree. Can you make it through the maze to the mighty tree of faith in Christ?

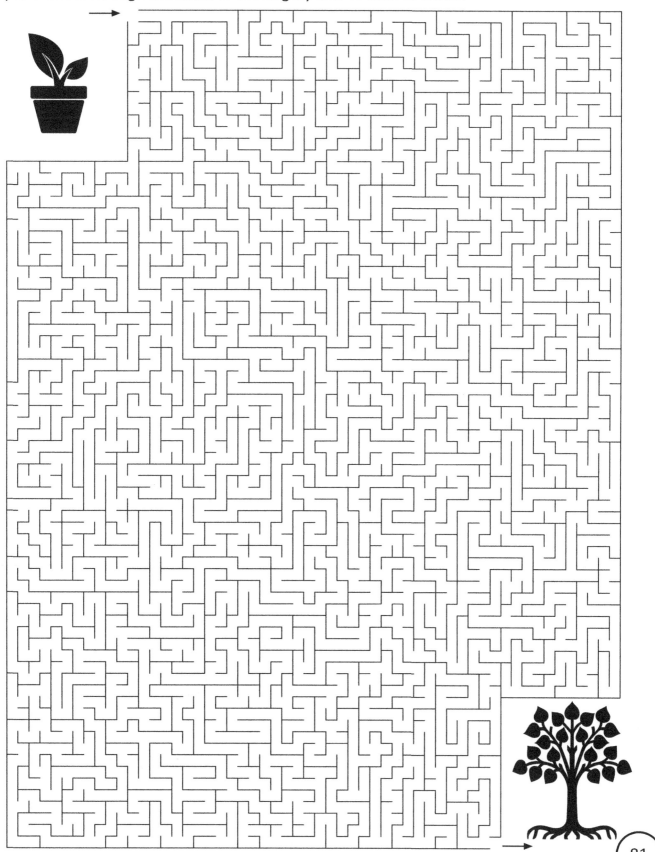

Jacob 1–4

Be Reconciled unto God through the Atonement of Christ

Instructions: Solve this word sudoku puzzle the same way that you'd solve a numeric sudoku. Each of the bold words in the scripture below is found once in every row, column and 3×3 box.

Jacob 4:6

Wherefore, we search the prophets, and we have many **revelations** and the spirit of **prophecy**; and having all these witnesses we obtain a **hope**, and our **faith** becometh **unshaken**, insomuch that we truly can **command** in the name of Jesus and the very **trees** obey us, or the **mountains**, or the waves of the **sea**.

sea	hope			trees	mountains		revelations	
	faith			prophecy	unshaken	sea	command	mountains
mountains			revelations	command		hope		trees
prophecy	revelations	faith				mountains	trees	hope
			prophecy	mountains	hope	faith		revelations
	mountains		trees	faith	revelations		prophecy	sea
revelations		mountains	sea	unshaken				faith
unshaken	prophecy	trees			faith	revelations	sea	
	sea	hope	command		trees	prophecy		unshaken

Jacob 1–4

Be Reconciled unto God through the Atonement of Christ

Instructions: Fill in the blank puzzle grid using the word bank with the bold words from the scripture below. Place the words in the correct place on the grid.

Neil L. Andersen, "Spiritual Whirlwinds" (Ensign, May 2014)

You are infinitely more **precious** to God than a **tree**. You are His **son** or His **daughter**. He made your spirit **strong** and **capable** of being **resilient** to the **whirlwinds** of **life**. The whirlwinds in your youth, like the wind against a young tree, can **increase** your **spiritual strength**, preparing you for the years ahead. How do you prepare for your whirlwinds? "**Remember** … it is upon the rock of our **Redeemer**, who is Christ, the Son of God, that ye must **build** your **foundation**; that when the devil shall send forth his mighty winds, … his shafts in the whirlwind, … when all his hail and his mighty storm shall **beat** upon you, it shall have no **power** … to **drag** you down … because of the **rock** upon which ye are built." This is your **safety** in the whirlwind.

3 Letters	rock	strong	Remember	**10 Letters**
son			daughter	foundation
	5 Letters	**7 Letters**	Redeemer	whirlwinds
4 Letters	power	capable	strength	
drag	build			
tree		**8 Letters**	**9 Letters**	
beat	**6 Letters**	precious	spiritual	
life	safety	increase	resilient	

Jacob 1–4

Be Reconciled unto God through the Atonement of Christ

Handwriting Practice

Practice your handwriting by tracing the sentence below. Then use the blank lines to write the sentence on your own.

I can strengthen my faith in Jesus Christ.

Jacob 5–7

The Lord Labors with Us

Word Angles

Instructions: Find the bold words from the scripture. Each word path may run north, east, south, or west, may make one right-angled turn, and may cross another word path. A few words may make no right angle turn at all.

Jacob 6:4–5

And how **merciful** is our God unto us, for he **remembereth** the house of Israel, both **roots** and **branches**; and he stretches forth his **hands** unto them all the day **long**; and they are a **stiffnecked** and a **gainsaying** **people**; but as many as will not **harden** their **hearts** shall be **saved** in the **kingdom** of **God**. Wherefore, my beloved brethren, I **beseech** of you in words of **soberness** that ye would **repent**, and come with full **purpose** of heart, and **cleave** unto God as he cleaveth unto you. And while his arm of mercy is **extended** towards you in the **light** of the **day**, harden not your hearts.

```
K C E N F F I T S J A E L C R U U
E G P M I C Q R E O V L M E R C I
D D A R B K R F E R E L E P E U F
B K N X L N T W U R K P Y E Q Q U
T T C I G E C B Q H P H O O W J L
M Q H L M P M O D N F E L P M A G
T V E R A E M G I E T H Z H O Q A
V M S E Q R Y W X R P K N D A Y I
W M O D G R O O E E U W A C J D N
G X P D N K L T D B T A N E S S S
P C R O I I L S I M D E G N I Y A
H S U X K B O N G E W D W R S O P
X D P R Q H V Z Z M R N Y E D E T
H A R K L C E E S E B E G B J J H
X X D J G I L I T R M T W O E O A
W B E Y H Y G N R L R X I S S D N
F H N T T N H E A X D E V A S A N
```

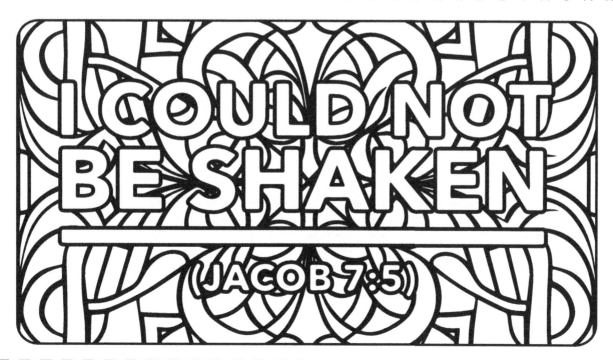

Jacob 5–7

The Lord Labors with Us

Translation Station

Instructions: Translate the Morse code below into English to discover the hidden message. Write the alphabet letter beneath each Morse Code letter.Each letter, number, and punctuation is separated by a slash: /.. Use the key at the back of the book to help you.

·—/—·/—··/　　··/—/　　—·—·/·—/——/·/　　—/———/　　·——·/·—/···/···/

—/····/·—/—/　　—/····/·/　　···/·/—·/····/—/—·/—·/···/　　—··/··/—·/

——/———/　　·—/—·/—··/　　·—·/·—/—···/——/·—/　　·——/··/—/····/

—/····/···/··/·—·/　　——/··/——/····/—/···/·—·—·　　·—/—·/—··/

—/····/·/　　·—··/———/·—/—/　　———/···—/　　—/····/·/

···—/··/—·/·—/——·/·—/·—·/—··/　　·—·/—·/——/———/·—/·/—··/

·—/·—·/···/———/　　·——/··/—/····/　　—/····/·/——/·—·—·—

·—/—·/—··/　　—/····/·/·—··/　　—··/··/—·/　　———/·—··/··/·—·—/

—/····/·/　　——·/———/——/——/·—/—·/—··/—··/——/·/—·/—/···/

———/··—/　　—/····/·/　　·—··/———/·—/—··/　　——/··—/

—/····/·/　　···—/··/—·/·/·—/·—·/—··/　　··/—·　　·—/—·—·/—··/

—/····/··/—·/—/···/··—·—·　　·—·—·—/·—/—···/———/·—·/

·····/　　: ——···/·—··—/

Jacob 5–7

The Lord Labors with Us

Instructions: Connect all of the letters in the phrase bolded below. Don't be tricked by letters that take you into a dead end! There is only one path through the maze.

___ __ ____ __ ____ ____ ____ ___ ___ ___ ___ ___

_____ _____ _____ ___ _____; ___ ____ _____ ___ _____,

___ _____ __ ____ __ ___ _____ __ ____ _____ ___.

Jacob 7:23

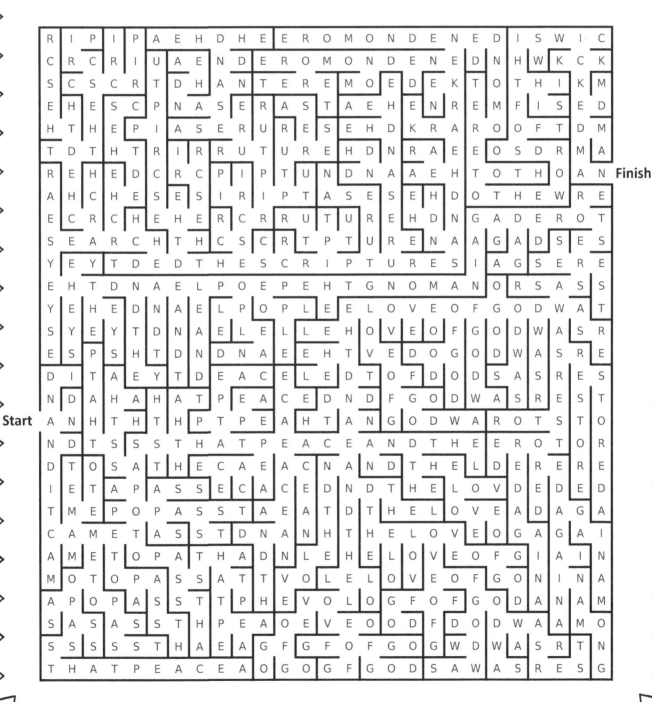

Jacob 5–7

The Lord Labors with Us

Instructions: Using the Across and Down clues, write the correct words in the numbered grid below. Hint: all of the words in the crossword come from the scripture below.

Jacob 5

ACROSS

3. underground tpart of the tree that lacks buds or leaves or nodes; gives nourishment to the tree
5. any piece of work that is undertaken or attempted
10. causing a sharp and acrid taste
11. original
13. quickly
14. fecal matter of animals
16. pass from physical life
17. a person working in the service of another
18. a small number
19. to throw or hurl; fling:
20. physical strength

DOWN

1. provide with sustenance
2. a farm of trees where olives are produced
4. a period of the year characterized by particular conditions of weather, temperature, etc.
6. quietly and steadily persevering in detail or exactness
7. part of the olive tree that grows leaves and fruit
8. dishonest or immoral or evasive
9. to break up, turn over, or remove earth, sand, etc., as with a shovel
12. Jesus Christ
15. when a branch is transplanted from one tree to another

Hidden Picture: Jacob stood up for Jesus Christ and what he knew was true. Can you find 4 pictures of him in the hidden picture below? It will be tricky; the picture may be smaller, on its side, or even upside down! Then, see if you can find one image of the animals as well.

89

Jacob 5–7

The Lord Labors with Us

Unscrambler

Instructions: Unscramble the words below; look at the bold words in the scripture for a hint.

Jacob 7:5

And he had **hope** to shake me from the **faith**, notwithstanding the many **revelations** and the many things which I had seen concerning these things; for I **truly** had **seen angels**, and they had **ministered** unto me. And also, I had **heard** the **voice** of the **Lord** speaking unto me in very word, from time to time; **wherefore**, I could not be **shaken**.

feoeerhwr _____   ciove _____

tifha _____   eesn _____

dearh _____   drol _____

nkeahs _____   uyrlt _____

tenidmirse _____   oehp _____

sneagl _____   evsenaotrli _____

Letter Sudoku

Instructions: Solve the letter sudoku puzzle the same way you'd solve a numeric sudoku. Check your puzzle against the answer key on ColorMeChristian.org. Every column, row, and group of nine must contain every letter in the word **NOURISHED.** Letters are used only once;

Jacob 5:47

But what could I have done more in my vineyard? Have I slackened mine hand, that I have not **nourished** it? Nay, I have nourished it, and I have digged about it, and I have pruned it, and I have dunged it; and I have stretched forth mine hand almost all the day long, and the end draweth nigh. And it grieveth me that I should hew down all the trees of my vineyard, and cast them into the fire that they should be burned. Who is it that has corrupted my vineyard?

S					H		O	U
	E	N	O					
	H							
E		I				S		
		U			R	D	I	
	U			E	O	R		
	N					E	D	
H								I

April 15–21
Enos–Words of Mormon
"He Worketh in Me to Do According to His Will"

Reverse Word Search

Instructions: Instead of looking for words in a grid, place the bold words in the scripture in the empty word search puzzle. The words may be forwards, backwards, up, down, or diagonally The start letter of the words have been placed in the grid to get you started.

Words of Mormon 1:4

And the **things** which are upon these **plates pleasing** me, because of the **prophecies** of the **coming** of **Christ**; and my **fathers** knowing that many of them have been **fulfilled**; yea, and I also know that as **many** things as have been **prophesied concerning** us **down** to this **day** have been fulfilled, and as many as go **beyond** this day **must surely** come to **pass**—

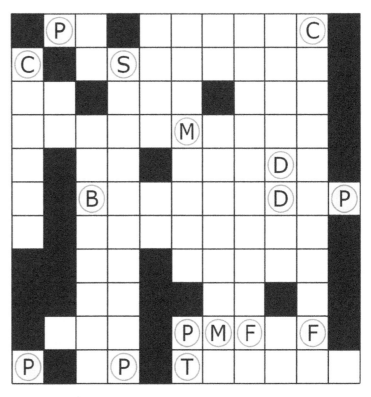

Mystery Picture Graph

Instructions: Find the mystery picture below by plotting and connecting the points of each line on the coordinate graph. Connect all the points in Line 1, stop, pick up your pencil, and then connect all the points in Line 2, and so on for the rest of the lines. The dot for the first (X,Y) coordinate pair on Line 1 has been placed for you.

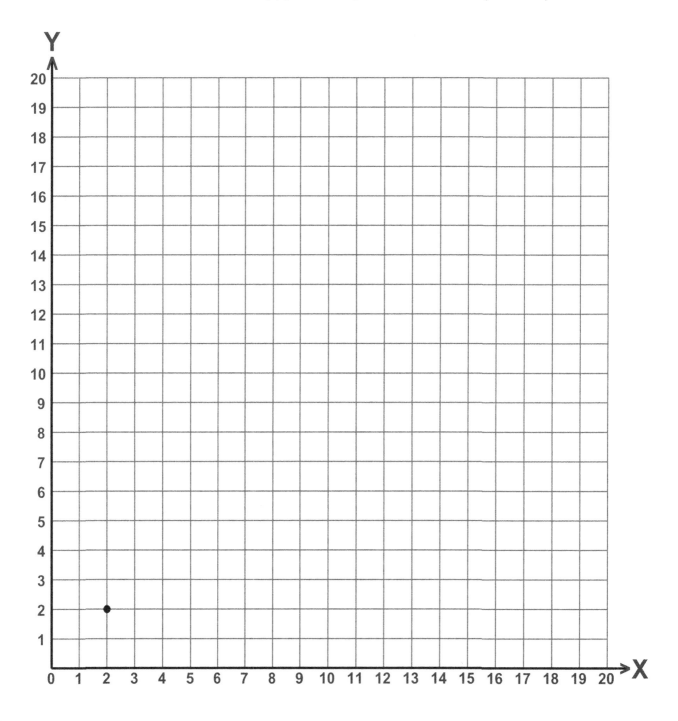

Line 1	(2, 2)	(3, 1)	(12, 1)	(14, 2)	(14, 4)	(8, 9)	(11, 11)	(14, 8)	(17, 11)	(17, 12)	(16, 13)	(15, 13)
(14, 12)	(10, 15)	(3, 9)	(6, 5)	(5, 4)	(3, 4)	(2, 3)	(2, 2)	**Line 2**	(11, 15)	(10, 16)	(10, 18)	(11, 19)
(13, 19)	(14, 18)	(14, 16)	(13, 15)	(11, 15)	**Line 3**	(16, 13)	(17, 14)	(18, 14)	(18, 13)	(17, 12)		

Enos–Words of Mormon

"He Worketh in Me to Do According to His Will"

Wacky Word Trails

Instructions: Start with the circled letter, use the clues to find and mark the trail of letters of all the connected bolded words from the scripture through the maze to the last letter. The path can wander up, down, left, and right at any point, even in the middle of the word.

Enos 1:4

And my soul **hungered**; and I **kneeled** down before my **Maker**, and I **cried** unto him in **mighty prayer** and **supplication** for mine own **soul**; and all the **day long** did I cry unto him; yea, and when the **night** came I did still **raise** my **voice high** that it reached the **heavens**.

```
N  Z  T  S  B  V  E  J  K  F  W  Q  D  S  P
C  L  E  P  B  G  Z  X  Z  A  F  J  D  J  Q
L  O  S  O  S  H  I  S  N  R  B  C  E  C  J
Y  N  I  A  R  T  H  G  I  E  U  R  A  M  D
K  G  H  V  O  I  C  E  D  K  J  G  R  R  D
N  I  G  X  I  V  A  D  M  A  N  U  G  O  Z
E  H  D  O  N  S  Y  H  D  J  G  H  X  L  N
E  L  E  X  E  V  A  E  E  R  E  D  W  M  P
H  K  Q  M  X  N  S  I  E  G  I  E  Y  O  B
G  T  C  Z  T  L  V  Y  M  M  R  C  N  G  I
C  Q  T  L  M  G  T  E  Z  O  E  R  T  H (M)
V  Y  Q  E  U  Q  E  Z  Q  Z  Y  A  Y  S  U
P  L  M  C  E  J  O  E  L  R  P  R  L  P  P
Q  V  Y  C  K  H  T  H  W  U  L  Y  I  C  A
N  T  O  N  L  U  M  V  Z  O  S  N  O  I  T
```

Knight Moves - Find a Word

Instructions: Start with the capital letter in the puzzle. To get to the next letter, jump two squares in any direction except diagonally, and then one square in a different direction. Your path will look like a capital L. To show you how it works, Only one route through the puzzle will make a word. Write the letters of the word you discover in the blanks below as you jump through the squares:

__ __ __ __ __ __ __ __
1 2 3 4 5 6 7 8

Now can you find this word in the following scripture?

Enos 1:6, 9, 11

U	h	e
k		n
s	n	a

Enos–Words of Mormon

"He Worketh in Me to Do According to His Will"

Handwriting Practice

Practice your handwriting by tracing the sentence below. Then use the blank lines to write the sentence on your own.

Heavenly Father hears and answers my sincere prayers.

ENOS, I DON'T GET HOW YOU CAN SAY YOUR TRIP WAS PRODUCTIVE WHEN YOU HUNTED PREY ALL DAY AND NIGHT BUT BROUGHT BACK NOTHING.

NO, NO. I HUNTED *AND* PRAYED ALL DAY AND NIGHT.

mormoncartoonist.com

Enos–Words of Mormon

"He Worketh in Me to Do According to His Will"

Heavenly Father hears and answers my prayers.

Come, Follow Me Manual, 2024

Start

End

Enos–Words of Mormon

"He Worketh in Me to Do According to His Will"

By Arie Van De Graaff

Can you find 9 differences between the two pictures of Enos praying?

Word Square

Instructions: Word squares are a liike Sudoku puzzles, but each letter can occur only once in each row and in each column. Check your puzzle against the answer key on ColorMeChristian.org. Every row and column must contain every letter in the word **KNOWETH.** This word can be written in the gray row.

Words of Mormon 1:7

And I do this for a wise purpose; for thus it whispereth me, according to the workings of the Spirit of the Lord which is in me. And now, I do not know all things; but the Lord **knoweth** all things which are to come; wherefore, he worketh in me to do according to his will.

			O	H		
E			K		W	T
W	O	E	T	K	H	N
T	E		H			O
H		W	N			
	T		E		K	

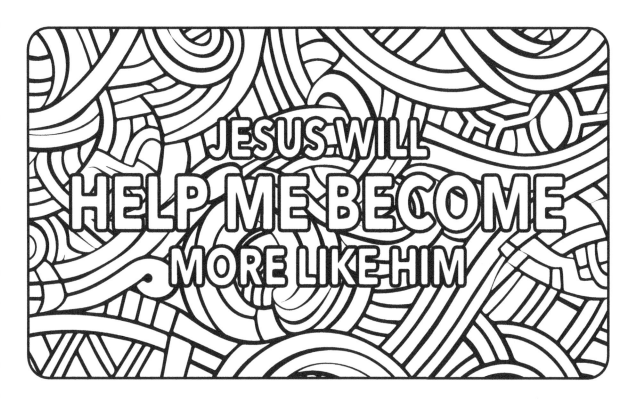

Mosiah 1–3

"Filled with Love towards God and All Men"

Missing Vowels Word Search

Instructions: Find the hidden words. The words have been placed horizontally, vertically, diagonally, forwards, or backwards, and the vowels have been removed. When you locate a word, draw an ellipse around it and fill the vowels in.

Mosiah 3:5

For behold, the **time cometh**, and is not far distant, that with **power**, the Lord **Omnipotent** who **reigneth**, who was, and is from all **eternity** to all eternity, shall come down from **heaven** among the **children** of men, and shall dwell in a **tabernacle** of **clay**, and shall go forth amongst men, working **mighty miracles**, such as **healing** the **sick**, **raising** the **dead**, causing the **lame** to **walk**, the **blind** to receive their **sight**, and the **deaf** to **hear**, and **curing** all manner of **diseases**.

```
H       V     N     W  S  D  D     Y  F
  Y  Q  B  H  B     M  N     L  V  M  C  S
F  R        H  Y  M     C  C  G  Q  N  H  X
  X        Q     T     K  H  Y           P
  Y  S  L  G  D  L  X  S  T  D     P  L  D
D  T  C  B  L     N  D     S     Z     D  K
S     G  H  T  K     M  L  Z     Z  T  R  S
D  N  N  K  H  Y     C  C  M  D  C
  R     Z  L  C  G              N  N  J
S     L  W     L  K  R  R     R  G  T  C  D
  T     W  N  D  Z        P     R  H  M
     N  X     L  N  M  L  H  H  H  T  Q
S  F  H  N  R        G  N     T  H  X  B  Y
  L  C     N  R     B     T  N  V  Y     L
S  X  G  N     S        R  R     W     P  V
```

Word Star

Instructions: Start with the capital letter in the puzzle. Then choose one of the two lines to the next letter. Only one route through the word star will make a word. Write the letters of the word you discover in the blanks below as you travel through the star:

_ _ _ _ _ _ _

Now can you find this word in the following scripture?

Mosiah 2:21

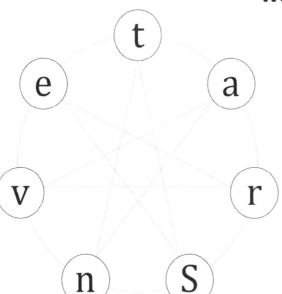

Serving Others, Serving God

When I serve others, I am serving God. Can you help the children find someone to serve at the end of the maze?

Mosiah 1–3

"Filled with Love towards God and All Men"

By Ari Van De Graaff

Find the hidden objects in the picture of King Benjamin teaching the people!

Cryptogram

Instructions: Each letter on the top stands for a letter in the alphabet. Solve the encrypted phrase by matching each letter on top to a letter in the alphabet on the bottom. Use the key to help you remember what the letters stand for so you can crack the code.

Y	X	W	G	U	L	R	N	V	I	P	Z	C	A	B	K	Q	D	E	F	O	T	H	M	J	S
A	B	C	D	E	F	G	H	I	J	K	L	M	N	O	P	Q	R	S	T	U	V	W	X	Y	Z

O S W U F R ,   A S   W N I S   M N F F S R   X S   A U E G

P J H D ;   N H R   J T   J ,   C W U X   A S   M N F F   A U E G

P J H D ,   R U   F N O U G   V U   Z S G I S   A U E ,   V W S H

U E D W V   H U V   A S   V U   F N O U G   V U   Z S G I S

U H S   N H U V W S G ?   X U Z J N W   2 : 1 8

Mosiah 1–3

"Filled with Love towards God and All Men"

Instructions: Solve this word sudoku puzzle the same way that you'd solve a numeric sudoku. Each of the bold words in the scripture below is found once in every row, column and 3×3 box.

Mosiah 3:19

For the **natural** man is an **enemy** to God, and has been from the fall of Adam, and will be, forever and ever, unless he yields to the enticings of the Holy Spirit, and putteth off the natural **man** and becometh a saint through the atonement of Christ the Lord, and becometh as a child, **submissive**, **meek**, **humble**, **patient**, full of **love**, willing to **submit** to all things which the Lord seeth fit to inflict upon him, even as a child doth submit to his father.

submit		enemy		meek			love	
love	submissive	humble			natural		meek	
	meek		man	love	humble			
	love		natural			submissive		meek
natural		submit	humble			love		
meek	enemy			patient		humble		
		meek	submit				enemy	patient
man	natural			humble			submissive	
	submit		submissive	man				natural

Mosiah 1–3

"Filled with Love towards God and All Men"

Fallen Phrase

Instructions: The letters in each column have fallen from the grid. Put them back correctly to rebuild the phrase. Cross out each letter in the jumble below once you place it in the grid. Pay attention because the letters in each column are scrambled. Start with simple 1 or 2 letter words and use the process of elimination. To check your answer, read **Mosiah 2:17**

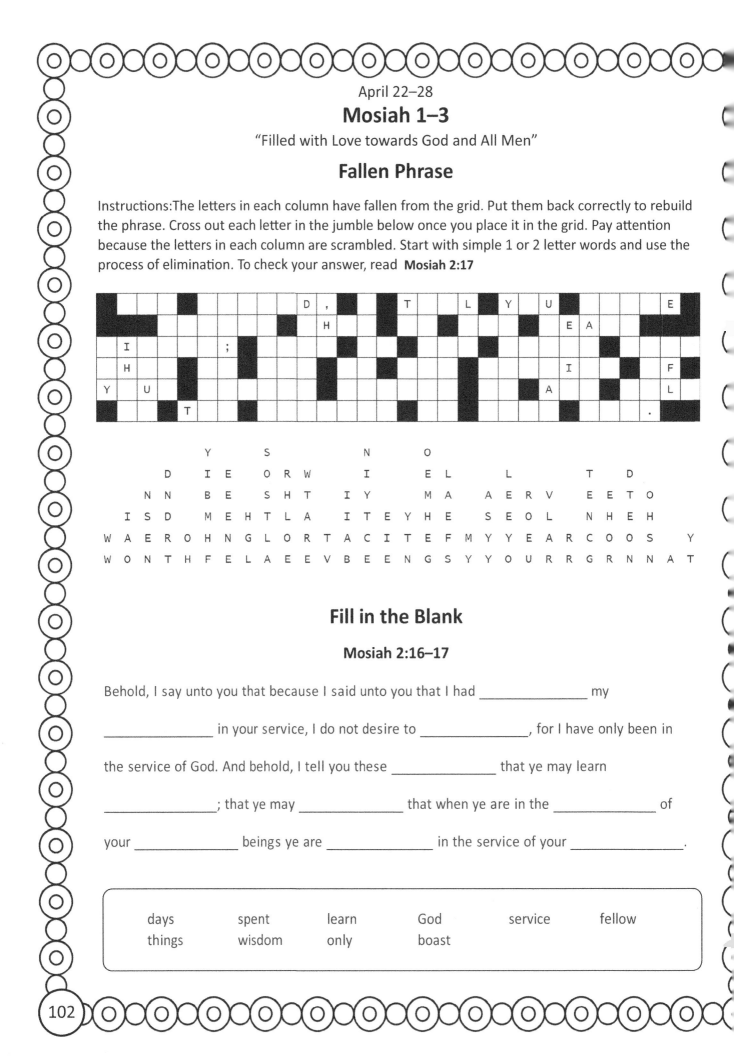

Fill in the Blank

Mosiah 2:16–17

Behold, I say unto you that because I said unto you that I had _____ my

_____ in your service, I do not desire to _____, for I have only been in

the service of God. And behold, I tell you these _____ that ye may learn

_____; that ye may _____ that when ye are in the _____ of

your _____ beings ye are _____ in the service of your _____.

days	spent	learn	God	service	fellow
things	wisdom	only	boast		

REPENTANCE BRINGS JOY

Mosiah 4–6

"A Mighty Change"

Word Search

Instructions: Find the bold words from the scripture in the word search puzzle. Each word could be hidden forwards, backwards, up, down, or diagonally.

Mosiah 4:16

I say unto you, I **would** that ye **should remember** to **retain** the **name written always** in your **hearts**, that ye are not **found** on the **left hand** of **God**, but that ye **hear** and **know** the **voice** by which ye **shall** be **called**, and also, the name by which he shall call **you**.

E	N	E	B	W	A	F	N	E	T	T	I	R	W	K
N	I	A	T	E	R	O	L	T	N	U	W	H	Z	P
P	E	S	M	D	R	U	E	T	R	O	S	C	D	M
Z	D	F	A	V	U	N	F	O	E	G	Y	M	T	W
K	K	N	H	T	C	D	T	W	M	H	B	Y	L	K
Q	L	N	A	D	V	V	L	G	E	Q	E	U	V	B
Y	K	B	F	H	T	S	V	S	M	Z	O	A	I	A
A	C	W	I	H	C	Y	O	W	B	Y	X	K	R	R
S	R	D	R	B	G	A	I	I	E	T	M	N	R	Y
H	N	T	V	R	O	W	C	V	R	X	U	O	M	S
S	E	A	Z	F	D	L	E	O	I	D	B	W	H	Q
K	H	A	M	J	N	A	P	E	V	T	Y	O	N	P
Y	D	A	R	E	D	L	U	O	W	X	U	G	J	S
L	G	B	L	T	B	P	D	E	L	L	A	C	F	J
G	Y	N	V	L	S	C	Q	I	D	I	O	Q	N	H

Word Bricks

Instructions: A sentence is written on the wall. But brick layers built the wall in the wrong order. Your job is to put the bricks in the right order. Hint: **Mosiah 4:3**

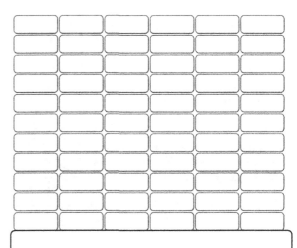

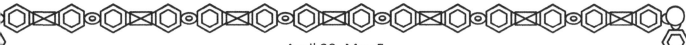

Mosiah 4–6

"A Mighty Change"

Instructions: Using the Across and Down clues, write the correct words in the numbered grid below. Hint: all of the words in the crossword come from the scripture below.

Mosiah 4:13–16, 26

ACROSS

5. a personal foe
6. completely unclothed
9. devote one's life or efforts to, as of countries or ideas
10. a strong positive emotion of regard and affection
13. affected by impairment of normal physical or mental function
15. an abatement in intensity or degree
16. to furnish; provide
18. an angry dispute
19. feeling a need or desire to eat food

DOWN

1. act in disregard of laws, rules, contracts, or promises
2. quiet or sedate in demeanor
3. cause harm to
4. "food, clothing, shelter in this case"
7. the act of reducing something unpleasant
8. that which is deserved or owed
9. assistance in time of difficulty
11. an impoverished person who lives by asking for charity
12. be engaged in a contest or struggle
14. a factual statement
17. ineffectual or unsuccessful; futile

Mosiah 4–6

"A Mighty Change"

Handwriting Practice

Practice your handwriting by tracing the sentence below. Then use the blank lines to write the sentence on your own.

The gospel of Christ inspires me to treat others with love and kindness.

Translation Station

Instructions: Translate the sign language letters below into English to discover the hidden message. Write the alphabet letter beneath each hand sign. Use the key at the back of the book to help you.

The gospel of Jesus Christ inspires me to treat others with **love** and kindness.

Come, Follow Me Manual, 2024

Start

End →

Mosiah 4–6

"A Mighty Change"

Letter Sudoku

Instructions: Solve the letter sudoku puzzle the same way you'd solve a numeric sudoku. Check your puzzle against the answer key on ColorMeChristian.org. Every column, row, and group of nine must contain every letter in the worda **WOULD GIVE.** Letters are used only once;

Mosiah 4:24

And again, I say unto the poor, ye who have not and yet have sufficient, that ye remain from day to day; I mean all you who deny the beggar, because ye have not; I would that ye say in your hearts that: I give not because I have not, but if I had I **would give**.

	L	I	W		V		G	O
D	G	V		O				L
	D					V	W	
L	I			W				
			E	L				I
O						E	D	
I			G				U	
	U	D	V					

May 6–12

Mosiah 7–10

"In the Strength of the Lord"

Word Angles

Instructions: Find the bold words from the scripture. Each word path may run north, east, south, or west, may make one right-angled turn, and may cross another word path. A few words may make no right angle turn at all.

Mosiah 9:17–18

Yea, in the **strength** of the **Lord** did we go forth to **battle** against the **Lamanites**; for I and my people did cry **mightily** to the Lord that he would **deliver** us out of the **hands** of our **enemies**, for we were **awakened** to a **remembrance** of the **deliverance** of our **fathers**. And God did hear our cries and did **answer** our **prayers**; and we did go **forth** in his might; yea, we did go forth against the Lamanites, and in one day and a night we did slay three thousand and forty-three; we did slay them even until we had **driven** them out of our **land**.

```
C P Y E Z D E L I V E U P K D I
F T K C D Y I I O F R E L R M L
D Y A K R S D N A H A H T N J Y
D Q O N I N S W A I N B T T A A
D L N E V O L Y E M C W A X X E
E D F J R L A A E O E N B A S R
L C A F E O M M I E S F W N P E
I G L I G E A E X L R E W S K Y
V S D R O J N N B G V R M A Z A
E R N I L E I E V G W V T N R R
A L A N D V T E S G A T I W P P
L O X A Y S T R E N G T I X H T
R D M W I S K F O R T H T A F O
E F I A K E N E D E B E W R T Z
P N G H T I L Y M C Q R F L O M
I R E M E M B R A N H S Y Y B A
```

Secret Code

Instructions: The secret message is written in symbols. In the code key you can find what each symbol means. Write the letter above the symbol and you can read the secret message.

a	b	c	d	e	f	g	h	i	j	k	l	m
□	◇	△	◁	⬠	▷	◣	✕	◸	▽	◺	▷	◿

n	o	p	q	r	s	t	u	v	w	x	y	z
◁	▱	▽	▯	○	▭	⊡	⋈	⋃	△	◁	△	⊐

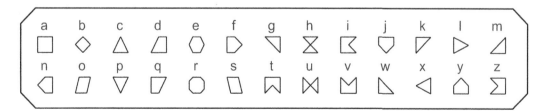

Mosiah 7–10

"In the Strength of the Lord"

Instructions: Connect all of the letters in the phrase bolded below. Don't be tricked by letters that take you into a dead end! There is only one path through the maze.

____ ___ ___ _____ _ _____ ____ ___, _____ _____, _____
____ _____ _____; _____ __ _____ _ _____
_____ __ ___ _____ _____.

Mosiah 8:18

Finish

Start

Mosiah 7–10

"In the Strength of the Lord"

Handwriting Practice

Practice your handwriting by tracing the sentence below. Then use the blank lines to write the sentence on your own.

When I am weak, the Lord can strengthen me.

JUST ANOTHER DAY AT THE PRESCHOOL OF THE PROPHETS.

Mosiah 7–10

"In the Strength of the Lord"

Instructions: Fit the bold words from the scripture below into the encircled squares. Words will read forward, backward, up, down, and diagonally and will normally cross other words. Start with the hints provided.

Mosiah 7:19

Therefore, **lift** up your **heads**, and **rejoice**, and put your **trust** in **God**, in that God who was the God of **Abraham**, and **Isaac**, and **Jacob**; and also, that God who brought the children of **Israel** out of the land of **Egypt**, and caused that they should **walk** through the **Red Sea** on **dry ground**, and fed them with **manna** that they might not **perish** in the **wilderness**; and **many** more **things** did he do for them.

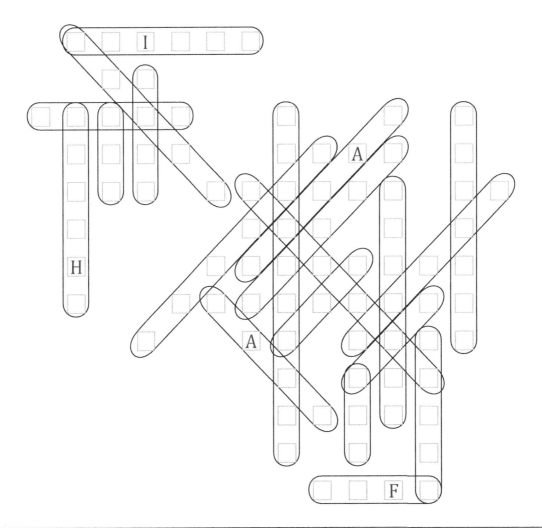

lift	heads	rejoice	trust	God	Abraham
Isaac	Jacob	Israel	Egypt	walk	Red
Sea	dry	ground	manna	perish	wilderness
many	things				

Hidden Picture: When I am weak, the Lord can strengthen me, like he did King Zeniff and his people when the went to battle against the Lamanites. Can you find 6 pictures of the soldier in the hidden picture below? It will be tricky; the picture may be smaller, on its side, or even upside down! Then, see if you can find one image of the animals as well.

Mosiah 7–10

"In the Strength of the Lord"

Unscrambler

Instructions: Unscramble the words below; look at the bold words in the scripture for a hint.

Mosiah 10:10–11

And it came to pass that we did go up to **battle** against the **Lamanites**; and I, even I, in my **old** age, did go up to battle against the Lamanites. And it came to **pass** that we did go up in the **strength** of the **Lord** to battle. Now, the Lamanites knew **nothing concerning** the Lord, nor the strength of the Lord, therefore they **depended** upon their own strength. Yet they were a **strong people**, as to the strength of **men**.

dedneped _____	elttab _____
ssap _____	drol _____
dlo _____	gninrecnoc _____
elpoep _____	setinamal _____
gnihton _____	nem _____
gnorts _____	htgnerts _____

Word Square

Instructions: Word squares are a liike Sudoku puzzles, but each letter can occur only once in each row and in each column. Check your puzzle against the answer key on ColorMeChristian.org. Every row and column must contain every letter in the word **MANIFEST.** This word can be written in the gray row.

Mosiah 8:17

But a seer can know of things which are past, and also of things which are to come, and by them shall all things be revealed, or, rather, shall secret things be made **manifest**, and hidden things shall come to light, and things which are not known shall be made known by them, and also things shall be made known by them which otherwise could not be known.

	I			S			
E			A		T		
A	F		T	M		S	
	T	E	M	S	A		N
I		T	S			F	
S		A	F		T		E
	S		A	N		E	I

May 13–19

Mosiah 11–17

"A Light … That Can Never Be Darkened"

Wacky Word Trails

Instructions: Start with the circled letter, use the clues to find and mark the trail of letters of all the connected bolded words from the scripture through the maze to the last letter. The path can wander up, down, left, and right at any point, even in the middle of the word.

Mosiah 17:9–10

Now **Abinadi** said unto him: I say unto you, I will **not recall** the **words** which I have **spoken** unto you concerning this **people**, for they are **true**; and that ye may know of their **surety** I have suffered myself that I have **fallen** into your **hands**. Yea, and I will **suffer** even until death, and I will not recall my words, and they shall **stand** as a **testimony** against **you**. And if ye **slay** me ye will **shed innocent blood**, and this shall also stand as a testimony **against** you at the **last day**.

```
C  Z  U  V  I  S  P  T  W  Z  Y  Z  Y  K  O
X  I  D  S  D  S  O  Y  J  L  W  A  Z  C  H
E  D  A  B  A  E  K  E  X  B  Y  W  G  M  S
H  S  Y  I  N  N  S  E  D  S  L  J  A  I  U
L  L  A  I  N  S  U  U  P  U  D  S  A  Z  Z
A  C  G  V  U  T  R  A  H  A  N  P  V  I  S
R  E  A  T  X  T  E  T  Y  C  O  E  A  S  N
T  C  O  O (N) E  P  Z  Y  L  P  Z  C  S  Y
N  E  N  F  F  S  T  A  Y  E  V  Z  D  A  A
E  N  N  E  U  S  I  D  Y  L  A  S  H  P  J
L  S  I  R  D  S  M  O  A  L  S  T  B  G  K
L  T  H  H  F  D  Y  N  X  G  E  W  K  E  A
A  A  A  O  U  R  B  C  C  Z  X  T  A  J  V
F  N  D  Y  W  O  L  R  W  W  E  Z  W  V  T
E  U  R  T  D  O  O  T  F  Y  P  W  V  Q  K
```

Mystery Picture Graph

Instructions: Find the mystery picture below by plotting and connecting the points of each line on the coordinate graph. Connect all the points in Line 1, stop, pick up your pencil, and then connect all the points in Line 2, and so on for the rest of the lines. The dot for the first (X,Y) coordinate pair on Line 1 has been placed for you.

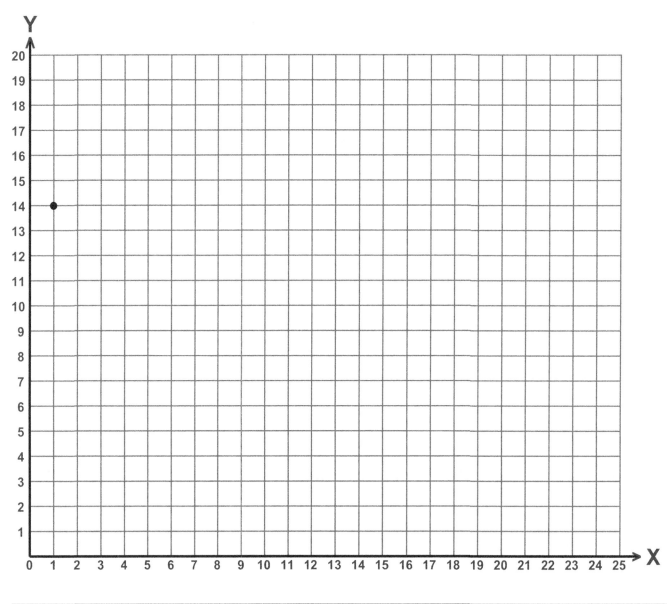

Line 1	(1, 14)	(2, 12)	(4, 12)	(5, 10)	(4, 9)	(4, 7)	(5, 6)	(5, 4)	(6, 4)	(6, 3)	(8, 3)	(9, 2)
(10, 2)	(11, 3)	(12, 2)	(13, 2)	(14, 3)	(16, 3)	(16, 4)	(17, 4)	(17, 6)	(18, 7)	(18, 9)	(17, 10)	(18, 12)
(20, 12)	(21, 14)	(17, 14)	(17, 16)	(16, 17)	(15, 17)	(14, 18)	(12, 18)	(11, 17)	(10, 18)	(8, 18)	(7, 17)	(6, 17)
(5, 16)	(5, 14)	(1, 14)	**Line 2**	(10, 6)	(11, 5)	(12, 6)	**Line 3**	(11, 5)	(11, 7)	(12, 8)	**Line 4**	(11, 7)
(10, 8)	(12, 8)	**Line 5**	(8, 12)	(8, 11)	(9, 11)	(9, 12)	(8, 12)	**Line 6**	(13, 12)	(13, 11)	(14, 11)	(14, 12)
(13, 12)	**Line 7**	(7, 13)	(7, 9)	(8, 7)	(9, 4)	(13, 4)	(14, 7)	(15, 9)	(15, 13)	(14, 14)	(13, 14)	(12, 15)
(11, 14)	(10, 15)	(9, 14)	(8, 14)	(7, 13)	**Line 8**	(8, 3)	(7, 0)	**Line 9**	(14, 3)	(15, 0)		

Mosiah 11–17

"A Light ... That Can Never Be Darkened"

Instructions: Fill in the blank puzzle grid using the word bank with the bold words from the scripture below. Place the words in the correct place on the grid.

Mosiah 16:7–9

And now if Christ had not come into the **world**, **speaking** of **things** to come as **though** they had already **come**, there could have been no **redemption**. And if Christ had not risen from the dead, or have **broken** the **bands** of **death** that the grave should have no victory, and that death should have no sting, there could have been no resurrection. But there is a **resurrection**, therefore the **grave** hath no **victory**, and the **sting** of **death** is **swallowed** up in **Christ**. He is the **light** and the **life** of the **world**; yea, a light that is **endless**, that can **never** be **darkened**; yea, and also a life which is endless, that there can be no more death.

4 Letters	light	broken	8 Letters	10 Letters
life	bands	though	speaking	redemption
come	world		darkened	
	death	7 Letters		12 Letters
5 Letters		endless	9 Letters	resurrection
never	6 Letters	victory	swallowed	
grave	things			
sting	Christ			

Messenger From The Lord

Help Abinidi reach King Noah so he can give the king his message from the Lord.

KING ZEDEKIAH

Mosiah 11–17

"A Light … That Can Never Be Darkened"

Instructions: Solve this word sudoku puzzle the same way that you'd solve a numeric sudoku. Each of the bold words in the scripture below is found once in every row, column and 3×3 box.

Mosiah 14:6

All we, like **sheep**, have **gone astray**; we have **turned every** one to his own **way**; and the **Lord** hath **laid** on him the **iniquities** of **us** all.

	astray		Lord				sheep	
		way	laid		astray			gone
gone							laid	astray
	turned	gone			every	astray		
	iniquities				laid		turned	every
sheep	every	Lord						iniquities
turned			way				Lord	sheep
Lord	way						astray	laid
		sheep			Lord	way		turned

Mosiah 11–17

"A Light … That Can Never Be Darkened"

Fill in the Blank

Mosiah 13:11

And now I _____ unto you the _____ of the _____ of

_____, for I _____ that they are not _____ in your

_____; I perceive that ye have _____ and taught _____ the most

part of your _____.

| commandments | written | perceive | studied | remainder | read |
| hearts | iniquity | God | lives | | |

Mosiah 18–24

We Have Entered into a Covenant with Him

Missing Vowels Word Search

Instructions: Find the hidden words. The words have been placed horizontally, vertically, diagonally, forwards, or backwards, and the vowels have been removed. When you locate a word, draw an ellipse around it and fill the vowels in.

Mosiah 24:13-14

And it came to pass that the voice of the Lord came to them in their **afflictions**, saying: **Lift** up your **heads** and be of good **comfort**, for I know of the **covenant** which ye have made unto me; and I will covenant with my people and **deliver** them out of **bondage**. And I will also **ease** the **burdens** which are put upon your **shoulders**, that even you cannot feel them upon your **backs**, even while you are in **bondage**; and this will I do that ye may stand as **witnesses** for me hereafter, and that ye may know of a **surety** that I, the Lord God, do **visit** my **people** in their afflictions.

```
H   F P K   W H D B V K     L S
H N B   F F L   C T     N S R
  T X M S J L T H T T B   N
  S       L D R Z G R N S D
D K Y Y   H M R       B H   L
S P     P L   P H T F X L
W Q Y W Q W S W Y M V M C
B   N D   G   M B W   C     H
S S   L W H S   P D D P V C S
K N G   P Z S B V   J     Y
C   F   Q     C L H J N   R
  D D T B   N B L     Z   Z P
B R N S B F T F S V Z W N W
G     Y V   V M   W N T R
W B B S T S W S G R V   S   T
```

Word Star

Instructions: Start with the capital letter in the puzzle. Then choose one of the two lines to the next letter. Only one route through the word star will make a word. Write the letters of the word you discover in the blanks below as you travel through the star:

u h r

y t

i A

o t

＿ ＿ ＿ ＿ ＿ ＿ ＿ ＿

Now can you find this word in the following scripture?

Mosiah 18:17

Mosiah 18–24

We Have Entered into a Covenant with Him

Handwriting Practice

Practice your handwriting by tracing the sentence below. Then use the blank lines to write the sentence on your own.

God can make my burdens light.

WHY DO I NEED A BATH TONIGHT? AT MY BAPTISM EARLIER TODAY, YOU SAID I HAVE NEVER BEEN MORE CLEAN.

mormoncartoonist.com

© Arie Van De Graaff

Mosiah 18–24

We Have Entered into a Covenant with Him

Instructions: Using the Across and Down clues, write the correct words in the numbered grid below. Hint: all of the words in the crossword come from the scripture below.

Mosiah 24:8–17

ACROSS

5. an agreement between God and his people
6. the state of being under the control of another person
8. a cause of great suffering and distress
10. weight to be carried or borne
16. cause to suffer
17. any piece of work that is undertaken or attempted
18. the act of going to see some person or place or thing for a short time
19. a state of being relaxed and feeling no pain
20. vehemently angry, incensed and condemnatory

DOWN

1. not as heavy as before
2. the posterior part of a human (or animal) body
3. watch over or shield from danger or harm
4. to issue, move, or proceed in great quantity or number
7. freedom from difficulty or hardship or effort
9. pleasantly optimistic and happy
11. the power or right to give orders or make decisions
12. good-natured tolerance of delay
13. bring to a destination
14. watch over or shield from danger or harm
15. bring to a destination

May 20–26

Mosiah 18–24

We Have Entered into a Covenant with Him

When I am baptized, I become a **member** of the Church of Jesus Christ.

Come, Follow Me Manual, 2024

Start →

End →

Mosiah 18–24

We Have Entered into a Covenant with Him

Translation Station

Instructions: Translate the Morse code below into English to discover the hidden message. Write the alphabet letter beneath each Morse Code letter. Each letter, number, and punctuation is separated by a slash: /. Use the key at the back of the book to help you.

·-/-·/-··/ ····/·/ -··-/---/--/--/·-/-·/-··/·/-··/

-/····/·/--/ -/····/·-/-/ -/····/·/-·--/

···/····/---/··-/·-··/-··/ ---/····/···/·/·-·/···-/·/ -/····/·/

···/·-/--·/·-/·-·/-/····/ -·/·-/--·/--·/--- ·-/-·/-··/

-··/·/·/·--/ ··/-/ ····/---/·-··/--·/--- ·-/-·/-··/

·-/·-··/···/---/ ·/····-/·/··-/·-··/-··/ -···/·-/-·--/

-/····/·/--·/ ···/····/---/··-/·-··/-··/ --·/··/···-/·/

-/····/·-/-/·--/···/ -/---/ -/····/·/ ·-·/---/·-·/-··/

-/····/·/··/·-·/ --·/---/-··/·-·-·- --/---/···/··/·-/····/

·----/-----/---··/ : ·----/·····-/

Letter Sudoku

Instructions: Solve the letter sudoku puzzle the same way you'd solve a numeric sudoku. Check your puzzle against the answer key on ColorMeChristian.org. Every column, row, and group of nine must contain every letter in the worda **MOURN WITH.** Letters are used only once;

Mosiah 18:9

Yea, and are willing to **mourn with** those that mourn; yea, and comfort those that stand in need of comfort, and to stand as witnesses of God at all times and in all things, and in all places that ye may be in, even until death, that ye may be redeemed of God, and be numbered with those of the first resurrection, that ye may have eternal life

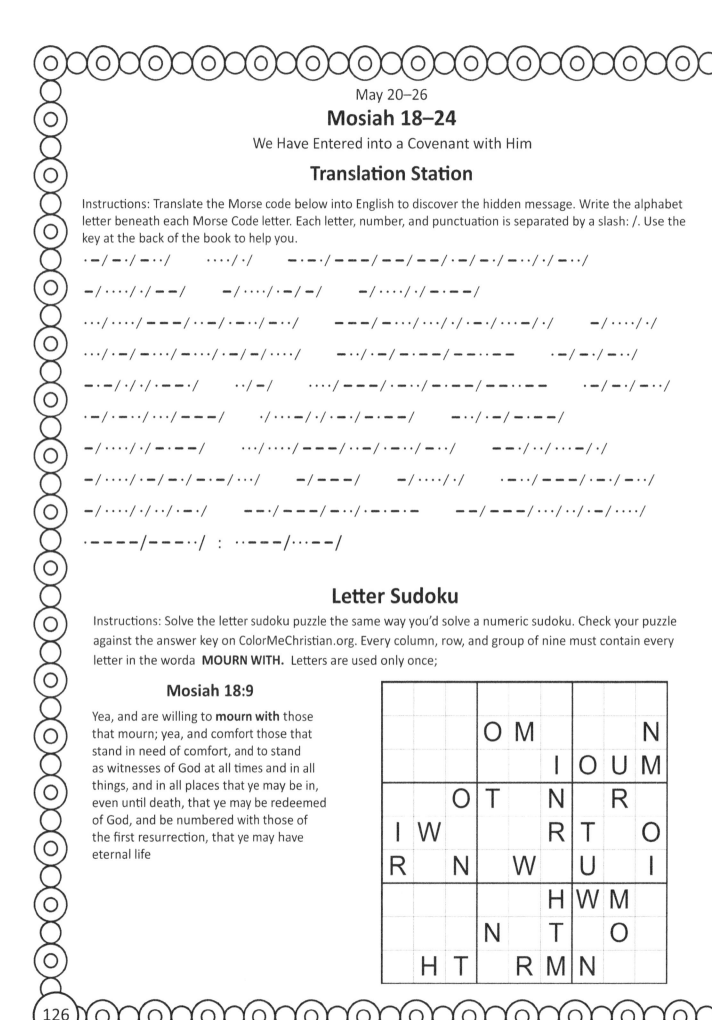

Mosiah 25–28

"They Were Called the People of God"

Reverse Word Search

Instructions: Instead of looking for words in a grid, place the bold words in the scripture in the empty word search puzzle. The words may be forwards, backwards, up, down, or diagonally The start letter of the words have been placed in the grid to get you started.

Mosiah 27:14

And again, the **angel** said: **Behold**, the Lord hath **heard** the **prayers** of his **people**, and also the prayers of his **servant**, **Alma**, who is thy **father**; for he has prayed with much **faith** concerning thee that thou mightest be **brought** to the **knowledge** of the **truth**; therefore, for this **purpose** have I **come** to **convince** thee of the **power** and **authority** of **God**, that the prayers of his **servants** might be **answered** according to their faith.

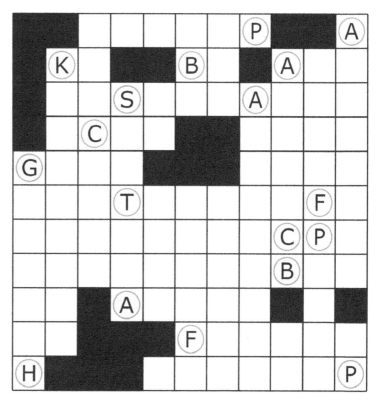

Hidden Picture: The conversion of Alma the Younger and the sons of Mosiah shows that, with the Savior's power, anyone can change. Can you find 6 pictures of Alma in the hidden picture below? It will be tricky; the picture may be smaller, on its side, or even upside down! Then, see if you can find 1 image of the animals as well.

Handwriting Practice

Practice your handwriting by tracing the sentence below. Then use the blank lines to write the sentence on your own.

I can pray and fast for God to bless those I love.

COMPARING THE COST OF COLLEGE TUITION AND A MISSION, I NOW UNDERSTAND WHY KING MOSIAH SENT HIS FOUR SONS ON A 14-YEAR MISSION.

wardcartoonist.com

©Arie Van De Graaff

Mosiah 25–28

"They Were Called the People of God"

Word Angles

Instructions: Find the bold words from the scripture. Each word path may run north, east, south, or west, may make one right-angled turn, and may cross another word path. A few words may make no right angle turn at all.

Mosiah 26:29–31

Therefore I say unto you, Go; and whosoever **transgresseth** against me, him shall ye **judge** according to the **sins** which he has **committed**; and if he **confess** his sins before thee and me, and **repenteth** in the **sincerity** of his **heart**, him shall ye **forgive**, and I will forgive him also. Yea, and as **often** as my **people repent** will I forgive them their **trespasses** against me. And ye shall also forgive one **another** your trespasses; for verily I say unto you, he that forgiveth not his **neighbor**'s trespasses when he **says** that he repents, the **same** hath brought **himself** under **condemnation**.

```
G H A X K T H E R N E M K Z J N
G I H M C O S N A R T A E H F O
P M C B H N G A S S E S A S T I
B S E L F A R P L Z Z W R S E T
Z F N D L N E S P O E P T H N A
C E P G K T S E L C L G Q F A N
H R E P E N S R E U X N L D B M
F O R G I V E T N B U C O N D E
E S A Y S E T U A H X N U F G X
W F E S S Y H D S T Z J Y L J S
Z N W L K F Y E R E T N E P E R
C O V L U J C T I R E C N I S S
X C M N X K O T T E G D U J I A
W S H G Z T J I Y C N P U N E M
P I A U C O M M I O E E I U O C
F N S L Y T M N T A I G H B O R
```

Knight Moves - Find a Word

Instructions: Start with the capital letter in the puzzle. To get to the next letter, jump two squares in any direction except diagonally, and then one square in a different direction. Your path will look like a capital L. To show you how it works, Only one route through the puzzle will make a word. Write the letters of the word you discover in the blanks below as you jump through the squares:

$\underline{}\ \underline{}\ \underline{}\ \underline{}\ \underline{}\ \underline{}\ \underline{}\ \underline{}$
1 2 3 4 5 6 7 8

Now can you find this word in the following scripture?

Mosiah 27:24

e	n	d
e		p
e	R	t

Mosiah 25–28

"They Were Called the People of God"

Instructions: Connect all of the letters in the phrase bolded below. Don't be tricked by letters that take you into a dead end! There is only one path through the maze.

___ _____, ____ __ __ _____; _____ __ _____ _____ __
_____ ____ _____. ___ _____ __ _____ _____
_____ __ __ ____; ___ ___ ____ _ _____ _____.

Mosiah 26:22

Finish

Start

Mosiah 25–28

"They Were Called the People of God"

Cryptogram

Instructions: Each letter on the top stands for a letter in the alphabet. Solve the encrypted phrase by matching each letter on top to a letter in the alphabet on the bottom. Use the key to help you remember what the letters stand for so you can crack the code.

K	Y	D	B	X	I	A	O	F	M	E	L	T	H	Q	Z	S	U	J	G	R	V	P	C	W	N
A	B	C	D	E	F	G	H	I	J	K	L	M	N	O	P	Q	R	S	T	U	V	W	X	Y	Z

I H U , Q G F C N K , F N G V K U K W K Z M K C H I

J B Q F Z Q , G Z C N G V K D K K Z U K C K K J K C

H I M N K L H U C ; D K N H L C F G J D H U Z H I

M N K Q W F U F M . J H Q F G N 2 7 : 2 4

Word Square

Instructions: Word squares are a liike Sudoku puzzles, but each letter can occur only once in each row and in each column. Check your puzzle against the answer key on ColorMeChristian.org. Every row and column must contain every letter in the word **SNATCH.** This word can be written in the gray row.

Mosiah 27:28-29

Nevertheless, after wading through much tribulation, repenting nigh unto death, the Lord in mercy hath seen fit to **snatch** me out of an everlasting burning, and I am born of God.

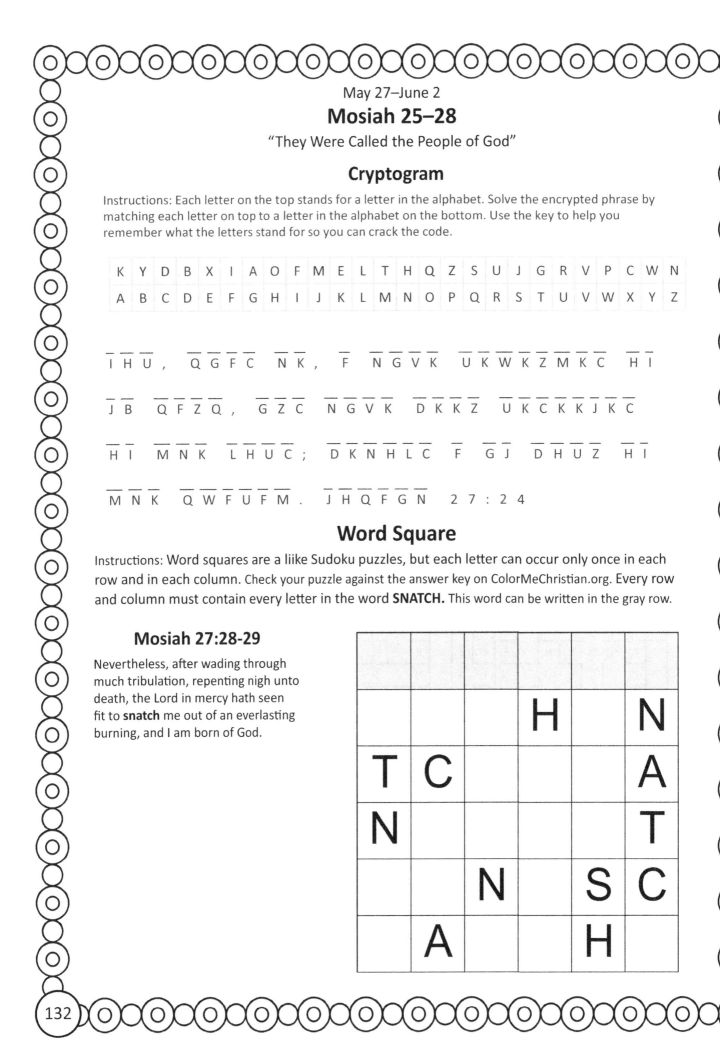

Testimony

Help the children through the maze to reach the things and people to base their testimony on.

June 3–9
Mosiah 29–Alma 4
"They Were Steadfast and Immovable"

Word Search

Instructions: Find the bold words from the scripture in the word search puzzle. Each word could be hidden forwards, backwards, up, down, or diagonally.

Alma 1:2–4

And it came to pass that in the first year of the reign of Alma in the judgment-seat, there was a man brought before him to be **judged**, a man who was large, and was **noted** for his much **strength**. And he had gone about among the people, **preaching** to them that which he **termed** to be the word of God, bearing down **against** the **church**; declaring unto the people that every priest and teacher ought to become **popular**; and they ought not to **labor** with their hands, but that they ought to be **supported** by the people. And he also testified unto the people that all **mankind** should be saved at the last day, and that they need not fear nor tremble, but that they might lift up their heads and rejoice; for the Lord had **created** all men, and had also **redeemed** all men; and, in the end, all men should have **eternal life**.

```
G E S P I P L E T E R N A L Z
D N Y W C R E A T E D P X A L
E C I S P W F T N M Z J L R A
B W W H U R X Y W R V G P O U
M M N A C P G R E D E E M E D
Y O F J G A P O P U L A R T M
S J U E L A E O P W R S F W D
T Y K I X H I R R O B A L E H
R B F E R C Y N P T D U T J V
E E Z I L R G J S B E O Y T L
N X L R H U J U N T N D X T J
G A Z C B H S D M A N K I N D
T Q J P F C L G B G Q C P K Q
H J M T I V T E Z T Z M T Q X
O H Y O D U H D E M R E T U H
```

Translation Station

Instructions: Translate the sign language letters below into English to discover the hidden message. Write the alphabet letter beneath each hand sign. Use the key at the back of the book to help you.

Mosiah 29–Alma 4

"They Were Steadfast and Immovable"

Instructions: Solve this word sudoku puzzle the same way that you'd solve a numeric sudoku. Each of the bold words in the scripture below is found once in every row, column and 3×3 box.

Alma 4:19

And this he did that he himself might go forth among his people, or among the people of Nephi, that he might **preach** the **word** of **God** unto them, to stir them up in remembrance of their **duty**, and that he might pull down, by the word of God, all the **pride** and craftiness and all the contentions which were among his people, seeing no way that he might **reclaim** them **save** it were in bearing down in **pure testimony** against them.

				reclaim		pride	pure	
pride				pure	duty			God
			pride	testimony	God			
	testimony		reclaim		pride		word	
		save		God		duty		
	pride	God					save	reclaim
		preach	God					save
word		pure	testimony		save			
	duty	pride		preach				testimony

Mystery Picture Graph

Instructions: Find the mystery picture below by plotting and connecting the points of each line on the coordinate graph. Connect all the points in Line 1, stop, pick up your pencil, and then connect all the points in Line 2, and so on for the rest of the lines. The dot for the first (X,Y) coordinate pair on Line 1 has been placed for you.

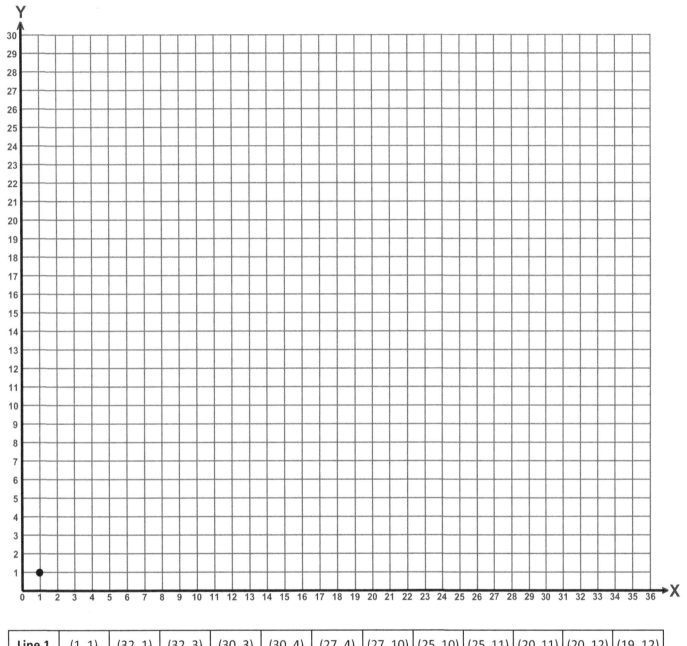

Line 1	(1, 1)	(32, 1)	(32, 3)	(30, 3)	(30, 4)	(27, 4)	(27, 10)	(25, 10)	(25, 11)	(20, 11)	(20, 12)	(19, 12)
(19, 13)	(18, 13)	(18, 18)	(17, 19)	(17, 25)	(16, 25)	(16, 19)	(15, 18)	(15, 13)	(14, 13)	(14, 12)	(13, 12)	(13, 11)
(8, 11)	(8, 10)	(6, 10)	(6, 4)	(3, 4)	(3, 3)	(1, 3)	(1, 1)	**Line 2**	(15, 1)	(15, 4)	(18, 4)	(18, 1)
Line 3	(6, 4)	(27, 4)	**Line 4**	(8, 10)	(25, 10)	**Line 5**	(8, 9)	(8, 7)	(10, 7)	(10, 9)	(8, 9)	**Line 6**
(12, 9)	(12, 7)	(14, 7)	(14, 9)	(12, 9)	**Line 7**	(16, 9)	(16, 7)	(18, 7)	(18, 9)	(16, 9)	**Line 8**	(20, 9)
(20, 7)	(22, 7)	(22, 9)	(20, 9)	**Line 9**	(23, 9)	(23, 7)	(25, 7)	(25, 9)	(23, 9)	**Line 10**	(16, 1)	(16, 3)
(17, 3)	(17, 1)											

137

Mosiah 29–Alma 4

"They Were Steadfast and Immovable"

Fallen Phrase

Instructions: The letters in each column have fallen from the grid. Put them back correctly to rebuild the phrase. Cross out each letter in the jumble below once you place it in the grid. Pay attention because the letters in each column are scrambled. Start with simple 1 or 2 letter words and use the process of elimination. To check your answer, read **Alma 1:30**

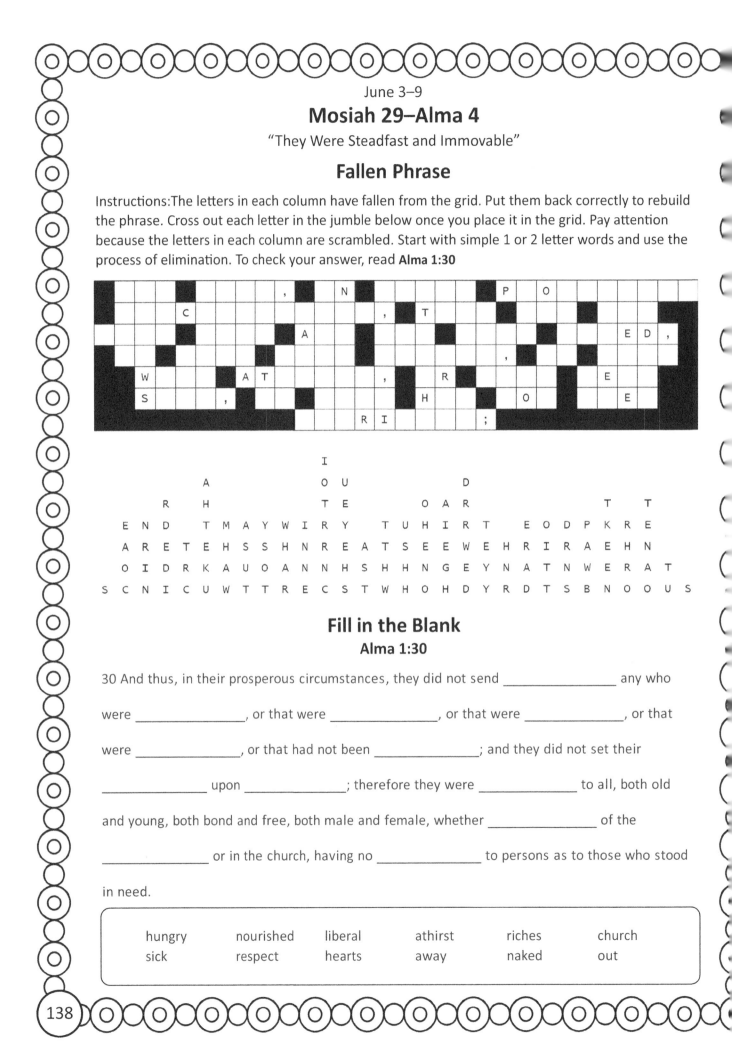

Fill in the Blank
Alma 1:30

30 And thus, in their prosperous circumstances, they did not send _____ any who

were _____, or that were _____, or that were _____, or that

were _____, or that had not been _____; and they did not set their

_____ upon _____; therefore they were _____ to all, both old

and young, both bond and free, both male and female, whether _____ of the

_____ or in the church, having no _____ to persons as to those who stood

in need.

hungry	nourished	liberal	athirst	riches	church
sick	respect	hearts	away	naked	out

Alma 5–7

"Have Ye Experienced This Mighty Change in Your Hearts?"

Wacky Word Trails

Instructions: Start with the circled letter, use the clues to find and mark the trail of letters of all the connected bolded words from the scripture through the maze to the last letter. The path can wander up, down, left, and right at any point, even in the middle of the word.

Alma 5:46

Behold, I say unto you they are **made known** unto me by the Holy Spirit of God. Behold, I have **fasted** and **prayed many days** that I might know these **things** of myself. And now I do know of **myself** that they are **true**; for the **Lord** God hath made them **manifest** unto me by his **Holy Spirit**; and this is the spirit of **revelation** which is in me.

```
Q Q Q X E V Z T I O Z Z D L Q
B P S P R E L A V N R H K D K
B I W Y D E R P S B R S E K E
S U T C S T A Y G E H O E Q V
Y V S O A F D E N I A L Q H H
C J Q S L B E E Q H T D M A D
H I U S F H U P Z T Y W Y N I
M N Z Z T L S O K K L O B O V
I B M Y C N F D A P C H Z W H
B F Q K U K L E Y E S T R N L
T W D T M M Y S S F H S L C S
X G F W X T I F M I I Q W G G
G N Q R X N R I A N A M V D R
H U A T N C B P U R D N L K O
Y S M V U E A S E T E W O N (L)
```

Word Bricks

Instructions: A sentence is written on the wall. But brick layers built the wall in the wrong order. Your job is to put the bricks in the right order. Hint: **Alma 5:44–48**

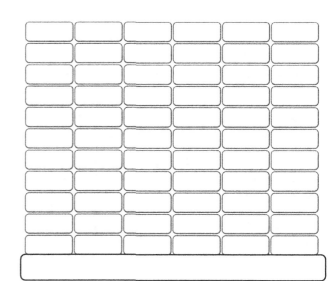

Alma 5–7

"Have Ye Experienced This Mighty Change in Your Hearts?"

Secret Code

Instructions: The secret message is written in symbols. In the code key you can find what each symbol means. Write the letter above the symbol and you can read the secret message.

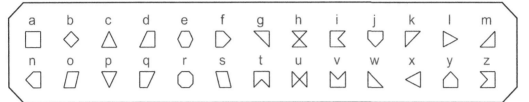

5 : 1 4

APPARENTLY, MY GIRLFRIEND EXPERIENCED WHAT ALMA CALLED "A MIGHTY CHANGE OF HEART."

THAT'S GREAT.

NO. SHE'S DUMPING ME.

mormoncartoonist.com

© Arie Van De Graaff

Alma 5–7

"Have Ye Experienced This Mighty Change in Your Hearts?"

Instructions: Fit the bold words from the scripture below into the encircled squares. Words will read forward, backward, up, down, and diagonally and will normally cross other words. Start with the hints provided.

Alma 7:19–20

For I **perceive** that ye are in the **paths** of **righteousness**; I perceive that ye are in the path which **leads** to the kingdom of **God**; yea, I perceive that ye are making his paths **straight**. I perceive that it has been made **known** unto you, by the **testimony** of his **word**, that he **cannot walk** in **crooked** paths; neither doth he **vary** from that which he hath **said**; neither hath he a **shadow** of **turning** from the **right** to the **left**, or from that which is **right** to that which is **wrong**; therefore, his **course** is **one eternal round**.

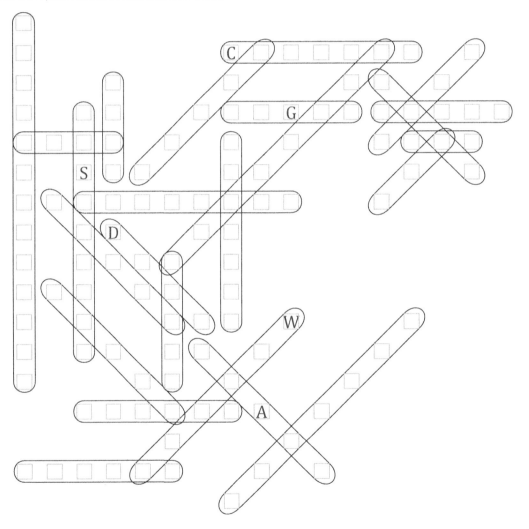

perceive	paths	righteousness	leads	God
straight	known	testimony	word	cannot
walk	crooked	vary	said	shadow
turning	right	left	right	wrong
course	one	eternal	round	

June 10–16
Alma 5–7
"Have Ye Experienced This Mighty Change in Your Hearts?"

I can gain my own **testimony** through the Holy Ghost.

Come, Follow Me Manual, 2024

Alma 5–7

"Have Ye Experienced This Mighty Change in Your Hearts?"

Handwriting Practice

Practice your handwriting by tracing the sentence below. Then use the blank lines to write the sentence on your own.

I can gain my own testimony through the Holy Ghost.

Letter Sudoku

Instructions: Solve the letter sudoku puzzle the same way you'd solve a numeric sudoku. Check your puzzle against the answer key on ColorMeChristian.org. Every column, row, and group of nine must contain every letter in the worda **PAIN MERCY.** Letters are used only once;

Alma 7:11–13

And he shall go forth, suffering pains and afflictions and temptations of every kind; and this that the word might be fulfilled which saith he will take upon him the **pain**s and the sicknesses of his people. And he will take upon him death, that he may loose the bands of death which bind his people; and he will take upon him their infirmities, that his bowels may be filled with **mercy**, according to the flesh, that he may know according to the flesh how to succor his people according to their infirmities. Now the Spirit knoweth all things; nevertheless the Son of God suffereth according to the flesh that he might take upon him the sins of his people, that he might blot out their transgressions according to the power of his deliverance; and now behold, this is the testimony which is in me.

R	E						A	I
C	Y					P	E	N
					C		M	
A		R	E					
Y		N			M		I	E
	E	A	Y	N		I		
						A	E	
I			M		R	Y	N	

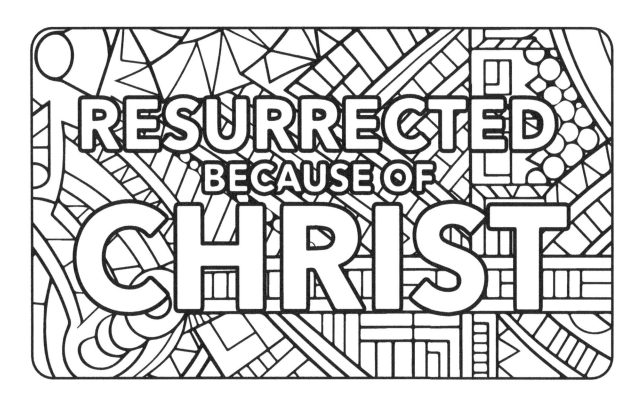

June 17–23
Alma 8–12
Jesus Christ Will Come to Redeem His People

Missing Vowels Word Search

Instructions: Find the hidden words. The words have been placed horizontally, vertically, diagonally, forwards, or backwards, and the vowels have been removed. When you locate a word, draw an ellipse around it and fill the vowels in.

Alma 9:26–27

And not many days hence the **Son** of **God** shall **come** in his **glory**; and his glory shall be the glory of the **Only Begotten** of the **Father**, **full** of **grace**, **equity**, and **truth**, full of **patience**, **mercy**, and long-suffering, quick to **hear** the **cries** of his **people** and to **answer** their **prayers**. And behold, he cometh to redeem those who will be **baptized** unto **repentance**, through **faith** on his **name**.

```
  S  Z  W        S  P  R  F  Y  Z  L  G  F
C  S  H  B  S  R  D     R  W     C  V     N
   D        C  B        H  Z     R  D  B
R  M     Y  F  R  W  B     G     T  T     N
G  R     G  S  S  H     N  L  Y  G  L  H  M
C  R  K  W  N  B  Y  Z  X  W  N  R  W  R  X
P     V     C  T  R     T  H     J  S     M
L  L     F           B  K     L        P  G
R        P  T  M  L  C  L  N     H
N  K  Q     P  T        P  V  W  M  Q  N
Y     Q  L     R        H     X     Z  T  D
G  R  D  T  P  W  X  V  C  F     N  S     R
M  K        C  N        T     P  T  N  B
J  S  K  L  X  R     H  T     F  V     C  P
   G  N     G  B     P  T     Z     D  D
```

Translation Station

Instructions: Translate the Morse code below into English to discover the hidden message. Write the alphabet letter beneath each Morse Code letter. Each letter, number, and punctuation is separated by a slash: /. Use the key at the back of the book to help you.

··/   ·−−/·−/−·/−/   −/−−−/   −···/·/   ·−/

−−/··/···/···/··/−−−/−·/·−/·−/−·/−−/   −·/−−−/·−−/·−·−·−   ··/

−···/−−−/−·/ '−/   ·−−/·−/−·/−/   −/−−−/   ·−−/·−/··/−/

··−/−·/−/··/·−·/   ··/ '−−/   −−·/·−/−−−/−−·/−·/·−·−·−

··/   ·−−/·−/−·/−/   −/−−−/   ···/····/·−/·−·/·/   −/····/·/

−−·/−−−/···/·−−·/·/·−/   −−·/····/··/·−·/·/   ··/ '−−/

−·−·/·−·/··/·−−/−·/−−   ··−/−−−/·−·/   ··/   ····/·−/···−/·/

·−/   −/··/···/−/··/−−/−−−/−·/··−−/   −−−/··−/   −−/·−···/

−−−/·−−/−·/·−·−·−

Mission Call

This young woman just received her mission call. Can you find the hidden objects in the picture?

ILLUSTRATIONS BY ARIE VAN DE GRAAF

BANANA   BASEBALL BAT   BUTTERFLY   CANDLE   CARROT   CRAYON   HORSESHOE   LADYBUG

LEAF   LOLLYPOP   PAINTBRUSH   PEAR   PENCIL   RULER   SCREWDRIVER   TOOTHBRUSH

Alma 8–12

Jesus Christ Will Come to Redeem His People

Instructions: Fill in the blank puzzle grid using the word bank with the bold words from the scripture below. Place the words in the correct place on the grid.

Alma 8:19-20

And as he **entered** the **city** he was an **hungered**, and he said to a man: Will ye give to an **humble servant** of God **something** to **eat**? And the man said unto him: I am a **Nephite**, and I know that thou art a **holy prophet** of God, for thou art the **man** whom an **angel** said in a **vision**: Thou shalt **receive**. Therefore, go with me into my **house** and I will **impart** unto **thee** of my **food**; and I **know** that thou wilt be a **blessing** unto me and my house.

3 Letters	holy	**6 Letters**	receive	blessing
eat	food	impart	Nephite	
man	know	vision	prophet	**9 Letters**
		humble	entered	something
4 Letters	**5 Letters**			
thee	house	**7 Letters**	8 Letters	
city	angel	servant	hungered	

Alma 8–12

Jesus Christ Will Come to Redeem His People

Instructions: Connect all of the letters in the phrase bolded below. Don't be tricked by letters that take you into a dead end! There is only one path through the maze.

___ _____ ___ ___ ____ _____ __ _____ _____ __ ___ _____ ____···

___ __ _____ __ _____ __ _____ _____ ___···

___ ____ _ _____ _____ __ ___ ___ ____.

Alma 11:43

Start

Finish

Alma 8–12
Jesus Christ Will Come to Redeem His People

Unscrambler

Instructions: Unscramble the words below; look at the bold words in the scripture for a hint.

Alma 12:33-34

But God did call on men, in the name of his **Son**, (this being the **plan** of **redemption** which was laid) saying: If ye will **repent**, and harden not your **hearts**, then will I have **mercy** upon you, through mine **Only Begotten** Son; Therefore, whosoever repenteth, and hardeneth not his heart, he shall have **claim** on mercy through mine Only Begotten Son, unto a **remission** of his **sins**; and these shall enter into my **rest**.

tres _____

nso _____

ntrepe _____

yonl _____

ssin _____

ttenbego _____

onremissi _____

mclai _____

tshear _____

onredempti _____

ymerc _____

npla _____

Word Square

Instructions: Word squares are a liike Sudoku puzzles, but each letter can occur only once in each row and in each column. Check your puzzle against the answer key on ColorMeChristian.org. Every row and column must contain every letter in the word **AMULEK.** This word can be written in the gray row.

Alma 10:12

And now, when **Amulek** had spoken these words the people began to be astonished, seeing there was more than one witness who testified of the things whereof they were accused, and also of the things which were to come, according to the spirit of prophecy which was in them.

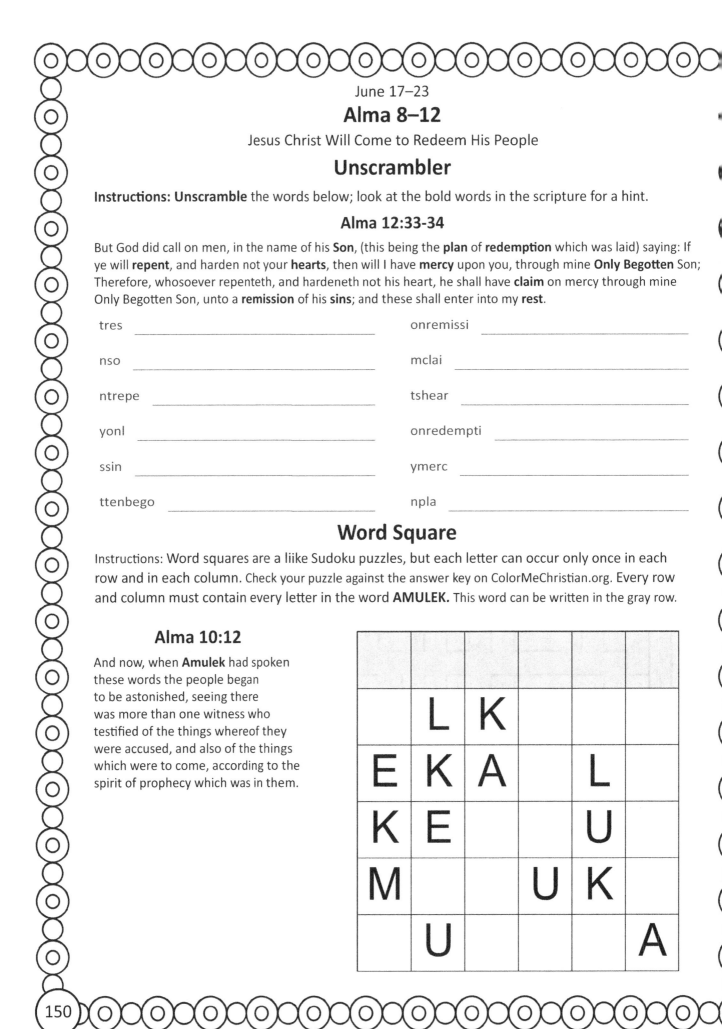

Alma 13–16

"Enter into the Rest of the Lord"

Word Angles

Instructions: Find the bold words from the scripture. Each word path may run north, east, south, or west, may make one right-angled turn, and may cross another word path. A few words may make no right angle turn at all.

Alma 13:10–12

Now, as I said concerning the holy order, or this **high priesthood**, there were many who were **ordained** and became high **priests** of God; and it was on account of their exceeding **faith** and **repentance**, and their **righteousness** before God, they choosing to **repent** and **work** righteousness rather than to **perish**; Therefore they were called after this **holy order**, and were **sanctified**, and their garments were washed **white** through the **blood** of the **Lamb**. Now they, after being sanctified by the Holy Ghost, having their garments made white, being pure and spotless before God, could not **look** upon **sin** save it were with **abhorrence**; and there were many, **exceedingly great many**, who were made **pure** and **entered** into the **rest** of the **Lord** their God.

```
C M A A I E N T A N C E E R G Q
C H Y R E P E N L U I C A C T H
H O L I T E S P A R G Z T V Y H
Y L O I F R T N M I S X G R L I
V D O O L B S X B G A Z G Y G G
D Y K P R I E U J H X Y I O N H
E A B H O R R G C T A U P R I F
I Q O U T P E C D E N I A D D A
F E C S S E N S U O D H U H E I
I N H L P K C L M Y X E X C E T
T N I S R H E D R N A M W U W H
C N A S I D R O E S T I N S H I
R O W K E E S I D E R E R I O T
K D R V S R I P L X B T I R M E
D O O H T Y G U R E V N W E X D
R E L M W P N Y V Q C E M P M U
```

Word Star

Instructions: Start with the capital letter in the puzzle. Then choose one of the two lines to the next letter. Only one route through the word star will make a word. Write the letters of the word you discover in the blanks below as you travel through the star:

_ _ _ _ _ _ _ _

Now can you find this word in the following scripture?

Alma 13:2

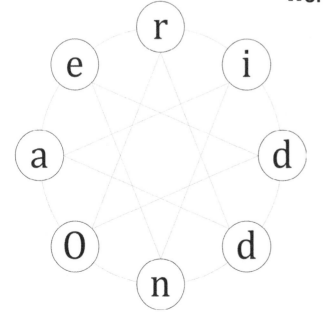

Hidden Picture: Alma had great faith in Jesus, which is why he went on a mission to Ammonihah. Can you find 7 pictures of Alma in the hidden picture below? It will be tricky; the picture may be smaller, on its side, or even upside down! Then, see if you can find 1 image of the animals as well.

Alma 13–16

"Enter into the Rest of the Lord"

Reverse Word Search

Instructions: Instead of looking for words in a grid, place the bold words in the scripture in the empty word search puzzle. The words may be forwards, backwards, up, down, or diagonally The start letter of the words have been placed in the grid to get you started.

Alma 13:16

Now these **ordinances** were **given after** this **manner**, that thereby the **people** might **look forward** on the **Son** of **God**, it being a **type** of his **order**, or it being his order, and this that they might look forward to him for a **remission** of their **sins**, that they might **enter** into the **rest** of the **Lord**.

PLEASE DON'T TELL ME THAT PROPERLY SPELLING IT IS A REQUIREMENT FOR RECEIVING THE MELCHIZEDEK PRIESTHOOD.

Zeezrom And The Change Of Heart

Zeezrom experienced a great change of heart through Jesus Christ. Can you help the unhappy Zeezrom through the maze so he can be happy?

Alma 13–16

"Enter into the Rest of the Lord"

Instructions: Solve this word sudoku puzzle the same way that you'd solve a numeric sudoku. Each of the bold words in the scripture below is found once in every row, column and 3×3 box.

Alma 14:26

And **Alma** cried, saying: How long shall we suffer these great **afflictions**, O Lord? O Lord, give us **strength** according to our **faith** which is in **Christ**, even unto **deliverance**. And they **broke** the **cords** with which they were bound; and when the people saw this, they began to **flee**, for the fear of destruction had come upon them.

	broke	faith				flee	strength	Christ
Christ		deliverance	strength			faith	Alma	afflictions
	flee	Alma	faith	Christ			deliverance	
Alma	Christ	broke	flee	afflictions			cords	
	afflictions	flee		strength		Alma		faith
	strength	cords		deliverance		Christ	afflictions	flee
broke		Christ	cords	faith	strength			
flee		strength			Christ		faith	broke
cords			deliverance			strength	Christ	Alma

Alma 13–16

"Enter into the Rest of the Lord"

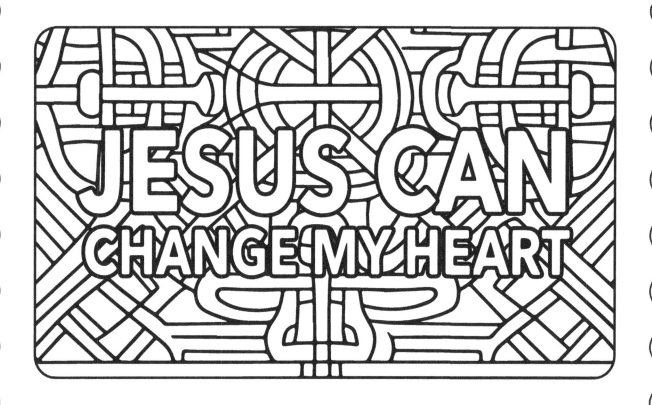

Cryptogram

Instructions: Each letter on the top stands for a letter in the alphabet. Solve the encrypted phrase by matching each letter on top to a letter in the alphabet on the bottom. Use the key to help you remember what the letters stand for so you can crack the code.

D	R	V	Q	G	B	J	K	N	Z	O	H	A	Y	P	F	C	W	X	I	M	L	T	S	E	U
A	B	C	D	E	F	G	H	I	J	K	L	M	N	O	P	Q	R	S	T	U	V	W	X	Y	Z

M I A M V U M X M T A : T P W L K Z F Y V T Y C Y X W

T I W L Y B Y A Y U O W T K I K P Q L B T X W W L K Z

Q M I X W F Y L Y M V Y A . M I A L Y X M T A :

N Y M , T F Y V T Y C Y M Q Q K B A T I E W K W L N

R K B A X . M V U M 15 : 8 - 9

Alma 17–22

"I Will Make an Instrument of Thee"

Word Search

Instructions: Find the bold words from the scripture in the word search puzzle. Each word could be hidden forwards, backwards, up, down, or diagonally.

Alma 20:25-26

Now when **Ammon** had said these words, the **king** began to **rejoice** because of his **life**. And when he saw that Ammon had no desire to **destroy** him, and when he also saw the **great love** he had for his son **Lamoni**, he was **astonished exceedingly**, and said: **Because** this is all that thou hast **desired**, that I would **release** thy **brethren**, and suffer that my son Lamoni should **retain** his **kingdom**, behold, I will **grant** unto you that my son may retain his kingdom from this **time** and **forever**; and I will **govern** him no more.

```
M  G  Y  L  G  N  I  D  E  E  C  X  E  V  E
R  U  I  H  R  P  Q  E  Y  S  T  P  L  Y  O
H  G  V  E  G  K  D  C  V  A  U  K  T  U
X  F  V  V  T  K  I  N  G  I  C  E  A  C  C
G  G  Q  O  N  Y  A  E  D  J  O  E  L  R  J
R  N  L  L  E  D  M  F  J  E  R  J  G  E  W
A  R  A  P  R  E  M  I  T  G  S  R  E  P  R
N  E  M  Y  H  W  O  L  T  F  T  I  Q  R  D
T  V  O  B  T  D  N  Z  J  W  K  O  R  B  R
K  O  N  L  E  A  S  T  O  N  I  S  H  E  D
U  G  I  W  R  E  V  E  R  O  F  W  T  C  D
R  M  F  H  B  Q  X  O  M  D  B  A  X  A  Z
K  I  N  G  D  O  M  G  D  V  I  V  A  U  L
P  A  M  Z  A  C  R  O  M  N  H  V  S  S  X
Y  O  R  T  S  E  D  M  A  S  A  C  T  E  O
```

Knight Moves - Find a Word

Instructions: Start with the capital letter in the puzzle. To get to the next letter, jump two squares in any direction except diagonally, and then one square in a different direction. Your path will look like a capital L. To show you how it works, Only one route through the puzzle will make a word. Write the letters of the word you discover in the blanks below as you jump through the squares:

_ _ _ _ _ _ _ _
1 2 3 4 5 6 7 8

Now can you find this word in the following scripture?

Alma 17:11

x	e	m
p		E
s	a	l

Mystery Picture Graph

Instructions: Find the mystery picture below by plotting and connecting the points of each line on the coordinate graph. Connect all the points in Line 1, stop, pick up your pencil, and then connect all the points in Line 2, and so on for the rest of the lines. The dot for the first (X,Y) coordinate pair on Line 1 has been placed for you.

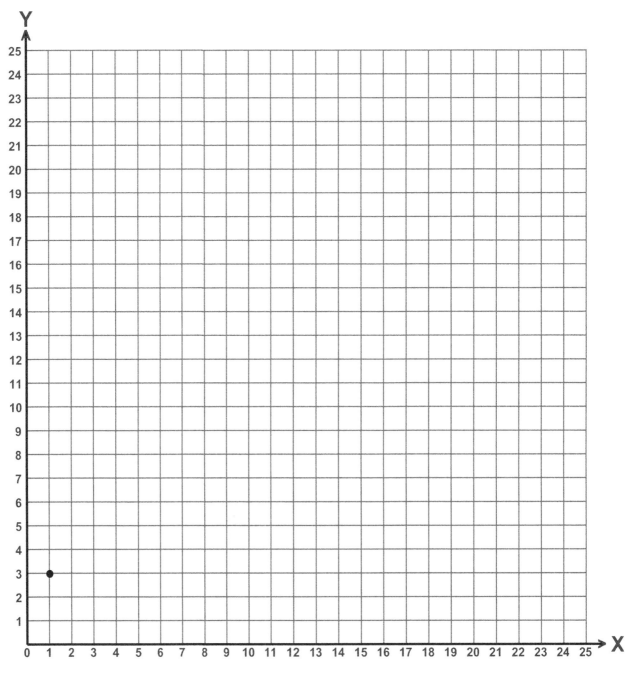

Line 1	(1, 3)	(10, 3)	(11, 2)	(14, 2)	(15, 3)	(24, 3)	(24, 20)	(22, 20)	(22, 22)	(14, 22)	(13, 21)	(12, 21)
(11, 22)	(3, 22)	(3, 20)	(1, 20)	(1, 3)	**Line 2**	(3, 20)	(3, 5)	(11, 5)	(12, 3)	(13, 3)	(14, 5)	(22, 5)
(22, 20)	**Line 3**	(12, 21)	(12, 3)	(13, 3)	(13, 21)	**Line 4**	(5, 20)	(10, 20)	**Line 5**	(5, 18)	(10, 18)	**Line 6**
(5, 16)	(10, 16)	**Line 7**	(5, 14)	(10, 14)	**Line 8**	(5, 12)	(10, 12)	**Line 9**	(5, 10)	(10, 10)	**Line 10**	(5, 8)
(10, 8)	**Line 11**	(15, 20)	(20, 20)	**Line 12**	(15, 18)	(20, 18)	**Line 13**	(15, 16)	(20, 16)	**Line 14**	(15, 14)	(20, 14)
Line 15	(15, 12)	(20, 12)	**Line 16**	(15, 10)	(20, 10)	**Line 17**	(15, 8)	(20, 8)				

Alma 17–22

"I Will Make an Instrument of Thee"

Translation Station

Instructions: Translate the sign language letters below into English to discover the hidden message. Write the alphabet letter beneath each hand sign. Use the key at the back of the book to help you.

Alma 17–22

"I Will Make an Instrument of Thee"

Instructions: Using the Across and Down clues, write the correct words in the numbered grid below. Hint: all of the words in the crossword come from the scripture below.

Alma 17:25-39

ACROSS

2. Groups of animals, especially sheep or birds, that are herded or kept together.
4. Heavy sticks or objects used as weapons or for striking.
5. A person who works for someone else, often performing household tasks or other duties.
8. Painful conditions, troubles, or hardships that cause suffering.
12. To bring or provide something, often to a specific person or place.
13. To form a circle around something or someone.
14. To give one's word or assurance to do something in the future.

DOWN

1. To be praised or complimented in a way that makes one feel pleased or honored.
3. Spread or dispersed in different directions.
5. A weapon with a long blade, typically used for cutting or thrusting.
6. A low, indistinct sound, often made by people talking quietly or expressing discontent.
7. To kill someone or something, usually in a violent or deliberate manner.
9. A simple weapon consisting of a strap or band with a pouch for holding and throwing stones.
10. To run away quickly, often to escape danger or a difficult situation.
11. To cry or shed tears, especially in sorrow or distress.

I can **help** others come unto Christ by showing my love for them.

Come, Follow Me Manual, 2024

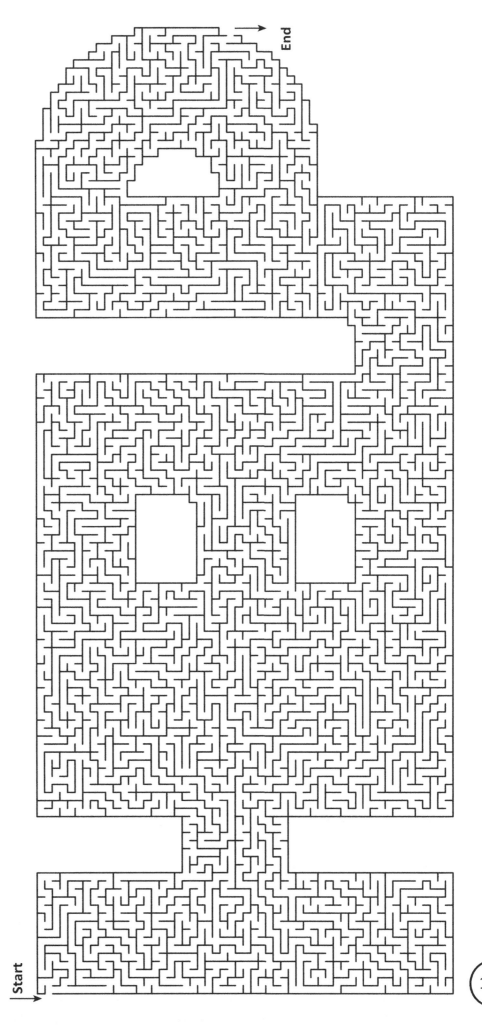

Start

End

Alma 17–22

"I Will Make an Instrument of Thee"

Letter Sudoku

Instructions: Solve the letter sudoku puzzle the same way you'd solve a numeric sudoku. Check your puzzle against the answer key on ColorMeChristian.org. Every column, row, and group of nine must contain every letter in the worda **IN THE LORD.** Letters are used only once;

Alma 17:2–3

Now these sons of Mosiah were with Alma at the time the angel first appeared unto him; therefore Alma did rejoice exceedingly to see his brethren; and what added more to his joy, they were still his brethren **in the Lord**; yea, and they had waxed strong in the knowledge of the truth; for they were men of a sound understanding and they had searched the scriptures diligently, that they might know the word of God. But this is not all; they had given themselves to much prayer, and fasting; therefore they had the spirit of prophecy, and the spirit of revelation, and when they taught, they taught with power and authority of God.

O	E	R		T		L		H
D			N	O		I		
L				H				
	H			I	N			O
N			D				T	
			T				O	
	D					E	H	N
			O	N			D	I

Alma 23–29

They "Never Did Fall Away"

Wacky Word Trails

Instructions: Start with the circled letter, use the clues to find and mark the trail of letters of all the connected bolded words from the scripture through the maze to the last letter. The path can wander up, down, left, and right at any point, even in the middle of the word.

Alma 27:22–23

And it came to pass that the **voice** of the **people** came, saying: Behold, we will **give** up the land of **Jershon**, which is on the east by the sea, which joins the land **Bountiful**, which is on the south of the land Bountiful; and this land Jershon is the land which we will give unto our **brethren** for an **inheritance**. And behold, we will set our **armies between** the land Jershon and the land **Nephi**, that we may **protect** our brethren in the land Jershon; and this we do for our brethren, on **account** of their **fear** to **take** up **arms against** their brethren lest they should **commit sin**; and this their **great** fear came because of their **sore repentance** which they had, on account of their **many murders** and their **awful wickedness**.

```
Y  D  R  E  Z  E  R (G) R  S  L  P  O  E  L
A  T  I  H  N  A  G  J  E  H  E  G  A  P  T
N  F  E  N  C  T  I  T  W  O  H  A  I  N  S
C  E  A  I  O  M  M  E  B  N  R  E  S  K  U
S  M  R  N  E  E  W  T  N  S  O  Q  U  I  X
A  R  A  V  R  A  A  C  E  R  H  K  B  E  C
W  F  U  T  P  H  I  C  X  F  T  E  R  C  I
S  W  L  N  E  G  T  O  W  L  S  Z  R  U  O
W  J  O  E  V  I  N  U  M  X  U  V  M  A  V
X  B  R  P  R  S  C  T  X  G  P  X  S  N  Y
Q  C  U  S  O  T  E  B  N  T  I  E  R  M  S
W  Z  A  C  X  A  Y  O  U  U  F  D  R  U  S
H  O  R  U  R  A  A  T  S  L  D  I  I  C  E
A  P  X  I  M  E  K  N  I  T  A  H  W  K  N
G  W  Z  E  S  R  E  P  E  N  N  C  E  E  D
```

Word Bricks

Instructions: A sentence is written on the wall. But brick layers built the wall in the wrong order. Your job is to put the bricks in the right order. Hint: **Alma 26:30**

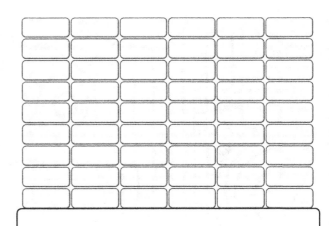

we	ve	ha	And
ed	suf	fer	all
man	ner		of
aff	. . and	lic	ns . tio
pos	sup	we ed	t	tha
y	would	bour	jo	e
aps	f pl i	we	ful	er h
the	me	could	be	ans
so	of	ing	me .	sav

Alma 23–29

They "Never Did Fall Away"

Fallen Phrase

Instructions:The letters in each column have fallen from the grid. Put them back correctly to rebuild the phrase. Cross out each letter in the jumble below once you place it in the grid. Pay attention because the letters in each column are scrambled. Start with simple 1 or 2 letter words and use the process of elimination. To check your answer, read **Alma 29:3**

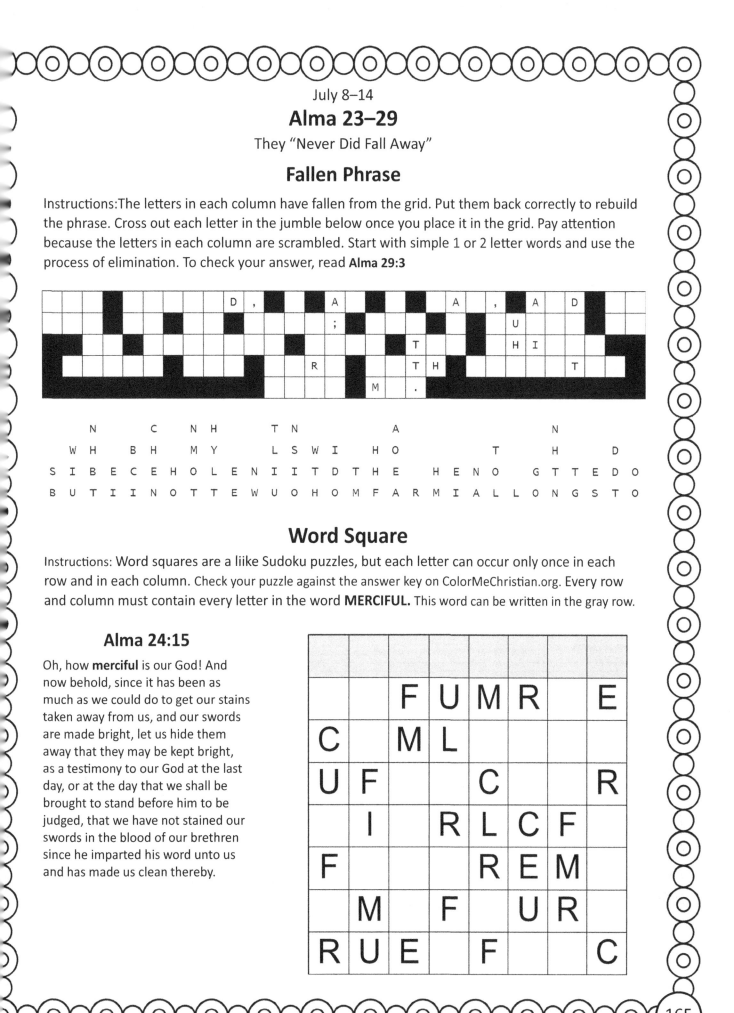

Word Square

Instructions: Word squares are a liike Sudoku puzzles, but each letter can occur only once in each row and in each column. Check your puzzle against the answer key on ColorMeChristian.org. Every row and column must contain every letter in the word **MERCIFUL.** This word can be written in the gray row.

Alma 24:15

Oh, how **merciful** is our God! And now behold, since it has been as much as we could do to get our stains taken away from us, and our swords are made bright, let us hide them away that they may be kept bright, as a testimony to our God at the last day, or at the day that we shall be brought to stand before him to be judged, that we have not stained our swords in the blood of our brethren since he imparted his word unto us and has made us clean thereby.

Alma 23–29

They "Never Did Fall Away"

Handwriting Practice

Practice your handwriting by tracing the sentence below. Then use the blank lines to write the sentence on your own.

The Lord blesses me as I strive to keep my promises to Him.

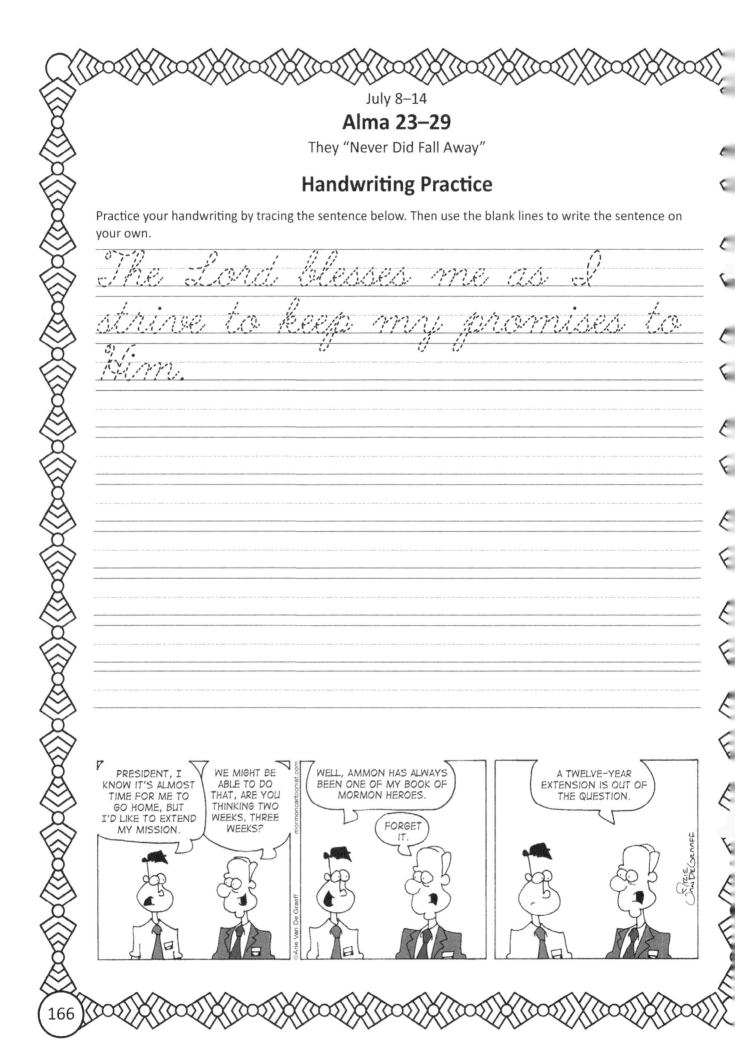

PRESIDENT, I KNOW IT'S ALMOST TIME FOR ME TO GO HOME, BUT I'D LIKE TO EXTEND MY MISSION.

WE MIGHT BE ABLE TO DO THAT, ARE YOU THINKING TWO WEEKS, THREE WEEKS?

WELL, AMMON HAS ALWAYS BEEN ONE OF MY BOOK OF MORMON HEROES.

FORGET IT.

A TWELVE-YEAR EXTENSION IS OUT OF THE QUESTION.

July 8–14

Alma 23–29

They "Never Did Fall Away"

Instructions: Connect all of the letters in the phrase bolded below. Don't be tricked by letters that take you into a dead end! There is only one path through the maze.

_ ____ _ ____ __ _____, ___ _____ ____ ___ ____ __ ____ _____, ____ _ _____ __ _____ ___ _____ ____ ___ _____ __ ___, ____ _ _____ __ _____ ___ _____, ___ ___ _____ ____ _____ _____!

Alma 29:1

Finish

Start

167

Alma 23–29
They "Never Did Fall Away"
Secret Code

Instructions: The secret message is written in symbols. In the code key you can find what each symbol means. Write the letter above the symbol and you can read the secret message.

a	b	c	d	e	f	g	h	i	j	k	l	m
□	◇	△	⏢	⬠	▷	◺	⊠	⟨	▽	▽	▷	◿
n	o	p	q	r	s	t	u	v	w	x	y	z
◁	▱	▽	▱	⬡	◠	⊔	⊠	M	⊔	◁	△	Σ

(Secret message written in symbols — Alma 26:11)

2 6 : 1 1

Fill in the Blank
Alma 24:7-9

I thank my God, my beloved people, that our great God has in _____ sent these our brethren, the Nephites, unto us to _____ unto us, and to _____ us of the _____ of our wicked fathers. And behold, I thank my great God that he has given us a _____ of his Spirit to _____ our _____, that we have opened a _____ with these brethren, the Nephites. And behold, I also thank my God, that by opening this correspondence we have been _____ of our _____, and of the many _____ which we have _____.

preach	committed	goodness	sins	portion	hearts
soften	convinced	murders	correspondence	convince	traditions

Alma 30–31

"The Virtue of the Word of God"

Missing Vowels Word Search

Instructions: Find the hidden words. The words have been placed horizontally, vertically, diagonally, forwards, or backwards, and the vowels have been removed. When you locate a word, draw an ellipse around it and fill the vowels in.

Alma 31:23-24

Now, after the people had all **offered** up **thanks** after this **manner**, they **returned** to their **homes**, **never** **speaking** of their **God again** until they had **assembled** themselves **together again** to the holy stand, to offer up thanks after their manner. Now when Alma saw this his **heart** was **grieved**; for he saw that they were a **wicked** and a **perverse** people; yea, he saw that their hearts were set upon **gold**, and upon **silver**, and upon all **manner** of **fine goods**.

```
T   N     G     L T L W V C F
G B S   M   H B S T     X L Z
W T W   G R J N R C M S S H D
P V H P R R M   K K   S     D
T     K   F     J M N   L G G
G G R Y   H D V R Y N M V   Z
S   D V V D     S   B     G
P L D P   R   K B N R L R W
  D Y S D R N R   H T   G   T
  R D F D   S P V S R D F X
K   X N     G   Q J K F M P K
  N Z G K Y   F   N   N   Z S
N N   N B   P G   R   C   G Z
G   D   N R   T   R D M   H
D M S B D X B D V G H H B L T
```

THAT WAS OUR LAST SET OF SCRIPTURES.

WE'LL HAVE TO GO BACK TO ZARAHEMLA FOR MORE.

THAT'S OUR LAST BOOK OF MORMON. I BET THE ANCIENT MISSIONARIES WERE NEVER THIS UNPREPARED.

WE'D BETTER GO BACK TO THE APARTMENT AND GET MORE.

Hidden Picture: Alma taught the Zoramites they didn't need to stand on a tall tower to pray to God. Can you find 5 pictures of this praying man in the hidden picture below? It will be tricky; the picture may be smaller, on its side, or even upside down! Then, see if you can find 1 image of the animals as well.

Alma 30–31

"The Virtue of the Word of God"

Instructions: Solve this word sudoku puzzle the same way that you'd solve a numeric sudoku. Each of the bold words in the scripture below is found once in every row, column and 3×3 box.

Alma 31:34-35

O Lord, wilt thou **grant** unto us that we may have **success** in bringing them again unto **thee** in Christ. Behold, O Lord, their **souls** are **precious**, and many of them are our brethren; therefore, give unto us, O Lord, **power** and **wisdom** that we may **bring** these, our brethren, again unto **thee**.

		precious				grant		bring
	power				thee	precious	wisdom	
	souls				wisdom		power	thee
	bring				success		grant	thee
wisdom	thee			power		thee		
		success	thee	precious	thee			
	precious			souls			thee	success
		grant	wisdom		precious	thee		
	thee			thee		souls	precious	

Alma 30–31

"The Virtue of the Word of God"

Instructions: Fit the bold words from the scripture below into the encircled squares. Words will read forward, backward, up, down, and diagonally and will normally cross other words. Start with the hints provided.

Alma 30:44

But **Alma** said unto him: Thou hast had **signs enough**; will ye **tempt** your **God**? Will ye say, **Show** unto me a **sign**, when ye have the **testimony** of all these thy **brethren**, and also all the **holy prophets**? The **scriptures** are **laid before** thee, yea, and all **things denote** there is a God; yea, even the **earth**, and all things that are upon the **face** of it, yea, and its **motion**, yea, and also all the **planets** which **move** in their **regular form** do **witness** that there is a **Supreme Creator**.

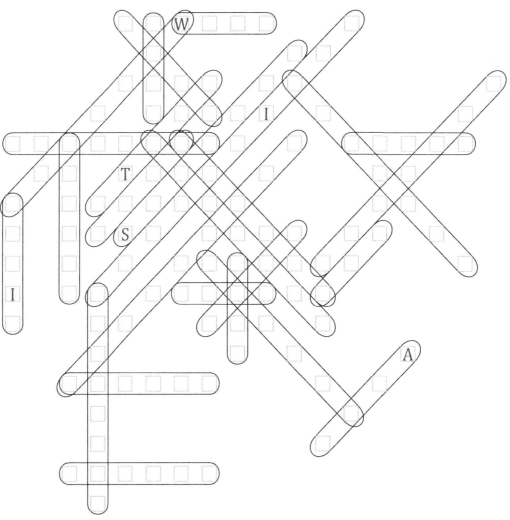

Alma	signs	enough	tempt	God	Show
sign	testimony	brethren	holy	prophets	scriptures
laid	before	things	denote	earth	face
motion	planets	move	regular	form	witness
Supreme	Creator				

July 15–21
Alma 30–31
"The Virtue of the Word of God"

Heavenly Father **hears** my prayers.

Come, Follow Me Manual, 2024

Start

End

Alma 30–31

"The Virtue of the Word of God"

Unscrambler

Instructions: Unscramble the words below; look at the bold words in the scripture for a hint.

Alma 30:34

And now, if we do not **receive anything** for our **labors** in the **church**, what doth it **profit** us to **labor** in the **church** save it were to **declare** the **truth**, that we may have **rejoicings** in the **joy** of our **brethren**?

arolb _____

irveece _____

hccurh _____

bsrola _____

fpoirt _____

ojy _____

rnherebt _____

hcruhc _____

ngyhntia _____

crdlaee _____

eijignrcos _____

thtur _____

Cryptogram

Instructions: Each letter on the top stands for a letter in the alphabet. Solve the encrypted phrase by matching each letter on top to a letter in the alphabet on the bottom. Use the key to help you remember what the letters stand for so you can crack the code.

K	P	Y	T	B	G	F	O	M	J	Q	E	V	X	I	A	Z	L	R	N	H	C	D	U	W	S
A	B	C	D	E	F	G	H	I	J	K	L	M	N	O	P	Q	R	S	T	U	V	W	X	Y	Z

P T W   T H Y ,   P Z   D U L   B S L P V U O T F   H G   D U L

Y H S W   U P W   P   F S L P D   D L T W L T V C   D H

R L P W   D U L   B L H B R L   D H   W H   D U P D   Y U O V U

Y P Z   J X Z D - C L P ,   O D   U P W   U P W   I H S L

B H Y L S G X R   L G G L V D   X B H T   D U L   I O T W Z

H G   D U L   B L H B R L   D U P T   D U L   Z Y H S W ,   H S

P T C D U O T F   L R Z L ,   Y U O V U   U P W

U P B B L T L W   X T D H   D U L I - D U L S L G H S L   P R I P

D U H X F U D   O D   Y P Z   L N B L W O L T D   D U P D

D U L C   Z U H X R W   D S C   D U L   M O S D X L   H G

D U L   Y H S W   H G   F H W .   P R I P   3 1 : 5

Alma 32–35

"Plant This Word in Your Hearts"

Word Angles

Instructions: Find the bold words from the scripture. Each word path may run north, east, south, or west, may make one right-angled turn, and may cross another word path. A few words may make no right angle turn at all.

Alma 32:41-42

But if ye will **nourish** the **word**, yea, nourish the tree as it beginneth to grow, by your **faith** with great **diligence**, and with **patience**, looking **forward** to the **fruit** thereof, it shall take **root**; and behold it shall be a tree springing up unto **everlasting life**. And because of your diligence and your faith and your patience with the word in nourishing it, that it may take root in you, behold, by and by ye shall **pluck** the fruit thereof, which is most **precious**, which is **sweet** above all that is sweet, and which is **white** above all that is white, yea, and **pure** above all that is pure; and ye shall **feast** upon this fruit even until ye are **filled**, that ye **hunger** not, **neither** shall ye **thirst**.

```
N O D F M H E K X W Z P V V I R
T S A E P T G F A I T H C K I V
A N P N I R W A R D E P J D E F
E E I O U O Q L P U R T Q B S I
C X X U A F R F G I U G L K K L
N I V R Z J U L E D X W T S S T
E O Q I X Z I L I T E O A T R S
I R U S H F T I H K P B N A I J
T A P E K C M F W P L U C K H S
F G D X F D A I E Y X U S A T W
I C E R P R O W T O O R B T E E
O R E G L V X J A M Q D L E G A
U V H N E V E R L A S T I C H Y
S A S U L R N E I T H E N N G I
J T B H I Z L O S X K R G E S O
Z C F L U K Q V C D I L I G V X
```

Translation Station

Instructions: Translate the Morse code below into English to discover the hidden message. Write the alphabet letter beneath each Morse Code letter. Each letter, number, and punctuation is separated by a slash: /. Use the key at the back of the book to help you.

```
−·−−/ ·/ ·−/ −−·−−    −/····/−−−/··−/    ·−/·−·/−/

−−/··/·−/−−·/··/−··−/··−·/·−·/    ··−/−·/−/−−−/    −/····/−·−−/

−·−·/····/··/·−·/−/−·/·−·/·/−·/    −−/····/··/−/    −/····/·/−·−−/

−·−/·/···/    ··−/−·/−/··/·−·/    −/····/·/·−−−−−    −/−−−/

−····/·/    ·····/·/·−·/−·/·−·/    −−−/··−/    −/····/·/·/    ·−/−·/−··/

−·/−−−/−/    −−−/··−/    −−/··/−·/−−−−−    ·−/−·/−··/

−/·−−−/−−·/··−/    ··−/·−·/·−·/·/·−/    ····/··/−/·−·/    −/····/··/−−·/··−

·−/·/·−/−−/··/    ···−/··/−·−/−−−/··/····
```

Nourishing The Plant Of Faith

Your testimony of Jesus Christ grows as you nourish it. Help these children walk through the garden maze so they can nourish their little plants with water.

Alma 32–35
"Plant This Word in Your Hearts"

Handwriting Practice

Practice your handwriting by tracing the sentence below. Then use the blank lines to write the sentence on your own.

My testimony of Jesus Christ grows as I nourish it.

Alma 32–35

"Plant This Word in Your Hearts"

Instructions: Fill in the blank puzzle grid using the word bank with the bold words from the scripture below. Place the words in the correct place on the grid.

Alma 32:28-29

Now, we will **compare** the **word** unto a seed. Now, if ye give **place**, that a seed may be **planted** in your **heart**, behold, if it be a **true seed**, or a **good** seed, if ye do not **cast** it **out** by your **unbelief**, that ye will **resist** the **Spirit** of the Lord, behold, it will begin to **swell** within your breasts; and when you feel these swelling **motions**, ye will begin to say within yourselves—It must needs be that this is a good seed, or that the word is good, for it beginneth to **enlarge** my **soul**; yea, it beginneth to **enlighten** my **understanding**, yea, it beginneth to be **delicious** to me. Now behold, would not this **increase** your **faith**? I say unto you, Yea; nevertheless it hath not **grown** up to a **perfect knowledge**.

3 Letters	word	**6 Letters**	motions	enlighten
out		resist		
	5 Letters	Spirit	**8 Letters**	**13 Letters**
4 Letters	place		increase	understanding
good	heart	**7 Letters**	unbelief	
seed	faith	compare		
true	swell	enlarge	**9 Letters**	
soul	grown	planted	knowledge	
cast		perfect	delicious	

Mystery Picture Graph

Instructions: Find the mystery picture below by plotting and connecting the points of each line on the coordinate graph. Connect all the points in Line 1, stop, pick up your pencil, and then connect all the points in Line 2, and so on for the rest of the lines. The dot for the first (X,Y) coordinate pair on Line 1 has been placed for you.

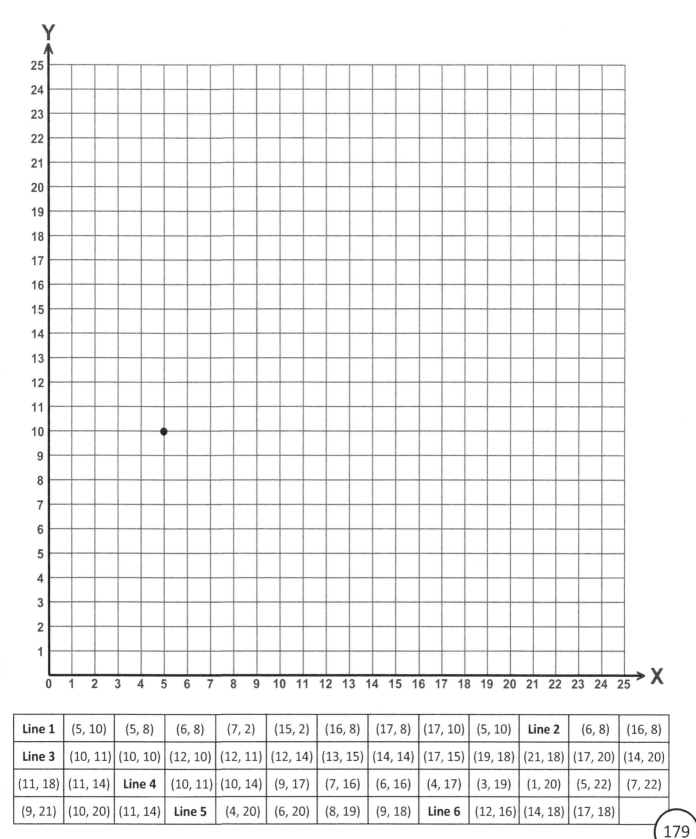

Line 1	(5, 10)	(5, 8)	(6, 8)	(7, 2)	(15, 2)	(16, 8)	(17, 8)	(17, 10)	(5, 10)	Line 2	(6, 8)	(16, 8)
Line 3	(10, 11)	(10, 10)	(12, 10)	(12, 11)	(12, 14)	(13, 15)	(14, 14)	(17, 15)	(19, 18)	(21, 18)	(17, 20)	(14, 20)
(11, 18)	(11, 14)	Line 4	(10, 11)	(10, 14)	(9, 17)	(7, 16)	(6, 16)	(4, 17)	(3, 19)	(1, 20)	(5, 22)	(7, 22)
(9, 21)	(10, 20)	(11, 14)	Line 5	(4, 20)	(6, 20)	(8, 19)	(9, 18)	Line 6	(12, 16)	(14, 18)	(17, 18)	

Alma 32–35

"Plant This Word in Your Hearts"

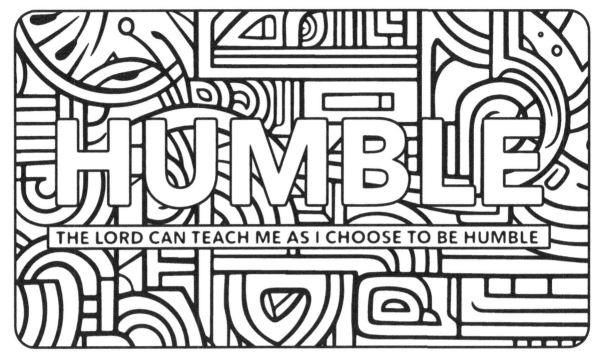

THE LORD CAN TEACH ME AS I CHOOSE TO BE HUMBLE

Letter Sudoku

Instructions: Solve the letter sudoku puzzle the same way you'd solve a numeric sudoku. Check your puzzle against the answer key on ColorMeChristian.org. Every column, row, and group of nine must contain every letter in the worda **FIND MERCY.** Letters are used only once;

Alma 32:13-14

And now, because ye are compelled to be humble blessed are ye; for a man sometimes, if he is compelled to be humble, seeketh repentance; and now surely, whosoever repenteth shall **find mercy**; and he that findeth mercy and endureth to the end the same shall be saved. And now, as I said unto you, that because ye were compelled to be humble ye were blessed, do ye not suppose that they are more blessed who truly humble themselves because of the word?

				I	N		M	D
Y			C		R	E		I
	F		R			I	N	
I		R		D				
E			M				F	
N		F						R
		M			R	F	C	
	E				M			

Alma 36–38

"Look to God and Live"

Word Search

Instructions: Find the bold words from the scripture in the word search puzzle. Each word could be hidden forwards, backwards, up, down, or diagonally.

Alma 37:6-7

Now ye may suppose that this is **foolishness** in me; but behold I say unto you, that by **small** and **simple things** are great things brought to **pass**; and **small means** in many instances doth **confound** the **wise**. And the Lord God doth work by means to bring about his **great** and **eternal purposes**; and by very small means the Lord doth confound the **wise** and bringeth about the **salvation** of many **souls**.

L	D	K	U	R	J	A	N	B	J	Y	S	R	C	M
L	B	E	S	N	A	E	M	P	Q	G	D	U	A	O
A	U	P	W	I	S	E	B	S	N	Y	N	G	H	U
M	S	U	K	Q	P	B	S	I	O	K	U	K	X	W
S	P	R	F	E	V	A	H	T	V	P	O	H	T	V
S	T	P	P	F	P	T	A	Q	V	C	F	U	P	U
B	L	O	N	K	O	E	I	D	S	L	N	T	W	L
C	S	S	B	D	R	I	A	K	A	P	O	F	A	S
F	U	E	F	G	K	S	O	B	L	D	C	N	E	Z
U	Z	S	U	U	E	L	Q	V	V	K	R	C	V	Q
N	S	E	N	L	X	U	T	A	A	E	R	L	W	S
Q	L	M	P	P	W	O	P	H	T	E	G	C	W	M
N	E	M	Y	M	Z	S	X	E	I	I	S	X	L	A
I	I	X	X	P	Z	R	A	B	O	G	I	I	R	L
S	O	F	O	O	L	I	S	H	N	E	S	S	W	L

Word Star

Instructions: Start with the capital letter in the puzzle. Then choose one of the two lines to the next letter. Only one route through the word star will make a word. Write the letters of the word you discover in the blanks below as you travel through the star:

_ _ _ _ _ _ _

Now can you find this word in the following scripture?

Alma 37:38

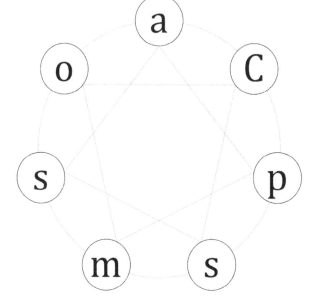

By small and simple things ARE GREAT THINGS brought to pass. ALMA 37:6

Alma 36–38

"Look to God and Live"

Reverse Word Search

Instructions: Instead of looking for words in a grid, place the bold words in the scripture in the empty word search puzzle. The words may be forwards, backwards, up, down, or diagonally The start letter of the words have been placed in the grid to get you started.

Alma 36:18-20

Now, as my mind caught **hold** upon this **thought**, I **cried** within my **heart**: O **Jesus**, thou Son of God, have **mercy** on me, who am in the **gall** of **bitterness**, and am **encircled** about by the **everlasting chains** of **death**. And now, behold, when I thought this, I could **remember** my **pains** no more; yea, I was **harrowed** up by the **memory** of my sins no more. And oh, what **joy**, and what **marvelous light** I did behold; yea, my soul was filled with **joy** as **exceeding** as was my **pain**!

A TESTIMONY TAKES TIME. LINE UPON LINE, PRECEPT UPON PRECEPT...BRICK UPON BRICK.

...AND THEN IT JUST CLICKS!

mormoncartoonist.com

Arie Van De Graaff

© Arie Van De Graaff

Alma 36–38

"Look to God and Live"

Handwriting Practice

Practice your handwriting by tracing the sentence below. Then use the blank lines to write the sentence on your own.

By small and simple things are great things brought to pass.

Translation Station

Instructions: Translate the sign language letters below into English to discover the hidden message. Write the alphabet letter beneath each hand sign. Use the key at the back of the book to help you.

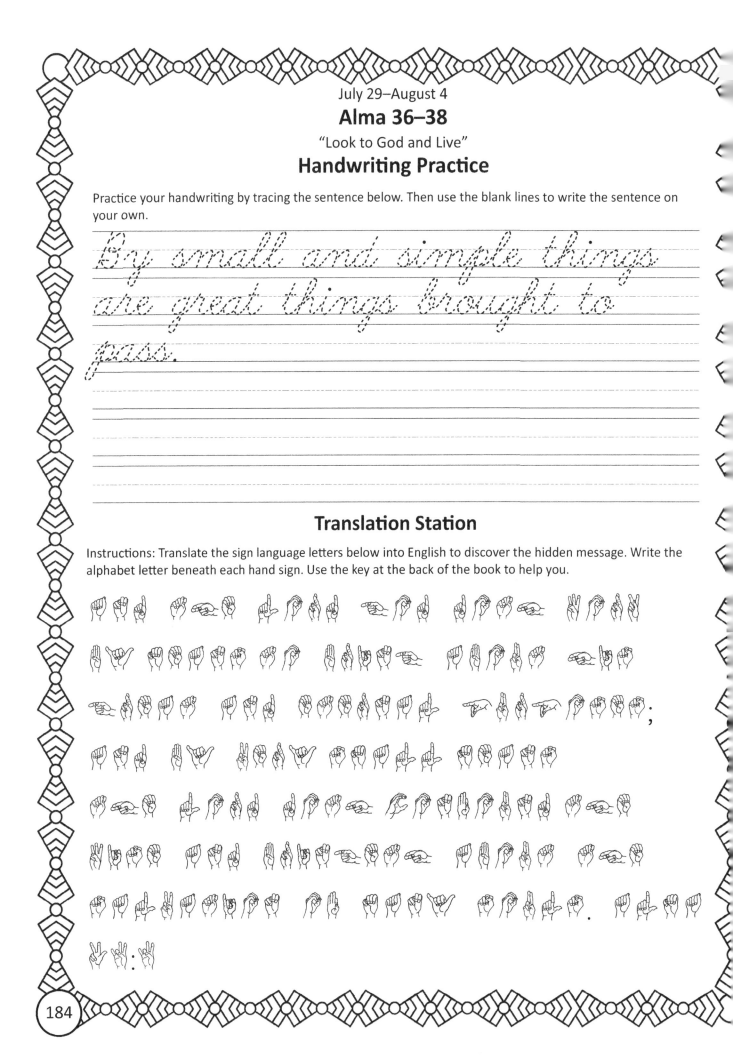

Repentance brings me **joy** in Jesus Christ.

Come, Follow Me Manual, 2024

Start ⟶

⟶ End

Alma 36–38

"Look to God and Live"

Fill in the Blank

Alma 36:18–19

Now, as my _____ caught hold upon this _____, I _____

within my _____ : O _____, thou Son of _____, have

_____ on me, who am in the gall of _____, and am encircled about by the

everlasting _____ of death. And now, behold, when I thought this, I could

_____ my _____ no more; yea, I was harrowed up by the

_____ of my sins no more.

memory	remember	Jesus	pains	mercy	mind
bitterness	cried	God	chains	thought	heart

Word Square

Instructions: Word squares are a liike Sudoku puzzles, but each letter can occur only once in each row and in each column. Check your puzzle against the answer key on ColorMeChristian.org. Every row and column must contain every letter in the word **COMING.** This word can be written in the gray row.

Alma 36:17

And it came to pass that as I was thus racked with torment, while I was harrowed up by the memory of my many sins, behold, I remembered also to have heard my father prophesy unto the people concerning the **coming** of one Jesus Christ, a Son of God, to atone for the sins of the world.

G				O	
		G	M		
O	G		N	C	
		O	G	M	C
M	I				N

August 5–11

Alma 39–42

"The Great Plan of Happiness"

Wacky Word Trails

Instructions: Start with the circled letter, use the clues to find and mark the trail of letters of all the connected bolded words from the scripture through the maze to the last letter. The path can wander up, down, left, and right at any point, even in the middle of the word.

Alma 40:11-12

Now, concerning the **state** of the **soul between death** and the **resurrection**—Behold, it has been made known unto me by an **angel**, that the **spirits** of all **men**, as soon as they are departed from this **mortal** body, yea, the spirits of all men, whether they be **good** or **evil**, are taken **home** to that God who gave them life. And then shall it come to pass, that the spirits of those who are **righteous** are **received** into a **state** of **happiness**, which is called **paradise**, a state of **rest**, a state of **peace**, where they shall rest from all their **troubles** and from all **care**, and **sorrow**.

```
N D Y Y Z B U I F I F A T F T
C T H Y J Z E O J R J T E P J
R U X L B K O R T E B S C A R
G Y X M K R D Z W E E N L U E
G I R P D K L L G N A E R O S
H V D O K S E P E L T S T W R
T E S O G S E L P S O R R O E
U O C E H J P K O H A K U H S
S R E I T A U E M L Q C V R U
V D E V D E K E T A L Y E R H
A M E P E C A V R U O Y C T I
R T N D R I E I O X V K P N O
O E H M I T P L M E T A A Q W
U Y C M P S H A P P I T R A D
B L E S S I D S S E N S E S I
```

Word Bricks

Instructions: A sentence is written on the wall. But brick layers built the wall in the wrong order. Your job is to put the bricks in the right order. Hint: **Alma 40:23**

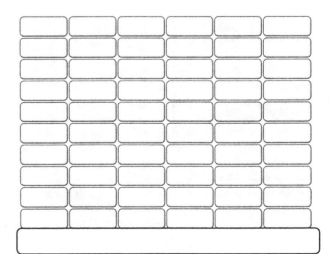

187

Hidden Picture: Just like the light of the sun helps us see, your good example can lead others to Christ. Can you find this 6 pictures of the sun in the hidden picture below? It will be tricky; the picture may be smaller, on its side, or even upside down! Then, see if you can find 1 image of the animals as well.

Alma 39–42

"The Great Plan of Happiness"

Instructions: Using the Across and Down clues, write the correct words in the numbered grid below. Hint: all of the words in the crossword come from the scripture below.

Alma 40:6–7, 11–14, 21–23

ACROSS

2. an official authorized to decide questions before a court
6. spiritual being attendant upon God
8. having desirable or positive qualities
11. state of well-being characterized by contentment and joy
13. returning something or someone to a satisfactory state
15. the place in which one's domestic affections are centered
16. experiencing or showing fear
19. between
20. junction by which parts or objects are linked together

DOWN

1. the permanent end of all life functions in an organism
3. having desirable or positive qualities
4. any place of complete bliss and delight and peace
5. a revival from death
7. junction by which parts or objects are linked together
9. shed tears because of sadness, rage, or pain
10. like or suggestive of a flame
12. being complete of its kind and without defect or blemish
14. spirits
17. morally bad or wrong
18. one of the jointed appendages of a body

Alma 39–42

"The Great Plan of Happiness"

Instructions: Connect all of the letters in the phrase bolded below. Don't be tricked by letters that take you into a dead end! There is only one path through the maze.

_____ _____, ___ _____ __ __ ___ _____ _____
_____ ___ _____ ___ _____.

Come, Follow Me 2024

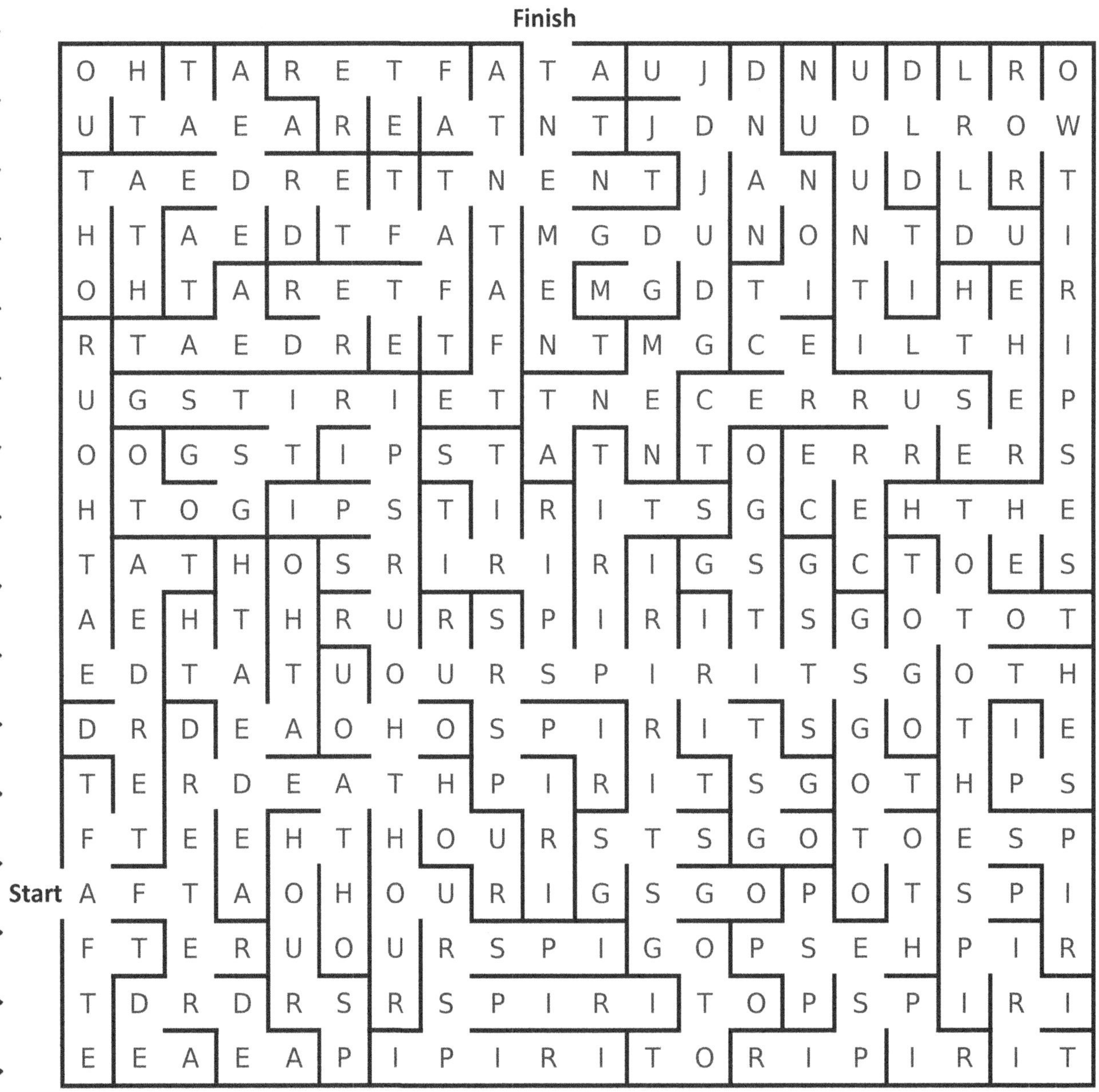

Finish

Start

August 5–11

Alma 39–42

"The Great Plan of Happiness"

Instructions: Solve this word sudoku puzzle the same way that you'd solve a numeric sudoku. Each of the bold words in the scripture below is found once in every row, column and 3×3 box.

Alma 39:1

And now, my son, I have somewhat more to say unto thee than what I said unto thy **brother**; for behold, have ye not observed the **steadiness** of thy brother, his **faithfulness**, and his **diligence** in **keeping** the **commandments** of God? Behold, has he not set a **good example** for **thee**?

				good	example	diligence		
keeping		example			diligence		good	
	brother	good						example
	keeping	brother			thee		commandments	
			diligence	keeping				faithfulness
faithfulness	example		brother		steadiness			
example	good				brother	commandments		
	steadiness			thee			example	keeping
thee	diligence					good	brother	

Knight Moves - Find a Word

Instructions: Start with the capital letter in the puzzle. To get to the next letter, jump two squares in any direction except diagonally, and then one square in a different direction. Your path will look like a capital L. To show you how it works, Only one route through the puzzle will make a word. Write the letters of the word you discover in the blanks below as you jump through the squares:

___ ___ ___ ___ ___ ___ ___ ___
1   2   3   4   5   6   7   8

Now can you find this word in the following scripture?

Alma 38:2–4

c	a	e
i		e
P	n	t

Alma 43–52

"Stand Fast in the Faith of Christ"

Secret Code

Instructions: The secret message is written in symbols. In the code key you can find what each symbol means. Write the letter above the symbol and you can read the secret message.

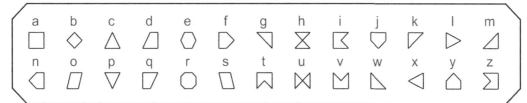

48 : 7

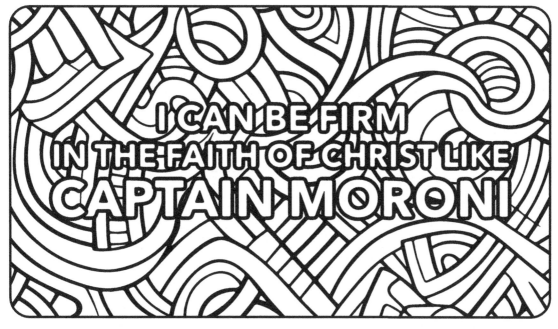

I CAN BE FIRM IN THE FAITH OF CHRIST LIKE CAPTAIN MORONI

Alma 43–52

"Stand Fast in the Faith of Christ"

Missing Vowels Word Search

Instructions: Find the hidden words. The words have been placed horizontally, vertically, diagonally, forwards, or backwards, and the vowels have been removed. When you locate a word, draw an ellipse around it and fill the vowels in.

Alma 46:12-13

And it came to pass that he rent his coat; and he took a piece thereof, and wrote upon it—In **memory** of our **God**, our **religion**, and **freedom**, and our **peace**, our **wives**, and our **children**—and he fastened it upon the end of a **pole**. And he fastened on his head-plate, and his **breastplate**, and his **shields**, and girded on his **armor** about his **loins**; and he took the pole, which had on the end thereof his **rent coat**, (and he called it the **title** of **liberty**) and he **bowed** himself to the earth, and he **prayed** mightily unto his God for the **blessings** of liberty to rest upon his **brethren**, so long as there should a band of **Christians** remain to **possess** the land—

```
T     L  P  T  S        R  B     P  G  V
   L  P  F  L  H  Y  S  T  L  H  X  R
T  K  J  T     W  V  P        C        D
P     L     S  N        L  S     W  Y  L  F
G  V  L     R  M     R  L  S  S  C     W  X
C  D  L  X  T  X  X  M  R  G  M     D  C  P
S  T  F  R     D     M  N        P  K  Z
L  J  X  J  K     C  T  N     M  Y  Q  J  B
   B  R     T  H  R     N  S        T     K
B     T  L  S     V     W  S  R  P  W  S
   T           J  M     N     Y     Z  H  G
R  T  T  N  G  D  C  H     L  D  R     N  C
T  V  L  D  D  X  C     X  B  K  D  T
Y  M     G  J  T  N     G     L     R  D
C  H  R     S  T     N  S  R     N  T  C
```

Unscrambler

Instructions: Unscramble the words below; look at the bold words in the scripture for a hint.

Alma 43:19

And when the **armies** of the **Lamanites** saw that the people of Nephi, or that **Moroni**, had **prepared** his **people** with **breastplates** and with arm-shields, yea, and also **shields** to **defend** their **heads**, and also they were **dressed** with **thick clothing.**

kciht _____

inorom _____

seimra _____

desserd _____

deraperp _____

sdaeh _____

setalptsaerb _____

sdleihs _____

dnefed _____

elpoep _____

gnihtolc _____

setinamal _____

Mystery Picture Graph

Instructions: Find the mystery picture below by plotting and connecting the points of each line on the coordinate graph. Connect all the points in Line 1, stop, pick up your pencil, and then connect all the points in Line 2, and so on for the rest of the lines. The dot for the first (X,Y) coordinate pair on Line 1 has been placed for you.

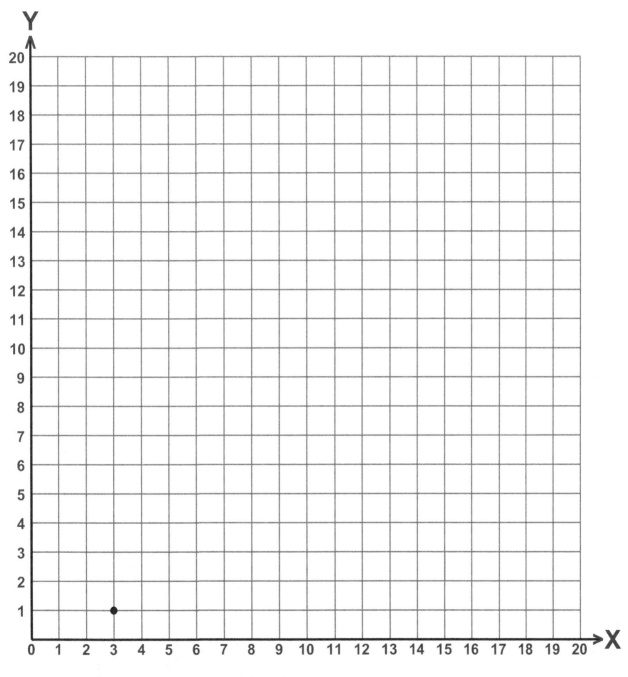

Line 1	(3, 1)	(19, 1)	(19, 12)	(20, 13)	(20, 16)	(18, 16)	(18, 15)	(17, 15)	(17, 16)	(16, 16)	(16, 15)	(15, 15)
(15, 16)	(13, 16)	(13, 13)	(14, 12)	(14, 10)	(13, 10)	(13, 9)	(12, 9)	(12, 10)	(10, 10)	(10, 9)	(9, 9)	(9, 10)
(8, 10)	(8, 12)	(9, 13)	(9, 16)	(7, 16)	(7, 15)	(6, 15)	(6, 16)	(5, 16)	(5, 15)	(4, 15)	(4, 16)	(2, 16)
(2, 13)	(3, 12)	(3, 1)	**Line 2**	(8, 10)	(8, 1)	**Line 3**	(14, 10)	(14, 1)	**Line 4**	(4, 7)	(5, 7)	(5, 9)
(4, 9)	(4, 7)	**Line 5**	(17, 7)	(18, 7)	(18, 9)	(17, 9)	(17, 7)	**Line 6**	(10, 1)	(10, 5)	(12, 5)	(12, 1)

195

Alma 43–52

"Stand Fast in the Faith of Christ"

Handwriting Practice

Practice your handwriting by tracing the sentence below. Then use the blank lines to write the sentence on your own.

Satan tempts and deceives us little by little.

AND WHICH SANDCASTLE IS YOURS, MORONI?

wardcartoonist.com

Arie Van De Graaff

©Arie Van De Graaff

Alma 43–52

"Stand Fast in the Faith of Christ"

Instructions: Connect all of the letters in the phrase bolded below. Don't be tricked by letters that take you into a dead end! There is only one path through the maze.

__ ___ ___ ___ ____' ___ ____' ___ ____ _____ __' ____ ____
_____' _____' ___ ____ _____ __ ____
_____ ____ ____ _____ _____;

Alma 48:17

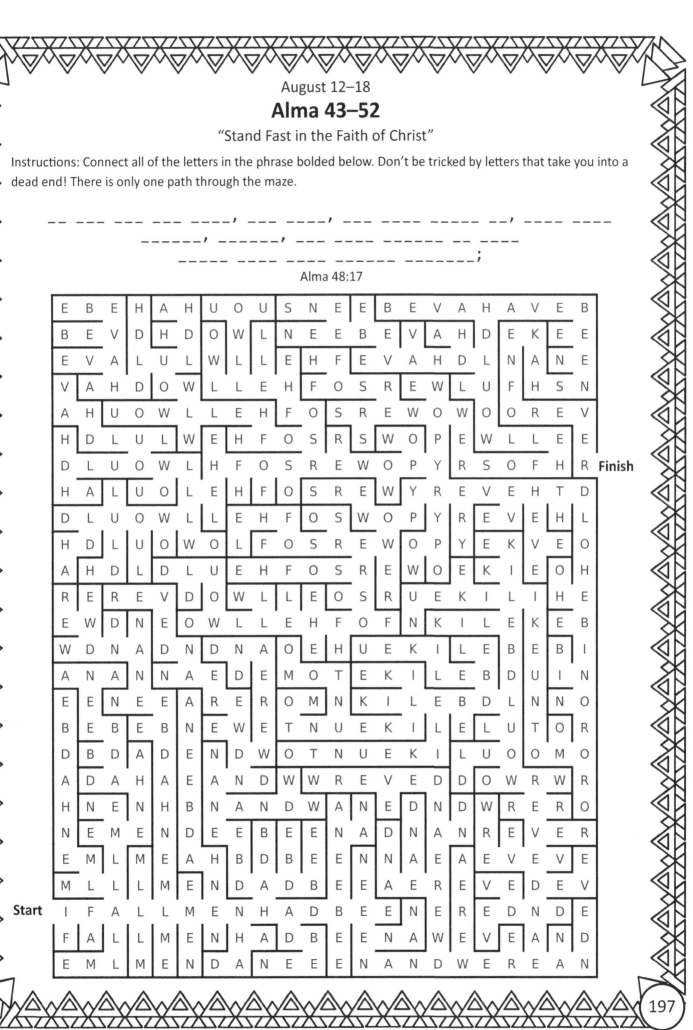

August 12–18

Alma 43–52

"Stand Fast in the Faith of Christ"

Fallen Phrase

Instructions: The letters in each column have fallen from the grid. Put them back correctly to rebuild the phrase. Cross out each letter in the jumble below once you place it in the grid. Pay attention because the letters in each column are scrambled. Start with simple 1 or 2 letter words and use the process of elimination. To check your answer, read **Alma 48:13**

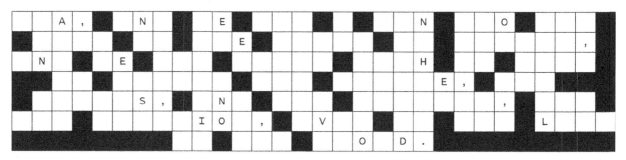

```
                F           F  I              T
      S         N  D         H  A     L  N  O  T        C  N        A  A
   I  I     H  D     D  E  N     S  W  I  R  S  P  H  M  A  O     A  H        S  N  H
H  R  D  O  M  E  E  H  G  A     N  I  S  E  B  E  C  O  U  L     W  Y  H  I  S  O  D
A  F  T  R  R  A  I  F  O  H  H  D  W  O  S  N  T  E  I  O  N     R  H  R  O  A  T  S
Y  E  I  G  H  T  L  I  A  T  D  H  H  A  S  I  A  W  O  P  F  T  T  H  E  I  W  T  S  S
```

Letter Sudoku

Instructions: Solve the letter sudoku puzzle the same way you'd solve a numeric sudoku. Check your puzzle against the answer key on ColorMeChristian.org. Every column, row, and group of nine must contain every letter in the worda **HEART SOUL.** Letters are used only once;

Alma 48:11–12

And Moroni was a strong and a mighty man; he was a man of a perfect understanding; yea, a man that did not delight in bloodshed; a man whose **soul** did joy in the liberty and the freedom of his country, and his brethren from bondage and slavery; Yea, a man whose **heart** did swell with thanksgiving to his God, for the many privileges and blessings which he bestowed upon his people; a man who did labor exceedingly for the welfare and safety of his people.

	O	E		L	A	T		
U		T	A			E	R	
L	O		U		T			
	T	H	L		A			
A	U			S			O	T
T			S		U			O
	S	U	O				A	
	H		T	A	E	S		U

I can be faithful to God like Helaman's young soldiers

August 19–25
Alma 53–63
"Preserved by His Marvelous Power"

Word Angles

Instructions: Find the bold words from the scripture. Each word path may run north, east, south, or west, may make one right-angled turn, and may cross another word path. A few words may make no right angle turn at all.

Alma 53:16-17

But behold, it came to pass they had many **sons**, who had not **entered** into a **covenant** that they would not take their **weapons** of **war** to **defend** themselves against their **enemies**; therefore they did **assemble** themselves **together** at this time, as many as were able to take up arms, and they called themselves **Nephites**. And they entered into a covenant to **fight** for the **liberty** of the Nephites, yea, to **protect** the **land** unto the laying **down** of their **lives**; yea, even they covenanted that they **never** would give up their **liberty**, but they would fight in all cases to protect the Nephites and themselves from **bondage**.

```
N Y T P M N E V U Y E A E J W Q
L C R P I B U E I C M S N O E N
L O E G S O Q R K V O S T K A I
A V B U L N C A U C I E E N P V
N E I S E D A G E L B M R Z O T
D N L W N N B O I G O D E S N C
E A R A E M I E S V W G R R G E
Z N T E G S A B Y T R E M E T G
Q Q N A H T M J M U Z B E D I D
H D M F N C Y E S E T I H P K I
O N X J J E O N W T A L Y E R B
X E F E D T V B O O Q X O N E O
N S J W E O R P D G W G A V W D
O K L O W Z G O W E G I F H C P
S Q I X Y J R E H T H O D Y G I
G M V E S J X B Y O T I F L H X
```

Word Star

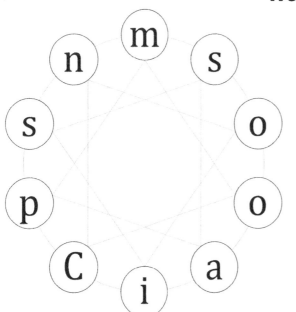

Instructions: Start with the capital letter in the puzzle. Then choose one of the two lines to the next letter. Only one route through the word star will make a word. Write the letters of the word you discover in the blanks below as you travel through the star:

— — — — — — — — — —

Now can you find this word in the following scripture?

Alma 53:13

Alma 53–63
"Preserved by His Marvelous Power"

Handwriting Practice

Practice your handwriting by tracing the sentence below. Then use the blank lines to write the sentence on your own.

I can choose to not be angry like Pahoran.

Cryptogram

Instructions: Each letter on the top stands for a letter in the alphabet. Solve the encrypted phrase by matching each letter on top to a letter in the alphabet on the bottom. Use the key to help you remember what the letters stand for so you can crack the code.

A	C	N	L	K	R	W	D	H	T	V	I	U	G	P	O	S	Z	Y	Q	E	B	J	X	M	F
A	B	C	D	E	F	G	H	I	J	K	L	M	N	O	P	Q	R	S	T	U	V	W	X	Y	Z

S U A ,   A C H   J I U S   H L H   P V U S   A C H

P V Q U F K U   J P   O U F Z P F Y   U K U F S   G P F H   P Z

B P Y Y A C H   G L J I   U X A B J C U Q Q ;   S U A ,   A C H

U K U C   A B B P F H L C N   J P   J I U L F   Z A L J I   L J

G A Q   H P C U   M C J P   J I U Y ;   A C H   L   H L H

F U Y U Y V U F   J I U   G P F H Q   G I L B I   J I U S   Q A L H

M C J P   Y U   J I A J   J I U L F   Y P J I U F Q   I A H

J A M N I J   J I U Y .   A D Y A   5 7 : 2 1

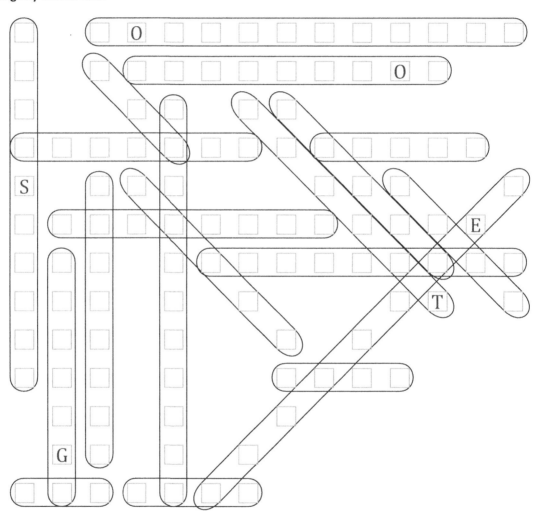

Alma 53–63

"Preserved by His Marvelous Power"

Instructions: Fit the bold words from the scripture below into the encircled squares. Words will read forward, backward, up, down, and diagonally and will normally cross other words. Start with the hints provided.

Alma 53:20–21

And they were all **young men**, and they were **exceedingly valiant** for **courage**, and also for **strength** and **activity**; but behold, this was not all—they were men who were **true** at **all times** in **whatsoever** thing they were **entrusted**. Yea, they were men of **truth** and **soberness**, for they had been **taught** to **keep** the **commandments** of God and to **walk uprightly** before him.

young	men	exceedingly	valiant
courage	strength	activity	true
all	times	whatsoever	entrusted
truth	soberness	taught	keep
commandments	walk	uprightly	

The Stripling Warriors

Help the these Stripling Warriors reach the battlefield so they can defend their families.

Alma 53–63

"Preserved by His Marvelous Power"

Word Square

Instructions: Word squares are a liike Sudoku puzzles, but each letter can occur only once in each row and in each column. Check your puzzle against the answer key on ColorMeChristian.org. Every row and column must contain every letter in the word **LIBERTY.** This word can be written in the gray row.

Alma 61:9

And now, in your epistle you have censured me, but it mattereth not; I am not angry, but do rejoice in the greatness of your heart. I, Pahoran, do not seek for power, save only to retain my judgment-seat that I may preserve the rights and the **liberty** of my people. My soul standeth fast in that liberty in the which God hath made us free.

			T		I	B
I	T		R	B	E	L
	B	T				E
E				L		T
		I		L		R
T	E			Y		I

Helaman 1–6

"The Rock of Our Redeemer"

Word Search

Instructions: Find the bold words from the scripture in the word search puzzle. Each word could be hidden forwards, backwards, up, down, or diagonally.

Helaman 5:29–30

And it came to pass that there came a **voice** as if it were above the **cloud** of **darkness**, saying: **Repent** ye, repent ye, and **seek** no more to **destroy** my **servants** whom I have sent unto you to **declare good tidings**. And it came to pass when they **heard** this voice, and beheld that it was not a voice of **thunder**, neither was it a voice of a **great tumultuous noise**, but behold, it was a **still** voice of **perfect mildness**, as if it had been a **whisper**, and it did **pierce** even to the very **soul**—

```
K  K  E  J  I  P  R  P  E  R  F  E  C  T  Q
S  E  E  K  I  B  I  E  E  N  D  R  M  J  D
N  C  O  E  L  U  O  S  D  R  O  I  J  A  U
G  L  R  D  E  Z  S  T  P  N  L  I  R  K  L
S  C  D  X  U  T  I  S  L  D  U  K  S  P  Z
E  W  F  E  V  D  C  P  N  B  N  H  Y  E  F
I  L  V  E  I  L  R  E  P  E  N  T  T  S  Y
O  O  A  N  O  U  S  D  S  E  U  F  K  T  O
L  U  G  U  X  S  F  S  V  O  I  C  E  N  R
J  S  D  F  G  J  Y  Q  C  M  P  U  S  A  T
D  D  E  C  L  A  R  E  G  R  E  A  T  V  S
P  K  W  C  F  T  J  E  P  G  D  O  I  R  E
X  Z  Q  N  D  R  A  E  H  Q  K  O  L  E  D
L  T  U  M  U  L  T  U  O  U  S  L  L  S  H
P  F  W  D  O  O  G  R  E  P  S  I  H  W  S
```

HOW ABOUT YOU HOOK ME UP WITH A SECRET COMBO MEAL?

GADIANTON DINES OUT.

Hidden Picture: Buildings need strong foundations, just like this temple. Can you find 5 pictures of the temple in the hidden picture below? It will be tricky; the picture may be smaller, on its side, or even upside down! Then, see if you can find 1 image of the animals as well.

Helaman 1–6

"The Rock of Our Redeemer"

Instructions: Using the Across and Down clues, write the correct words in the numbered grid below. Hint: all of the words in the crossword come from the scripture below.

Helaman 5:12

ACROSS

2. a state of ill-being due to affliction or misfortune
3. strength; ability to do something
8. a state of ill-being due to affliction or misfortune
10. Jesus Christ
11. Heavenly Father
13. precipitation of ice pellets
17. the basis on which something is grounded
18. Messiah
19. hit repeatedly
20. make by combining materials and parts

DOWN

1. air moving from high pressure to low pressure
4. recall knowledge; have a recollection
5. a violent weather condition with winds and precipitation and thunder and lightning
6. pull, as against a resistance
7. Jesus Christ
9. something directed or barbed as in sharp attack:
12. an evil supernatural being
14. material consisting of stone
15. descend freely under the influence of gravity
16. sorrow or grief

Helaman 1–6

"The Rock of Our Redeemer"

Instructions: Solve this word sudoku puzzle the same way that you'd solve a numeric sudoku. Each of the bold words in the scripture below is found once in every row, column and 3×3 box.

Helaman 3:35

Nevertheless they did **fast** and **pray oft**, and did wax stronger and stronger in their humility, and firmer and firmer in the **faith** of **Christ**, unto the filling their souls with **joy** and consolation, yea, even to the **purifying** and the sanctification of their **hearts**, which sanctification cometh because of their **yielding** their hearts unto God.

	joy		yielding					fast
			joy			oft	purifying	faith
	Christ		fast			yielding		
faith	purifying			fast		pray		
Christ						fast	faith	
		fast		pray	joy		yielding	
		Christ				faith	oft	
oft		purifying	pray				fast	
joy	faith			yielding			Christ	

August 26–September 1

Helaman 1–6

"The Rock of Our Redeemer"

The Holy Ghost whispers with a **still**, small voice.

Come, Follow Me Manual, 2024

Start

End

Helaman 1–6

"The Rock of Our Redeemer"

Fill in the Blank

Helaman 5:41

And _____ said unto them: You must _____, and _____ unto

the voice, even until ye shall have faith in _____, who was taught unto you by Alma,

and _____, and _____; and when ye shall do this, the _____

of _____ shall be _____ from _____ you.

Christ	removed	Amulek	cry	darkness	overshadowing
Zeezrom	Aminadab	cloud	repent		

Translation Station

Instructions: Translate the sign language letters below into English to discover the hidden message. Write the alphabet letter beneath each hand sign. Use the key at the back of the book to help you.

Helaman 7–12

"Remember the Lord"

Wacky Word Trails

Instructions: Start with the circled letter, use the clues to find and mark the trail of letters of all the connected bolded words from the scripture through the maze to the last letter. The path can wander up, down, left, and right at any point, even in the middle of the word.

Helaman 10:11–12

And now behold, I **command** you, that ye shall go and **declare** unto this **people**, that thus saith the Lord God, who is the **Almighty**: Except ye **repent** ye shall be **smitten**, even unto **destruction**. And behold, now it came to pass that when the Lord had **spoken** these words unto **Nephi**, he did **stop** and did not **go** unto his own **house**, but did **return** unto the **multitudes** who were **scattered** about upon the **face** of the **land**, and **began** to declare unto them the **word** of the **Lord** which had been spoken unto him, **concerning** their destruction if they did not repent.

```
N N W G X Y D W P M Y Y X H T
S E I X N R W W J O O C I G Y
F U P A L T V P S Z H X M L G
G T U Q U I D E S D C I P A O
(R) E R N M T U S C B I K N D S
A E Y J R D N A O I Z M O R T
N E K O P L A M M E Y E W P O
S H D P S D N S E O A R W H U
M R E P E N T D E C L B E O W
I G N I N R F Z N A G E S U P
T T D E S E V Y S C A S F K O
N E N H T C I G E P T F E D N
P T C U R N Q Q D H T E R T E
M I R T H O C E C L E I I H P
P O N L O R D F A P O E P L Y
```

Translation Station

Instructions: Translate the Morse code below into English to discover the hidden message. Write the alphabet letter beneath each Morse Code letter. Each letter, number, and punctuation is separated by a slash: /. Use the key at the back of the book to help you.

−·/−−−/·−−/ ·−−/·/ ····/·−/·−−−/·/ ·−/ ·−−/−−−/·−·/−··/−−·/

·−−/····/·/·−·/ ·−−/·/−−−/·−·/·−·/·/ ·−/·−·/·/

−··/−−−/·−/·−·/·−/·/·/·−−− ··/····/ −··/−−−/·−−

·−·/−−−/·−//·/ ·−−·/·−/·−·/·/·/−·// ··/·−/−−·· −−·/−−−/

·−/·−/·−·/ ·−−/·−/·−/−−−/····/ ·/····/·/ ·−/·/·−−/·/·−−··

·−−/·/ ·−·/·−/·−·/ ·−−/·/·−/ ·−·/·/·−−·/·/·−·/·−·/−−−/·/

·−/·−−·/·/ ·−·/·−/·−·/·/·−·/ −−−/··/·−/

·−−/·/·−−−/−−− ··/·/ ·−−/·/ ····/·/·/−·/ ·−/····/·/

·−−/····/·/·−·/−·/ ·−/····/·/·−−/·/ ···/·−/·−·/−··
```
```

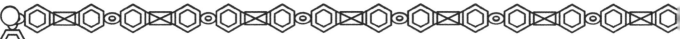

Helaman 7–12

"Remember the Lord"

Instructions: Fill in the blank puzzle grid using the word bank with the bold words from the scripture below. Place the words in the correct place on the grid.

Helaman 8:22–23

Our father **Lehi** was **driven** out of **Jerusalem** because he **testified** of these **things**. **Nephi** also testified of these things, and also almost all of our **fathers**, even down to this **time**; yea, they have testified of the **coming** of **Christ**, and have **looked forward**, and have **rejoiced** in his **day** which is to **come**. And behold, he is God, and he is **with** them, and he did **manifest himself** unto them, that they were **redeemed** by him; and they gave unto him **glory**, because of that which is to come.

3 Letters	Lehi	**6 Letters**	**7 Letters**	rejoiced
day		Christ	fathers	manifest
	5 Letters	driven	forward	
4 Letters	Nephi	coming	himself	**9 Letters**
with	glory	looked		testified
time		things	**8 Letters**	Jerusalem
come			redeemed	

This Is the Right Place

By Arie Van De Graaff

Brigham Young became sick during the trek west. When he arrived at the Salt Lake Valley, he was lying in the back of a wagon. Looking at the valley, he declared: "This is the right place," and the pioneers settled there because they followed the prophet. See if you can find the hidden objects in the picture.

BANANA   BASEBALL BAT   BELL   BOTTLE   BRUSH   CHEESE   ENVELOPE   ICE CREAM

MITT   OAR   PAINT BRUSH   PEN   SCREWDRIVER   TIE   WATCH   WATERMELON

Helaman 7–12

"Remember the Lord"

Handwriting Practice

Practice your handwriting by tracing the sentence below. Then use the blank lines to write the sentence on your own.

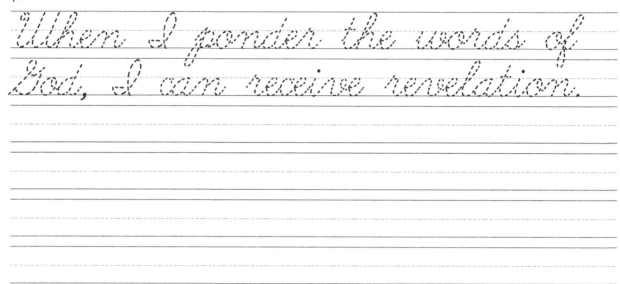

When I ponder the words of God, I can receive revelation.

PLEASE BLESS THIS FOOD THAT IT WILL NOURISH AND STRENGTHEN US.

BIRDS OF PRAY

September 2–8

Helaman 7–12

"Remember the Lord"

Instructions: Connect all of the letters in the phrase bolded below. Don't be tricked by letters that take you into a dead end! There is only one path through the maze.

______: __ ________ ___ _____ ______, _____ ____ ___ __________ __
_____ ______ __ ___. ____ ________ ____ ______, _________ ___
______ __ ___ ___ _____ __________ ___ _____________.

Guide to the Scriptures

Start

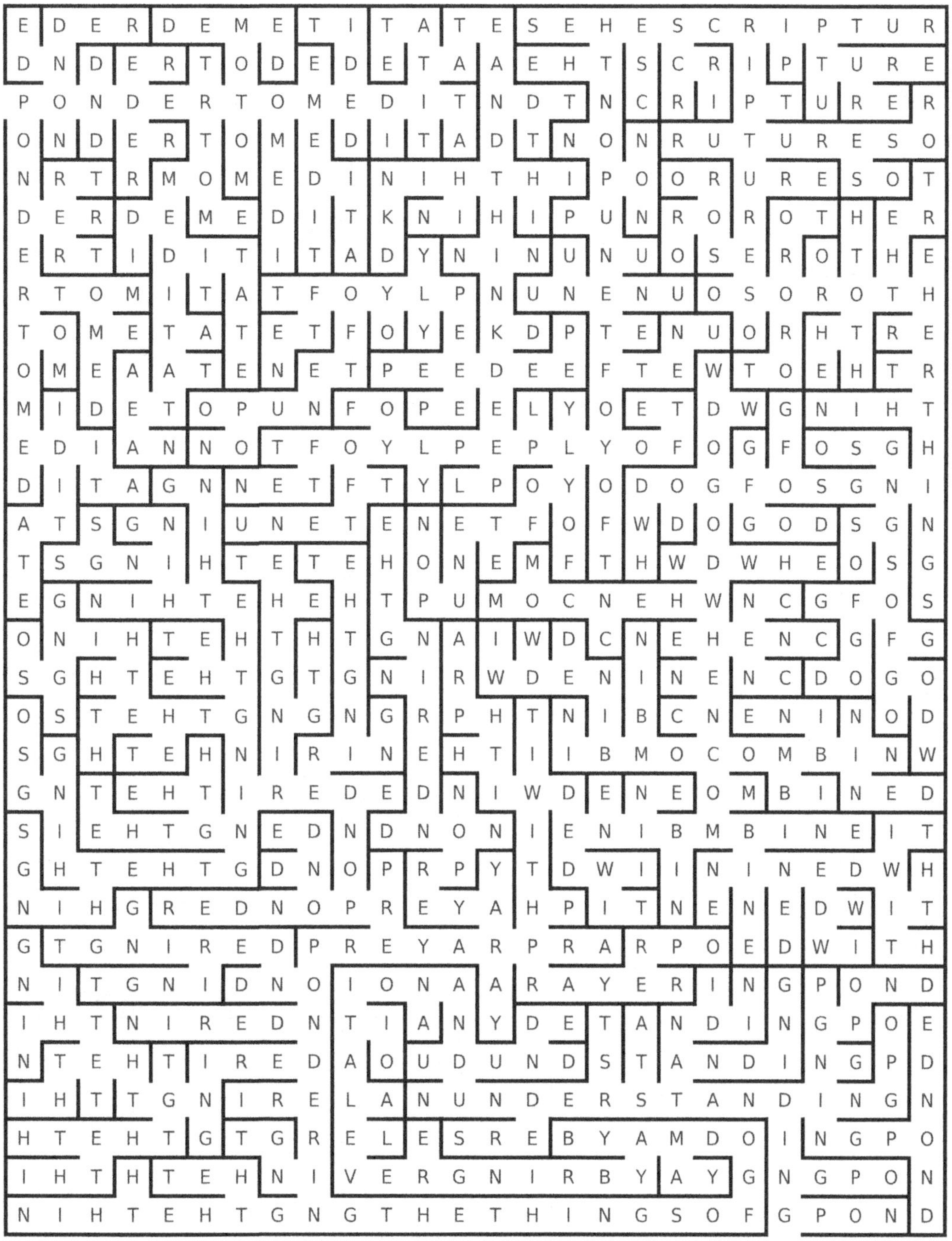

Finish

Helaman 7–12

"Remember the Lord"

Letter Sudoku

Instructions: Solve the letter sudoku puzzle the same way you'd solve a numeric sudoku. Check your puzzle against the answer key on ColorMeChristian.org. Every column, row, and group of nine must contain every letter in the worda **HEART UPON.** Letters are used only once;

Helaman 7:20–21

O, how could you have forgotten your God in the very day that he has delivered you? But behold, it is to get gain, to be praised of men, yea, and that ye might get gold and silver. And ye have set your **heart**s **upon** the riches and the vain things of this world, for the which ye do murder, and plunder, and steal, and bear false witness against your neighbor, and do all manner of iniquity.

			A	H	E	U		
			O				A	E
	P	U	E		T	N		
O		N	U		H		P	
E				N		O		T
T	R				O	A	N	
				A	P	R		
				E		T		O

September 9–15
Helaman 13–16
"Glad Tidings of Great Joy"

Missing Vowels Word Search

Instructions: Find the hidden words. The words have been placed horizontally, vertically, diagonally, forwards, or backwards, and the vowels have been removed. When you locate a word, draw an ellipse around it and fill the vowels in.

Helaman 16:1

And now, it came to pass that there were **many** who **heard** the **words** of **Samuel**, the **Lamanite**, which he **spake** upon the **walls** of the **city**. And as many as **believed** on his word went **forth** and **sought** for **Nephi**; and when they had come forth and **found** him they **confessed** unto him their **sins** and **denied not**, **desiring** that they might be **baptized** unto the **Lord**.

```
M L   M   N   T   L   T
  H D M Y T   C   S X   D M M
W P X J   S   M     L V R L T
D   N     D W   L L S K   D H
D T T W N   T   F W D R     H
Q Q C P F D G D R B S M B   S
    K   M Q S N   D       X S
S B R B N   B     B S N P   P
G T X   K F Q   D R W Y T H N
H X J T N     L B   S   R G
F   N D N   S Y     S Z X P
Y Y V D   N   S S     P   H P
C V L P L D N   G     V D D
H P H J F   H H L   D F   N T
Z   R T S T T J S P   K   D S
```

Knight Moves - Find a Word

Instructions: Start with the capital letter in the puzzle. To get to the next letter, jump two squares in any direction except diagonally, and then one square in a different direction. Your path will look like a capital L. To show you how it works, Only one route through the puzzle will make a word. Write the letters of the word you discover in the blanks below as you jump through the squares:

__ __ __ __ __ __ __
  2 3 4 5 6 7 8

Now can you find this word in the following scripture?

Helaman 14:20

e	d	r
a		n
e	k	D

217

Samuel The Lamanite

Samuel the Lamanite prophesied about Jesus' birth. Help Samuel through the maze so he can find and worship the Baby Jesus.

Helaman 13–16

"Glad Tidings of Great Joy"

Reverse Word Search

Instructions: Instead of looking for words in a grid, place the bold words in the scripture in the empty word search puzzle. The words may be forwards, backwards, up, down, or diagonally The start letter of the words have been placed in the grid to get you started.

Helaman 14:2–3

And behold, he said unto them: **Behold**, I **give** unto you a **sign**; for **five years** more **cometh**, and behold, then cometh the **Son** of **God** to **redeem** all those who shall **believe** on his **name**. And behold, this will I give unto you for a sign at the **time** of his **coming**; for behold, there shall be **great lights** in **heaven**, insomuch that in the **night before** he cometh there shall be no **darkness**, insomuch that it shall **appear** unto man as if it was **day**.

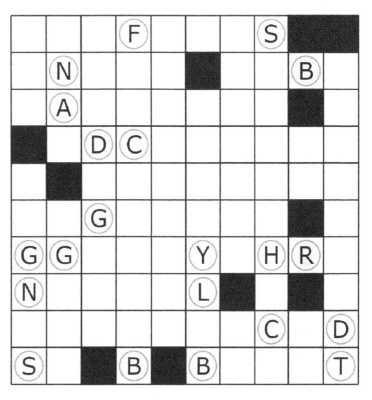

Helaman 13–16

"Glad Tidings of Great Joy"

Handwriting Practice

Practice your handwriting by tracing the sentence below. Then use the blank lines to write the sentence on your own.

Prophets teach about Jesus Christ.

Mystery Picture Graph

Instructions: Find the mystery picture below by plotting and connecting the points of each line on the coordinate graph. Connect all the points in Line 1, stop, pick up your pencil, and then connect all the points in Line 2, and so on for the rest of the lines. The dot for the first (X,Y) coordinate pair on Line 1 has been placed for you.

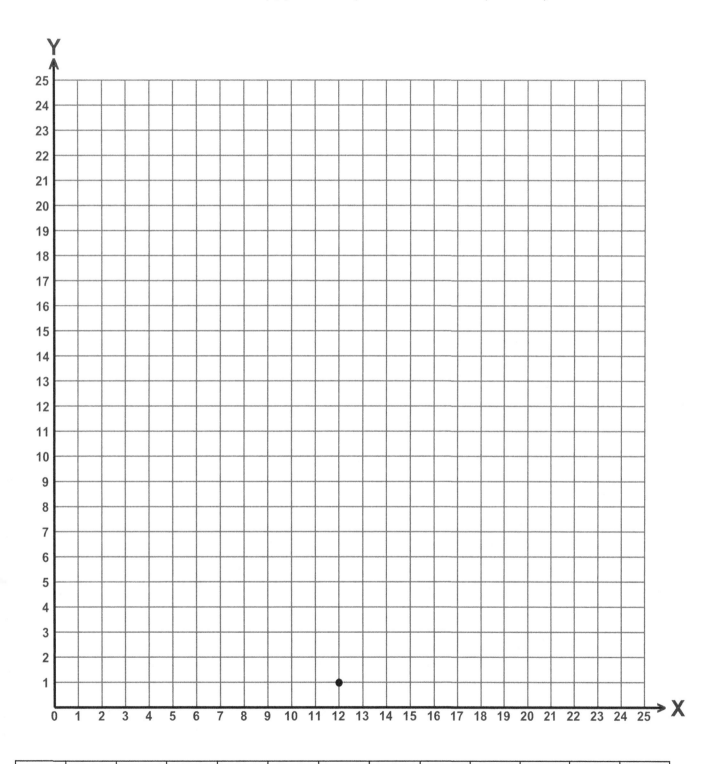

Line 1	(12, 1)	(23, 13)	(23, 20)	(20, 23)	(16, 23)	(12, 20)	(9, 23)	(4, 23)	(1, 20)	(1, 13)	(12, 1)	(20, 23)
Line 2	(23, 13)	(1, 20)	**Line 3**	(12, 20)	(17, 15)	**Line 4**	(1, 20)	(12, 1)				

Helaman 13–16

"Glad Tidings of Great Joy"

Secret Code

Instructions: The secret message is written in symbols. In the code key you can find what each symbol means. Write the letter above the symbol and you can read the secret message.

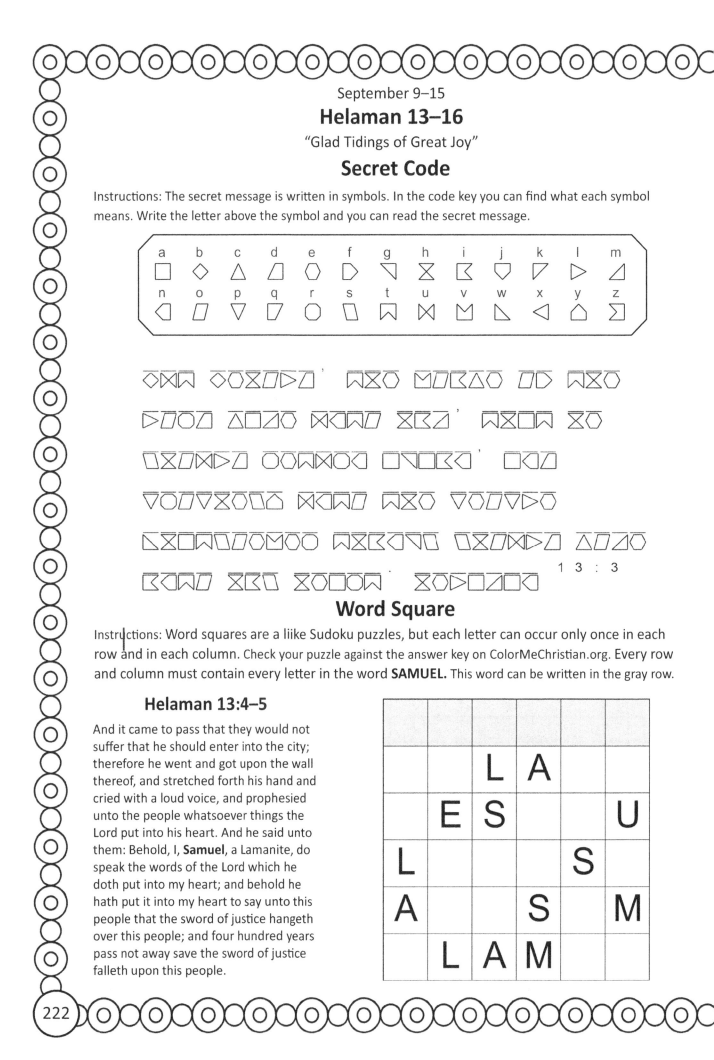

13 : 3

Word Square

Instructions: Word squares are a liike Sudoku puzzles, but each letter can occur only once in each row and in each column. Check your puzzle against the answer key on ColorMeChristian.org. Every row and column must contain every letter in the word **SAMUEL.** This word can be written in the gray row.

Helaman 13:4–5

And it came to pass that they would not suffer that he should enter into the city; therefore he went and got upon the wall thereof, and stretched forth his hand and cried with a loud voice, and prophesied unto the people whatsoever things the Lord put into his heart. And he said unto them: Behold, I, **Samuel**, a Lamanite, do speak the words of the Lord which he doth put into my heart; and behold he hath put it into my heart to say unto this people that the sword of justice hangeth over this people; and four hundred years pass not away save the sword of justice falleth upon this people.

3 Nephi 1–7

"Lift Up Your Head and Be of Good Cheer"

Word Angles

Instructions: Find the bold words from the scripture. Each word path may run north, east, south, or west, may make one right-angled turn, and may cross another word path. A few words may make no right angle turn at all.

3 Nephi 3:13–14

Yea, he sent a **proclamation** among all the **people**, that they should **gather together** their **women**, and their **children**, their **flocks** and their **herds**, and all their **substance**, save it were their land, unto one place. And he caused that **fortifications** should be built **round** about them, and the **strength** thereof should be **exceedingly great**. And he caused that **armies**, both of the **Nephites** and of the **Lamanites**, or of all them who were **numbered** among the Nephites, should be placed as **guards** round about to **watch** them, and to guard them from the **robbers** day and night.

```
K M N L I B L P O N S S H S O M
C D V N B E M A S D E L T H E R
K H W O C R S E V I Y B E C T P
P O Q C C T E W Z L T M G E B F
P E D Z Q Y L G D A R E O T S I
L R N K T K F L I B E S T O T J
T E G Q N C E O Q I X S X R X C
F T Q K A D O W M A X A F P O L
B N L A N J P N O C O E F J W T
I E Y I E Z B A I I N I G Y N S
B B J M V O C Z F S E I M Y D S
U Q T P A O T S N O T T E S N O
V E R S F L H L D B W H N E A G
E C N E T I H P E N C G E U L K
N C D E F E N V W A E I F M V T
J R V Q D S D G A R G A D N O B
```

Word Bricks

Instructions: A sentence is written on the wall. But brick layers built the wall in the wrong order. Your job is to put the bricks in the right order. Hint: **Hint: Song from the Primary Songbook, I'm Trying to be Like Jesus.**

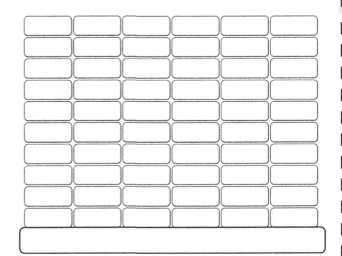

September 16–22

3 Nephi 1–7

"Lift Up Your Head and Be of Good Cheer"

Instructions: Using the Across and Down clues, write the correct words in the numbered grid below. Hint: all of the words in the crossword come from the scripture below.

3 Nephi 1:4–21

ACROSS

1. Behavior that is morally wrong, evil, or sinful.
6. The separation of the spirit from the mortal body.
8. A principle of action and power that must be centered on Jesus Christ to lead to salvation.
10. Being loyal, determined, and unwavering in purpose.
13. A person designated by God to be His spokesperson and to be a teacher, revelator and witness of gospel truths.
15. People who do not have faith or do not believe in a God..
16. To observe or keep an eye on something carefully.
17. Feeling annoyed or discouraged when one's efforts are not successful.
18. Bent forward or downward, often as a sign of respect or submission.
19. An extraordinary event caused by the power of God.
20. The absence of light; a state of being dark or dim.

DOWN

2. Shouts or expressions of joy, happiness, or encouragement.
3. When something promised or expected has been completed or achieved.
4. The base or support upon which something is built or established.
5. A tiny amount or small particle, often used in expressions like "not a whit," meaning not at all.

6. To cause severe damage or ruin something completely.
7. Having excessive pride in one's appearance or abilities; also, something done without success.
9. Extremely surprised or amazed.
10. Feeling deep sadness or grief.
11. To formally state or declare something as true, often in a legal or solemn manner.
12. A loud and chaotic noise, usually caused by a group of people.
14. The moment a person comes into this world

3 Nephi 1–7

"Lift Up Your Head and Be of Good Cheer"

Instructions: Solve this word sudoku puzzle the same way that you'd solve a numeric sudoku. Each of the bold words in the scripture below is found once in every row, column and 3×3 box.

3 Nephi 1:13-14

Lift up your head and be of good **cheer**; for behold, the **time** is at **hand**, and on this night shall the **sign** be **given**, and on the morrow come I into the **world**, to show unto the world that I will **fulfil** all that which I have caused to be **spoken** by the mouth of my holy prophets. Behold, I come unto my own, to fulfil all things which I have made known unto the children of men from the foundation of the world, and to do the **will**, both of the Father and of the Son—of the Father because of me, and of the Son because of my flesh. And behold, the time is at hand, and this night shall the sign be given.

spoken		time	hand					
given	cheer				spoken	fulfil		
	world	fulfil				sign		
time						hand	sign	spoken
	fulfil			sign				given
sign				will		cheer		fulfil
world						spoken	will	hand
will			time			world	fulfil	
		cheer	will	spoken	world			

September 16–22

3 Nephi 1–7

"Lift Up Your Head and Be of Good Cheer"

I am a **disciple** of Jesus Christ.

Come, Follow Me Manual, 2024

3 Nephi 1–7

"Lift Up Your Head and Be of Good Cheer"

WAIT, TITHING IS SUPPOSED TO BE FIRE INSURANCE, ISN'T IT? THEN, NOPE. NO WE DON'T HAVE FLOOD INSURANCE.

wardcartoonist.com

©Arie Van De Graaff

Cryptogram

Instructions: Each letter on the top stands for a letter in the alphabet. Solve the encrypted phrase by matching each letter on top to a letter in the alphabet on the bottom. Use the key to help you remember what the letters stand for so you can crack the code.

Y	S	O	V	R	T	W	Q	M	B	Z	P	K	U	I	X	N	L	G	H	J	D	C	A	E	F
A	B	C	D	E	F	G	H	I	J	K	L	M	N	O	P	Q	R	S	T	U	V	W	X	Y	Z

J Y T C R V ,   O   X I   X   V O B W O L R Y   C Z   U Y B N B

W T E O B F ,   F T Y   B C Q   C Z   S C V .   O   T X D Y

J Y Y Q   W X R R Y V   C Z   T O I   F C   V Y W R X E Y   T O B

G C E V   X I C Q S   T O B   L Y C L R Y ,   F T X F   F T Y A

I O S T F   T X D Y   Y D Y E R X B F O Q S   R O Z Y .   3

Q Y L T O   5 : 1 3

3 Nephi 8–11

"Arise and Come Forth unto Me"

Word Search

Instructions: Find the bold words from the scripture in the word search puzzle. Each word could be hidden forwards, backwards, up, down, or diagonally.

3 Nephi 11:14–15

Arise and **come forth** unto me, that ye may **thrust** your **hands** into my **side**, and also that ye may feel the **prints** of the **nails** in my hands and in my **feet**, that ye may **know** that I am the God of Israel, and the God of the whole earth, and have been **slain** for the **sins** of the **world**. And it came to pass that the **multitude** went forth, and thrust their hands into his side, and did feel the prints of the nails in his hands and in his feet; and this they did do, going forth **one** by one until they had all gone forth, and did **see** with their **eyes** and did **feel** with their hands, and did know of a **surety** and did bear **record**, that it was he, of whom it was **written** by the **prophets**, that should **come**.

W	K	M	Y	J	L	B	Z	S	G	Y	D	B	I	U
P	R	O	P	H	E	T	S	P	U	K	J	Z	S	U
D	C	M	W	E	M	O	C	G	M	R	W	X	N	U
V	V	I	S	B	H	P	I	U	Z	R	E	D	O	T
L	B	F	G	P	K	K	L	W	R	I	T	T	E	N
F	E	F	G	H	F	T	N	S	Z	O	U	X	Y	P
R	M	E	O	O	I	E	E	K	D	D	D	V	J	G
M	Z	E	F	T	N	B	N	K	L	N	W	O	N	K
H	P	T	U	G	A	K	O	R	D	A	A	H	H	T
S	Q	D	R	L	I	M	O	I	R	N	S	H	T	H
T	E	O	P	U	L	W	T	E	O	N	L	M	R	R
N	E	Y	R	S	S	H	D	E	C	O	A	S	O	U
I	E	M	E	A	O	I	Q	B	E	K	I	G	F	S
R	S	D	O	S	S	X	F	E	R	N	N	W	Y	T
P	X	T	D	C	U	P	Z	A	S	B	B	F	R	V

3 Nephi 8–11

"Arise and Come Forth unto Me"

Fill in the Blank

3 Nephi 11:3

And it came to pass that while they were thus conversing one with another, they

_____ a voice as if it came out of heaven; and they cast their eyes round about, for

they _____ not the voice which they heard; and it was not a _____ voice,

neither was it a _____ voice; nevertheless, and notwithstanding it being a

_____ voice it did _____ them that did _____ to the

_____, insomuch that there was no part of their _____ that it did not

cause to _____; yea, it did pierce them to the very _____, and did cause

their _____ to _____.

soul	quake	understood	burn	pierce	loud
center	heard	harsh	frame	hear	small
hearts					

Translation Station

Instructions: Translate the sign language letters below into English to discover the hidden message. Write the alphabet letter beneath each hand sign. Use the key at the back of the book to help you.

Hidden Picture: Jesus protects His people as a hen protects her chicks. Can you find the 7 chicks in the hidden picture below? It will be tricky; the picture may be smaller, on its side, or even upside down! Then, see if you can find 1 image of the other animals as well.

Handwriting Practice

Practice your handwriting by tracing the sentence below. Then use the blank lines to write the sentence on your own.

When I am in darkness, Jesus Christ can be my light.

3 Nephi 8–11

"Arise and Come Forth unto Me"

Instructions: Connect all of the letters in the phrase bolded below. Don't be tricked by letters that take you into a dead end! There is only one path through the maze.

– –– ––––– –– –––––– –––– – –––– ––––––, ––– ––– –––– – –––––– –––
–– – ––– –––––––––– ––– –––––––– ––––– ––– –––––, –– –– ––––
–––––– ––– –––––– –––– –– –––– –––– –––––– –– –––––.

3 Nephi 10:6

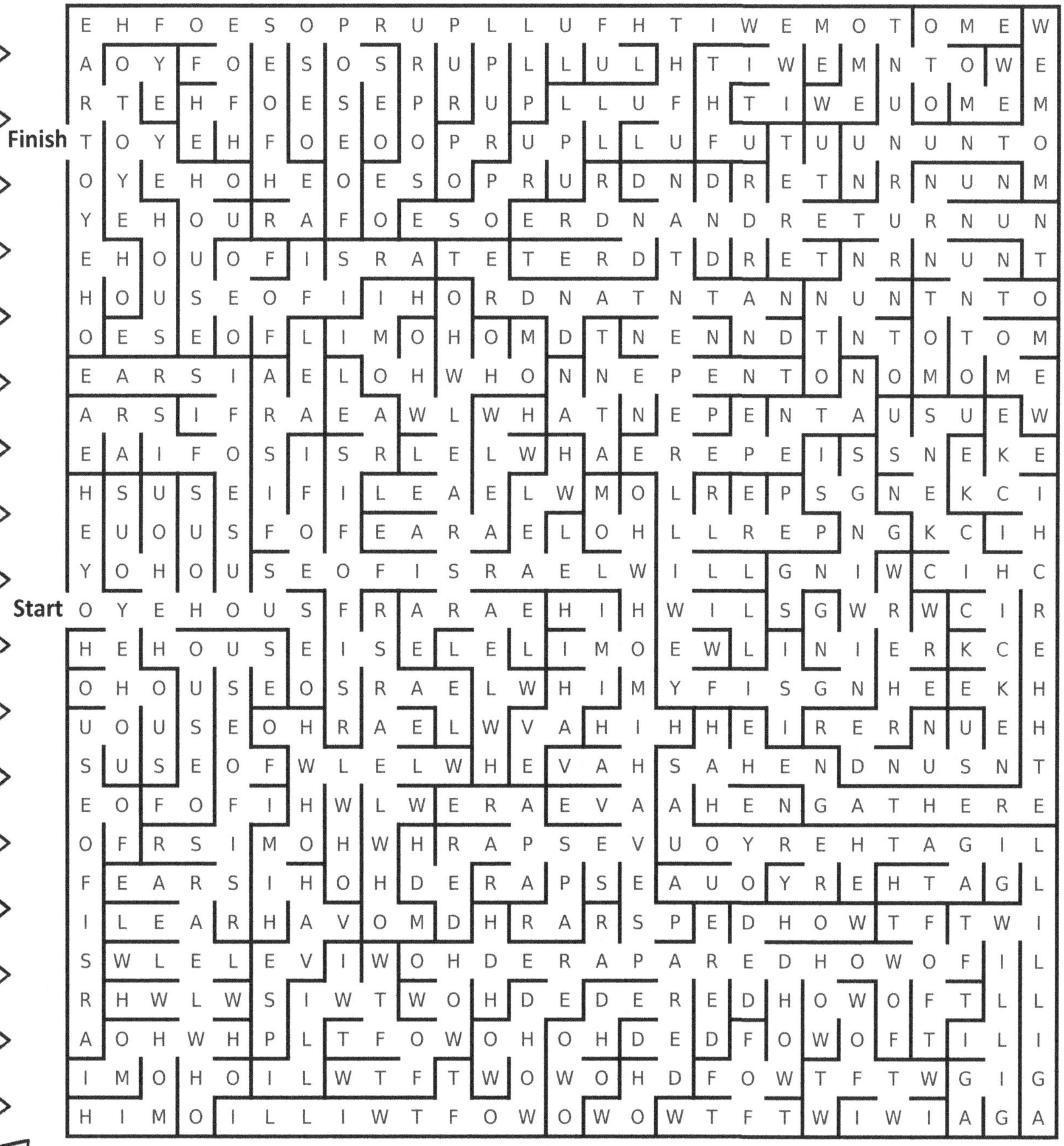

Finish

Start

3 Nephi 8–11

"Arise and Come Forth unto Me"

Fallen Phrase

Instructions: The letters in each column have fallen from the grid. Put them back correctly to rebuild the phrase. Cross out each letter in the jumble below once you place it in the grid. Pay attention because the letters in each column are scrambled. Start with simple 1 or 2 letter words and use the process of elimination. To check your answer, read **3 Nephi 9:18**

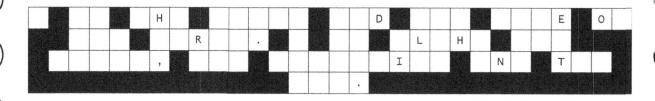

```
                              E   I
    A   M           H   I     I   A N         G         A
    M H G A     O   L   D   B T G A M     T H     A   I N
I O T E E T W E T L E G H E N D N N A N P E A L D F D H E F
```

Letter Sudoku

Instructions: Solve the letter sudoku puzzle the same way you'd solve a numeric sudoku. Check your puzzle against the answer key on ColorMeChristian.org. Every column, row, and group of nine must contain every letter in the worda **HEARS OUND.** Letters are used only once;

3 Nephi 11:5–7

And again the third time they did hear the voice, and did open their ears to **hear** it; and their eyes were towards the **sound** thereof; and they did look steadfastly towards heaven, from whence the sound came. And behold, the third time they did understand the voice which they heard; and it said unto them: Behold my Beloved Son, in whom I am well pleased, in whom I have glorified my name—hear ye him.

	R							A
	N	E		U			R	
A		D						
R	H			U		D		O
	U	D			A		H	
S				D		N	E	
	N	R		O			A	
D		H			R		S	

Setting A Good ExampleBy Following Jesus

You can be a good example by following Jesus. Help guide these children through the maze to Jesus .

September 30–October 6

3 Nephi 12–16

"I Am the Law, and the Light"

Wacky Word Trails

Instructions: Start with the circled letter, use the clues to find and mark the trail of letters of all the connected bolded words from the scripture through the maze to the last letter. The path can wander up, down, left, and right at any point, even in the middle of the word.

3 Nephi 12:14–16

Verily, verily, I say unto you, I **give** unto you to be the **light** of this **people**. A **city** that is set on a **hill** cannot be **hid**. Behold, do men light a **candle** and put it under a **bushel**? Nay, but on a **candlestick**, and it **giveth** light to all that are in the **house**; Therefore let your light so **shine** before this people, that they may **see** your **good works** and **glorify** your **Father** who is in **heaven**.

```
P A J I R G C V K P L O R I F
J B B F T O J S C T G A A H Y
E Q Q O G I V I G H L D N A C
Z C Q O D G E L P F E O D L E
E L G O X J T H M T S A N Q M
H B E S K F D I X I C C E V I
S U E S R O W H V X K H O U G
V U O N F A T R Y H A O X S E
A J H E S E H E H W T S C A D
L L A V T U Z D N D W H X X N
I H E F E C M K B S H G K E P
H I N E G Y W T B Q X T D X S
E H I C D B U L K D E H A D W
L (S) T Y C N B V M R Z U T S P
P O E P F T R K U Q A D K I
```

Translation Station

Instructions: Translate the Morse code below into English to discover the hidden message. Write the alphabet letter beneath each Morse Code letter. Each letter, number, and punctuation is separated by a slash: /. Use the key at the back of the book to help you.

·−/···/−·−·/−·−·· ·−/−·/−·−·/ ··/−· ···/····/·−···/·−···/

−···/·/ −−·/··/···−/·/−·/ ··−/·−·/·−/−−−/

−·−−/−−−/··−/·−·· ···/·/·/−−·/−−·−· ·−/−·/−··/

−·−−/·/ ···/····/·−/·−···/·−·/ ··−/··/−·/−·/−·−·

−·−/−·−·−/−·−·−/−·−−−·− ·−/−·−·/··−/·−·/ ··/·−·

···/····/·−/···−/·−···/ −···/·/ −−−/·−···/·−···/·−···/

··−/·−·/·−/−−−/ −·−·−/−−−/··−/·−·· ····−/ −··/·/−−·/····/··/

·−−−−/·····−/−−−−/·−− ·−·

3 Nephi 12–16

"I Am the Law, and the Light"

Instructions: Fit the bold words from the scripture below into the encircled squares. Words will read forward, backward, up, down, and diagonally and will normally cross other words. Start with the hints provided.

3 Nephi 14:24–27

Therefore, whoso **heareth** these **sayings** of mine and **doeth** them, I will liken him unto a **wise man**, who **built** his **house** upon a **rock**— And the **rain descended**, and the **floods came**, and the **winds blew**, and **beat** upon that **house**; and it **fell not**, for it was founded upon a rock. And every one that heareth these sayings of mine and doeth them not shall be likened unto a **foolish** man, who built his house upon the **sand**— And the rain descended, and the floods came, and the winds blew, and beat upon that house; and it fell, and **great** was the **fall** of it.

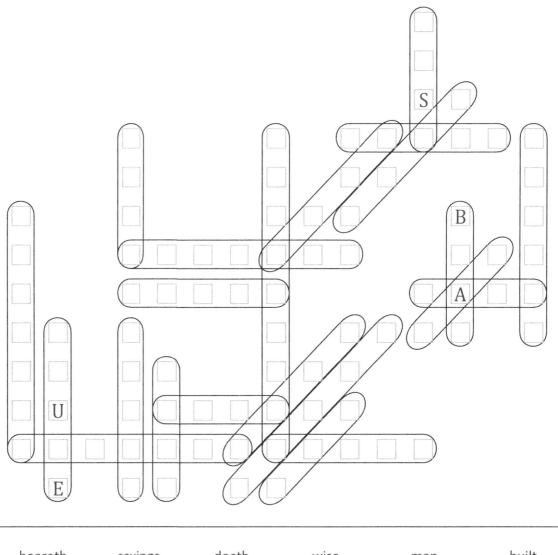

heareth	sayings	doeth	wise	man	built
house	rock	rain	descended	floods	came
winds	blew	beat	house	fell	not
foolish	sand	great	fall		

Mystery Picture Graph

Instructions: Find the mystery picture below by plotting and connecting the points of each line on the coordinate graph. Connect all the points in Line 1, stop, pick up your pencil, and then connect all the points in Line 2, and so on for the rest of the lines. The dot for the first (X,Y) coordinate pair on Line 1 has been placed for you.

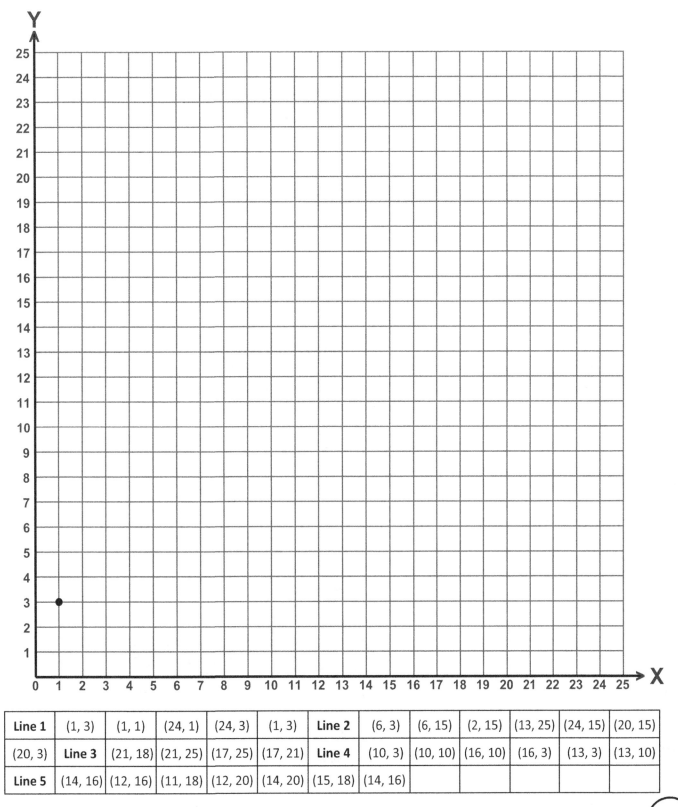

Line 1	(1, 3)	(1, 1)	(24, 1)	(24, 3)	(1, 3)	Line 2	(6, 3)	(6, 15)	(2, 15)	(13, 25)	(24, 15)	(20, 15)
(20, 3)	Line 3	(21, 18)	(21, 25)	(17, 25)	(17, 21)	Line 4	(10, 3)	(10, 10)	(16, 10)	(16, 3)	(13, 3)	(13, 10)
Line 5	(14, 16)	(12, 16)	(11, 18)	(12, 20)	(14, 20)	(15, 18)	(14, 16)					

3 Nephi 12–16

"I Am the Law, and the Light"

Unscrambler

Instructions: Unscramble the words below; look at the bold words in the scripture for a hint.

3 Nephi 13:19–21

Lay not up for **yourselves treasures** upon **earth**, where **moth** and **rust doth corrupt**, and **thieves break** through and **steal**; But lay up for yourselves treasures in **heaven**, where neither moth nor rust doth corrupt, and where thieves do not break through nor steal. For where your treasure is, there will your **heart** be also.

trus _____

sthieve _____

esyourselv _____

lstea _____

heart _____

thear _____

hdot _____

estreasur _____

akbre _____

thmo _____

enheav _____

ptcorru _____

Word Square

Instructions: Word squares are a liike Sudoku puzzles, but each letter can occur only once in each row and in each column. Check your puzzle against the answer key on ColorMeChristian.org. Every row and column must contain every letter in the word **DOETH.** This word can be written in the gray row.

3 Nephi 15:1

And now it came to pass that when Jesus had ended these sayings he cast his eyes round about on the multitude, and said unto them: Behold, ye have heard the things which I taught before I ascended to my Father; therefore, whoso remembereth these sayings of mine and **doeth** them, him will I raise up at the last day.

	D		E	
T				E
		H	D	
O	E			

3 Nephi 17–19

"Behold, My Joy Is Full"

Word Angles

Instructions: Find the bold words from the scripture. Each word path may run north, east, south, or west, may make one right-angled turn, and may cross another word path. A few words may make no right angle turn at all.

3 Nephi 18:7, 11

And this shall ye do in **remembrance** of my **body**, which I have **shown** unto you. And it shall be a **testimony** unto the Father that ye do always **remember** me. And if ye do always remember me ye **shall** have my **Spirit** to be **with** you. And this shall ye **always** do to those who **repent** and are **baptized** in my **name**; and ye shall do it in remembrance of my **blood**, which I have **shed** for you, that ye may **witness** unto the **Father** that ye do always remember me. And if ye do always remember me ye shall have my Spirit to be with you.

```
Z A F X C H G S Q G D A U E M P
V C Z W I T U J F Q X L T F W E
W P N T Q Z B V U G W W A Y S X
I T W X W L L O O D J E D Z M K
R N O H S S J K N C C O A I V B
I Y G Z B H Y J C E W E H T A F
P D O B D E P D Z C K R F S E R
S R E M E M B R A N Y E C I B A
A M Y G V I U M B R O K U L M L
V S Q X V T E S T I S S R N E Z
B H D H J I L D E M S E E P M X
Z A E Z I T P A B O G N P A E H
J L D A E S D X B N E T E B R T
E L Y U X H H H U Y A I N T Z F
O E M A X J F Q T M U W O E U D
C R Q N T D K B A C H P H E J V
```

Word Star

Instructions: Start with the capital letter in the puzzle. Then choose one of the two lines to the next letter. Only one route through the word star will make a word. Write the letters of the word you discover in the blanks below as you travel through the star:

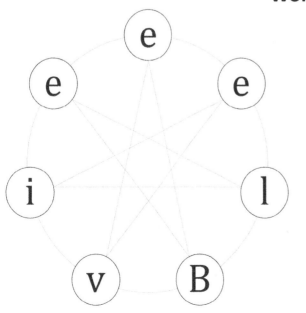

— — — — — — —

Now can you find this word in the following scripture?

3 Nephi 19:23

3 Nephi 17–19

"Behold, My Joy Is Full"

Instructions: Fill in the blank puzzle grid using the word bank with the bold words from the scripture below. Place the words in the correct place on the grid.

3 Nephi 18:18–21

Behold, verily, verily, I say unto you, ye must **watch** and **pray always** lest ye **enter** into **temptation**; for Satan **desireth** to have you, that he may **sift** you as **wheat**. Therefore ye must always pray unto the **Father** in my **name**; And **whatsoever** ye shall **ask** the Father in my name, which is **right**, **believing** that ye shall **receive**, behold it shall be **given** unto you. Pray in your **families** unto the Father, always in my name, that your **wives** and your **children** may be **blessed**.

3 Letters	5 Letters	6 Letters	8 Letters	10 Letters
ask	wives	always	desireth	temptation
	given	Father	families	whatsoever
4 Letters	right		children	
sift	watch	**7 Letters**		
pray	wheat	receive	**9 Letters**	
name	enter	blessed	believing	

3 Nephi 17–19

"Behold, My Joy Is Full"

Instructions: Solve this word sudoku puzzle the same way that you'd solve a numeric sudoku. Each of the bold words in the scripture below is found once in every row, column and 3×3 box.

3 Nephi 17:23-24

And he spake unto the multitude, and said unto them: Behold your **little ones**. And as they **looked** to behold they cast their eyes towards heaven, and they saw the heavens open, and they saw **angels** descending out of **heaven** as it were in the **midst** of **fire**; and they came down and **encircled** those little ones about, and they were encircled about with fire; and the angels did **minister** unto them.

angels				fire			heaven	
			angels		midst	fire		minister
	fire	encircled				angels	little	
	angels		ones	heaven	looked			
		fire			encircled		ones	angels
		heaven			minister		midst	little
	heaven		minister	ones	angels			
ones					fire	midst		heaven
little		angels		looked		ones		

3 Nephi 17–19

"Behold, My Joy Is Full"

Jesus taught me **how** to pray.

Come, Follow Me Manual, 2024

Start

End

3 Nephi 17–19

"Behold, My Joy Is Full"

Secret Code

Instructions: The secret message is written in symbols. In the code key you can find what each symbol means. Write the letter above the symbol and you can read the secret message.

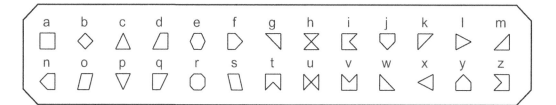

3   19 : 9

3 Nephi 20–26

"Ye Are the Children of the Covenant"

Reverse Word Search

Instructions: Instead of looking for words in a grid, place the bold words in the scripture in the empty word search puzzle. The words may be forwards, backwards, up, down, or diagonally The start letter of the words have been placed in the grid to get you started.

3 Nephi 22:7–8, 10

For a **small moment** have I **forsaken** thee, but with **great mercies** will I **gather** thee. In a little **wrath** I **hid** my **face** from thee for a moment, but with **everlasting kindness** will I have mercy on thee, saith the **Lord** thy **Redeemer**. For the **mountains** shall **depart** and the **hills** be **removed**, but my kindness shall not depart from thee, neither shall the **covenant** of my **peace** be **removed**, saith the Lord that hath mercy on thee.

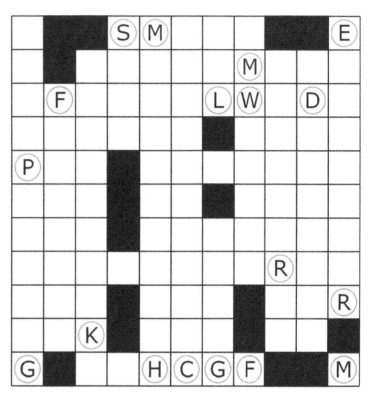

Cryptogram

Instructions: Each letter on the top stands for a letter in the alphabet. Solve the encrypted phrase by matching each letter on top to a letter in the alphabet on the bottom. Use the key to help you remember what the letters stand for so you can crack the code.

R	D	Q	M	K	G	W	A	E	P	I	C	B	H	O	N	Z	U	X	S	F	V	Y	T	L	J
A	B	C	D	E	F	G	H	I	J	K	L	M	N	O	P	Q	R	S	T	U	V	W	X	Y	Z

H P B   N I   T H K X N :   X N I T I   T L A K J X R A I T ,

G N K L N   W I   N H B   P O X   G K X N   W O R ,   X N I

U H X N I A   L O D D H P B I B   X N H X   K   T N O R Y B

F K V I   R P X O   W O R ;   U O A   K X   G H T   G K T B O D

K P   N K D   X N H X   X N I W   T N O R Y B   M I   F K V I P

R P X O   U R X R A I   F I P I A H X K O P T .   3   P I J N K   2 6 : 2

3 Nephi 20–26

"Ye Are the Children of the Covenant"

Missing Vowels Word Search

Instructions: Find the hidden words. The words have been placed horizontally, vertically, diagonally, forwards, or backwards, and the vowels have been removed. When you locate a word, draw an ellipse around it and fill the vowels in.

3 Nephi 20:11–12

Ye **remember** that I **spake** unto you, and said that **when** the **words** of **Isaiah** should be **fulfilled**—**behold** they are **written**, ye have them **before** you, **therefore search them**— And verily, verily, I say unto you, that when they **shall** be fulfilled then is the **fulfilling** of the **covenant** which the **Father** hath made unto his **people**, O **house** of **Israel**.

```
F D L   H   B   T R   V   L
  S D R   W N R H F G T L L
H L N   C K F R   R C W Q R
T F R   K   P S F F Q R X D H
H     Z C V       M Y   H S
  L M T N P T Z B L Y J W   J
R L   G   R   N S F S T   T S
  M T H P     Y   D H N R B
F N B W W T   Y P L C   K R
  G   T   B L K L N   C G M
R   R   S M   H T     V D
  M R   W   H Q V D Y S Y Y
J W   G K D S   N L B   D V Q
Z H N R V   C   G Q M G   Z T
L     R S   V F   T H   R Q
```

Word Bricks

Instructions: A sentence is written on the wall. But brick layers built the wall in the wrong order. Your job is to put the bricks in the right order. Hint: **3 Nephi 24:12**

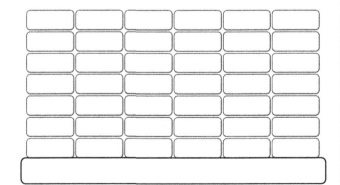

And	a l l	n		o n s	a t i
	o u	l l	l	y	c a l	s h a
f o r	s s e d ,		b l e	y e	
a		s h a		b e	l l
i g h	m e	l a n	d ,	d e l	t s o
t h		L o	t h e	s a i	o f	r d
			H o s	t s .	

Family History Fun

By Arie Van De Graaff

Help the boy at the bottom of this family tree identify his ancestors, Michael Cowdell and Elizabeth Reese. Michael Cowdell was bald and had facial hair and glasses. His wife wore a pendant around her neck. Elizabeth Reese wore earrings, but not glasses. She was married to a bald man with facial hair. Also answer these questions:

1. How many of the boy's ancestors wore glasses? ___

2. How many of the boy's ancestors had a bow tie? ___

3. How many of the boy's ancestors had facial hair? ___

4. How many of the boy's ancestors were bald? ___

3 Nephi 20–26

"Ye Are the Children of the Covenant"

Instructions: Connect all of the letters in the phrase bolded below. Don't be tricked by letters that take you into a dead end! There is only one path through the maze.

___ ___, _____, _ ___ ____ ___, ____ __ _____ __ _____ ____
_____. ___, _ _____ _ ____ ____ ___ ____ __ _____ ____
_____ _____; ___ _____ ___ ___ _____ __ _____.

3 Nephi 23:1

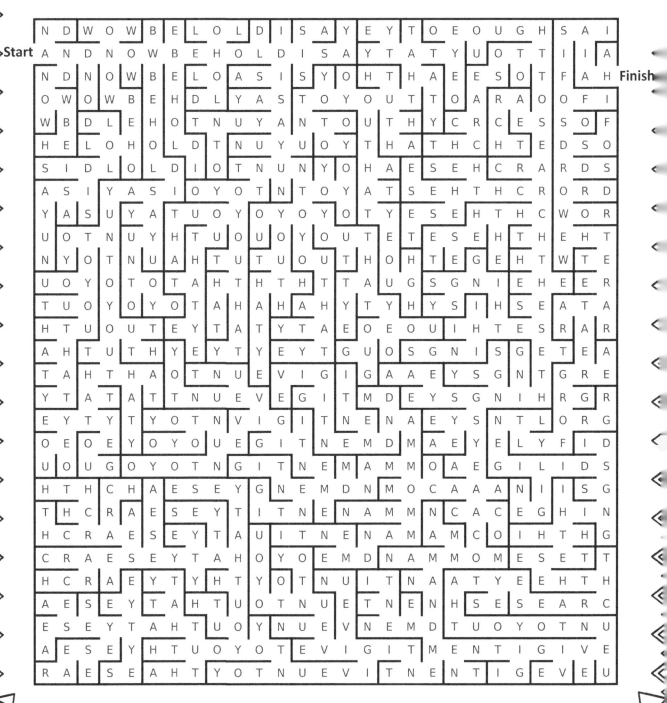

3 Nephi 20–26

"Ye Are the Children of the Covenant"

Handwriting Practice

Practice your handwriting by tracing the sentence below. Then use the blank lines to write the sentence on your own.

Paying tithing opens the windows of heaven.

3 Nephi 20–26
"Ye Are the Children of the Covenant"

Letter Sudoku

Instructions: Solve the letter sudoku puzzle the same way you'd solve a numeric sudoku. Check your puzzle against the answer key on ColorMeChristian.org. Every column, row, and group of nine must contain every letter in the worda **GLORY TIME.** Letters are used only once;

3 Nephi 26:3

And he did expound all things, even from the beginning until the **time** that he should come in his **glory**—yea, even all things which should come upon the face of the earth, even until the elements should melt with fervent heat, and the earth should be wrapt together as a scroll, and the heavens and the earth should pass away;

	E	O		L	R	Y		
M					I	L		T
		L						Y
R		I		Y			L	M
E		L		O				
O		I		R	G			
	G					Y	T	
Y		M					R	

October 21–27

3 Nephi 27–4 Nephi

"There Could Not Be a Happier People"

Word Search

Instructions: Find the bold words from the scripture in the word search puzzle. Each word could be hidden forwards, backwards, up, down, or diagonally.

3 Nephi 27:13 15–16

Behold I have given unto you my **gospel**, and this is the gospel which I have **given** unto you—that I came into the **world** to do the **will** of my **Father**, because my Father **sent** me....And for this cause have I been **lifted** up; therefore, according to the **power** of the Father I will **draw** all men unto me, that they may be **judged** according to their **works**. And it shall come to pass, that whoso **repenteth** and is **baptized** in my **name** shall be **filled**; and if he **endureth** to the **end**, behold, him will I hold **guiltless** before my Father at that **day** when I shall stand to judge the **world**.

```
M C Z T X C S L I F T E D P S
R H E N Z D S B I A Q L L W F
F T Z E Z J E B K S V R N A C
G E P S B Y L J A E N D A R U
C R J H T E T N E P E R M D N
M U E W O R L D G C T W E T V
G D J H U D I N V E O I M X A
I N A J T V U W W R P J Z D R
V E G B K A G M K O L U Y E C
E L C B T H F S W D F D A Q D
N E L D Z D F E C E M G D E P
P P H I F L R A N L Q E J P B
O S O X W R G G V L F D E S G
J O H R C O U N Z I V U A V H
I G S H O W K B B F W W C N B
```

Translation Station

Instructions: Translate the sign language letters below into English to discover the hidden message. Write the alphabet letter beneath each hand sign. Use the key at the back of the book to help you.

Hidden Picture: You belong to the Church of Jesus Christ. Can you find 4 pictures of the church building in the hidden picture below? It will be tricky; the picture may be smaller, on its side, or even upside down! Then, see if you can find 1 image of the animals as well.

3 Nephi 27–4 Nephi

"There Could Not Be a Happier People"

Instructions: Using the Across and Down clues, write the correct words in the numbered grid below. Hint: all of the words in the crossword come from the scripture below.

4 Nephi 1:2–3, 5, 15–17

ACROSS

1. possessing material wealth
3. disabled in the feet or legs
7. the deliberate act of deviating from the truth
11. having little money or few possessions
12. change the nature, purpose, or function of something
15. something acquired without compensation; a present
16. a strong positive emotion of regard and affection
17. having little money or few possessions
19. the deliberate act of deviating from the truth
20. a debate or argument

DOWN

2. a person entitled by law to inherit the estate of another
4. extraordinarily good or great
5. a slave
6. a person who can make their own choices
8. bitter conflict; heated or violent dissension
9. in accordance God's standards
10. Jesus Christ
13. smallest whole number or a numeral representing this number
14. to take action with respect to a thing or person
18. people who have severe hearing impairments

3 Nephi 27–4 Nephi

"There Could Not Be a Happier People"

Handwriting Practice

Practice your handwriting by tracing the sentence below. Then use the blank lines to write the sentence on your own.

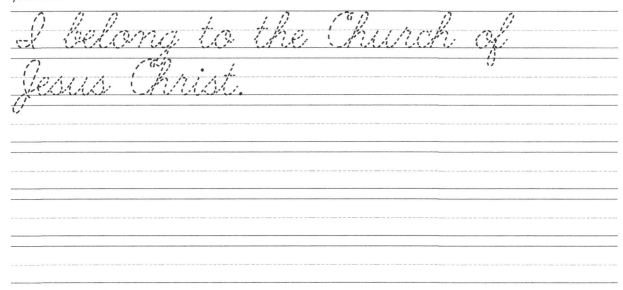

I belong to the Church of Jesus Christ.

SURE, I'D BE WILLING TO PRACTICE THE LAW OF CONSECRATION WITH THE CAR...AS SOON AS YOU START PRACTICING IT WITH THE MORTGAGE PAYMENT.

mormoncartoonist.com

© Arie Van De Graaff

Jesus Loves You

Help these people through the maze so they can also give Jesus a hug.

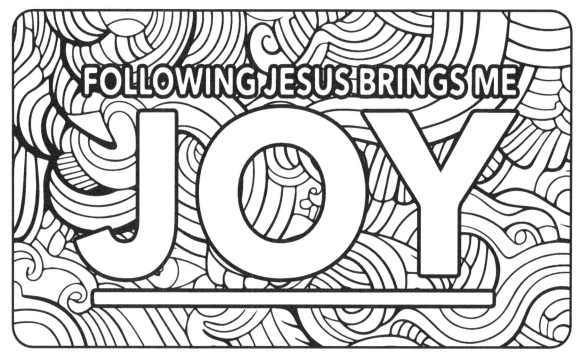

Word Square

Instructions: Word squares are a liike Sudoku puzzles, but each letter can occur only once in each row and in each column. Check your puzzle against the answer key on ColorMeChristian.org. Every row and column must contain every letter in the word **HEARTS.** This word can be written in the gray row.

4 Nephi 1:15–16

And it came to pass that there was no contention in the land, because of the love of God which did dwell in the **hearts** of the people. And there were no envyings, nor strifes, nor tumults, nor whoredoms, nor lyings, nor murders, nor any manner of lasciviousness; and surely there could not be a happier people among all the people who had been created by the hand of God.

	H	T	S	A	
	R			H	
		H			T
A	T	R			E
	A		E		

October 28–November 3
Mormon 1–6
"I Would That I Could Persuade All ... to Repent"

Wacky Word Trails

Instructions: Start with the circled letter, use the clues to find and mark the trail of letters of all the connected bolded words from the scripture through the maze to the last letter. The path can wander up, down, left, and right at any point, even in the middle of the word.

Mormon 2:8, 12-13

And it came to pass that when I, Mormon, saw their **lamentation** and their **mourning** and their **sorrow** before the Lord, my **heart** did begin to **rejoice** within me, **knowing** the **mercies** and the long-suffering of the Lord, therefore **supposing** that he would be **merciful** unto them that they would **again** become a **righteous people**. But behold this my joy was **vain**, for their sorrowing was not unto **repentance**, because of the **goodness** of God; but it was rather the sorrowing of the damned, because the Lord would not **always** **suffer** them to take **happiness** in **sin**.

```
Z  Q  D  Q  V  A  I  H  Q  V  M  Q  W  A  Y
J  V  R  K  G  P  N  P  E  O  P  A  L  E  S
B  G  M  K  N  I  P  V  K  W  L  E  X  E  M
I  N  O  U  R  N  H  Q  I  C  E  I  C  R  U
W  E  R  F  U  E  N  P  A  H  S  A  X  H  U
O (M) C  I  L  S  I  P  R  R  U  G  J  S  R
N  K  A  E  H  S  E  F  E  E  O  O  T  S  E
P  T  R  Y  O  S  U  F  O  J  G  D  N  E  P
B  S  Q  G  A  N  I  C  I  C  E  F  N  A  E
G  V  I  A  O  N  S  H  A  I  H  B  C  T  N
S  Y  N  S  I  T  N  E  D  N  C  S  E  J  N
I  E  V  U  U  A  T  M  O  J  R  O  O  B  L
A  L  L  P  P  M  M  A  A  T  R  O  S  G  U
C  J  I  S  O  M  U  L  T  E  T  W  R  S  Q
F  B  N  G  W  C  W  S  U  O  H  G  I  B  K
```

Knight Moves - Find a Word

Instructions: Start with the capital letter in the puzzle. To get to the next letter, jump two squares in any direction except diagonally, and then one square in a different direction. Your path will look like a capital L. To show you how it works, Only one route through the puzzle will make a word. Write the letters of the word you discover in the blanks below as you jump through the squares:

__ __ __ __ __ __ __
 2 3 4 5 6 7 8

Now can you find this word in the following scripture?

Mormon 1:1–3

b	m	r
R		m
e	e	e

Mormon 1–6

"I Would That I Could Persuade All … to Repent"

Instructions: Solve this word sudoku puzzle the same way that you'd solve a numeric sudoku. Each of the bold words in the scripture below is found once in every row, column and 3×3 box.

Mormon 3:12

Behold, I had **led** them, notwithstanding their **wickedness** I had led them many times to battle, and had **loved** them, according to the love of God which was in me, with all my **heart**; and my **soul** had been **poured** out in **prayer** unto my God all the day long for them; nevertheless, it was **without** faith, because of the **hardness** of their hearts.

			hardness	heart	loved		wickedness	prayer
prayer	heart	soul		without	wickedness		led	
	loved			led		poured	without	heart
	wickedness		led	soul	prayer		loved	without
			heart		without	led	soul	wickedness
	without	led		wickedness	hardness	prayer	heart	
wickedness		loved	without		poured	heart		
	prayer	hardness	wickedness		led		poured	soul
led	poured		soul	prayer	heart	wickedness		

Mystery Picture Graph

Instructions: Find the mystery picture below by plotting and connecting the points of each line on the coordinate graph. Connect all the points in Line 1, stop, pick up your pencil, and then connect all the points in Line 2, and so on for the rest of the lines. The dot for the first (X,Y) coordinate pair on Line 1 has been placed for you.

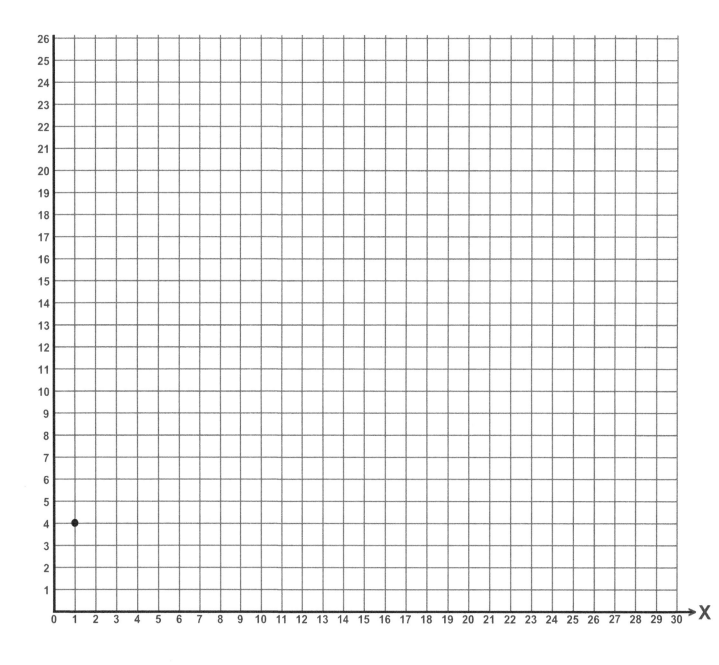

Line 1	(1, 4)	(6, 1)	(7, 3)	(7, 4)	(9, 7)	(10, 6)	(11, 8)	(14, 6)	(17, 9)	(13, 9)	(13, 11)	(22, 24)
(21, 28)	(16, 27)	(8, 14)	(6, 13)	(5, 17)	(3, 13)	(6, 11)	(5, 10)	(6, 9)	(4, 6)	(3, 6)	(1, 4)	Line 2
(8, 14)	(13, 11)	Line 3	(6, 11)	(11, 8)	Line 4	(21, 28)	(11, 13)					

Like Mormon, I can **follow** Jesus Christ.

Come, Follow Me Manual, 2024

End

Start

Mormon 1–6

"I Would That I Could Persuade All … to Repent"

Fallen Phrase

Instructions:The letters in each column have fallen from the grid. Put them back correctly to rebuild the phrase. Cross out each letter in the jumble below once you place it in the grid. Pay attention because the letters in each column are scrambled. Start with simple 1 or 2 letter words and use the process of elimination. To check your answer, read **Mormon 3:12.**

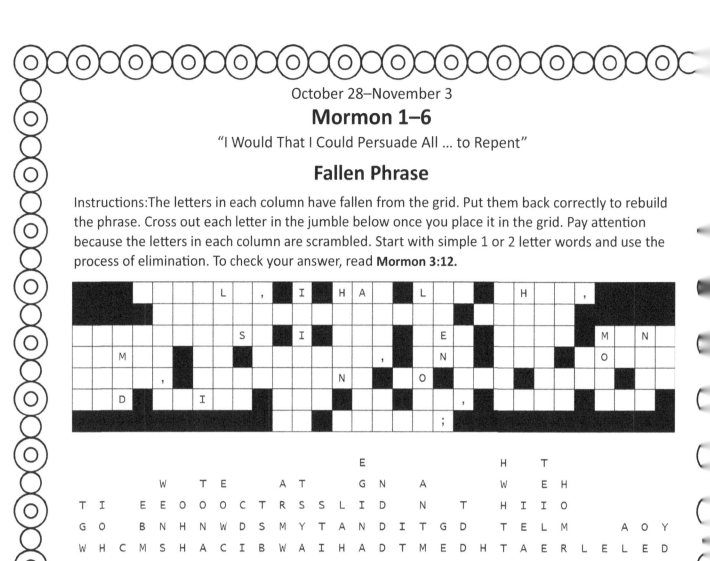

```
                           E                      H        T
        W      T    E            A    T        G   N        A           W        E   H
  T   I    E  E  O  O  O  C  T  R  S  S  L  I  D      N       T      H  I  I  O
  G   O    B  N  H  N  W  D  S  M  Y  T  A  N  D  I  T  G  D      T  E  L  M          A   O   Y
  W  H  C  M  S  H  A  C  I  B  W  A  I  H  A  D  T  M  E  D  H  T  A  E  R  L  E  L  E  D
  T  I  E  K  E  D  T  C  H  O  H  D  T  H  E  A  R  L  E  D  T  E  H  D  M  V  A  V  L  F
```

Translation Station

Instructions: Translate the Morse code below into English to discover the hidden message. Write the alphabet letter beneath each Morse Code letter. Each letter, number, and punctuation is separated by a slash: /. Use the key at the back of the book to help you.

.———/./.../..—/.../   .../.—/..—/—./   .—../———/...—/./

./...—/./.—./—.——/———/—./././—...—·   —/.—./././.—/—/

—/..../.—.—/   —.—/..—/—./—.../.—./—.—/

—/———/———/.—.—.—   .——/...././—./

.—.—/———/..../.—/—.—.—   ..../././.—/—./—/   ../.../

...—/..—/.—.—./.——./././—.../   .——/../—./..../

.—.—/———/..../.—/—.—.—   ———/—/.../././.—/.../

.——/..—/.—./—.—/   .—.../———/...././

—.—./———/..—/.—.—.—

Mormon 7–9

"I Speak unto You as If Ye Were Present"

Word Angles

Instructions: Find the bold words from the scripture. Each word path may run north, east, south, or west, may make one right-angled turn, and may cross another word path. A few words may make no right angle turn at all.

Mormon 8:24

And he **knoweth** their **prayers**, that they were in **behalf** of their **brethren**. And he knoweth their **faith**, for in his name could they **remove mountains**; and in his **name** could they cause the earth to **shake**; and by the **power** of his word did they cause **prisons** to **tumble** to the earth; yea, even the fiery **furnace** could not harm them, neither wild **beasts** nor poisonous **serpents**, because of the power of his **word**.

```
C H S N I T S X V Y G G L U B W
Z T N O S I R P S N I A T U R A
H E O S N V L D E V C L N Y E K
O W O N K F M E M X H W U I T T
A G W P O F A V F K I X O N H C
I A F R B T N L Z O U W M R R K
T D Y A P U L X O R A Y X N E O
H C M Y G M G H W Z Q Q Y T M E
Y V I E L B D G X C L E E Y P B
Q K B R S R R E S Q D K P O W E
L L E I K Q P V E R S A V G E W
S B H L K M E L N B G H S O R O
T U A L F B N U D X O Q E R L R
S H Z M T H T A W E N E M Z O D
A E B F H E S D E C A N R U F M
F P F X P K O J V O M E R K R E
```

ARE YOU SAYING THAT WHILE I WAS OVERCOME WITH THE SPIRIT, THERE WAS A SERIOUS DEBATE OVER WHETHER I SMELLED LIKE A TWO-DAY OLD ROTTING CORPSE?

THAT'S IT, I'M TAKING A BATH.

wardcartoonist.com

©Arie Van De Graaff

Mormon 7–9

"I Speak unto You as If Ye Were Present"

Secret Code

Instructions: The secret message is written in symbols. In the code key you can find what each symbol means. Write the letter above the symbol and you can read the secret message.

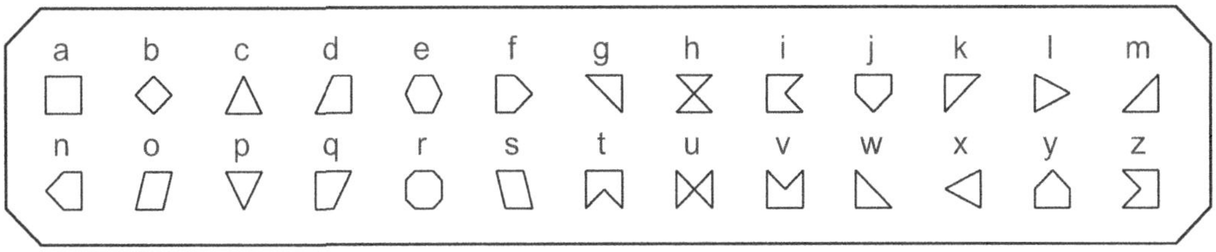

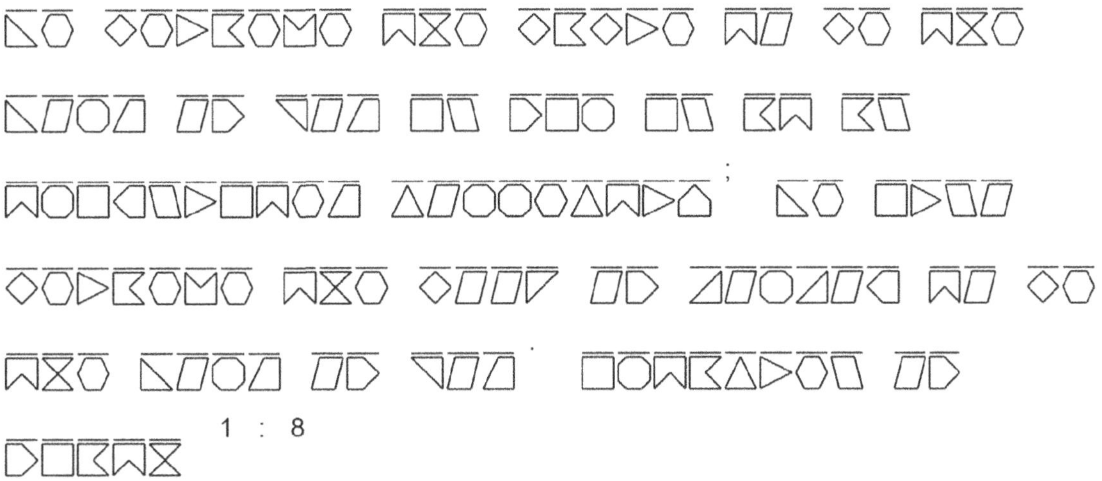

a	b	c	d	e	f	g	h	i	j	k	l	m
□	◇	△	⏢	⬡	⌂	◺	✕	⊏	▽	▷	◹	◿

n	o	p	q	r	s	t	u	v	w	x	y	z
◂	▱	▽	⏢	○	⊐	⊟	⋈	Ｍ	⋈	◁	△	⊵

(A secret message written in the symbols above appears here, with the scripture reference "1 : 8".)

Handwriting Practice

Practice your handwriting by tracing the sentence below. Then use the blank lines to write the sentence on your own.

Jesus Christ is a God of miracles.

Mormon 7–9

"I Speak unto You as If Ye Were Present"

Instructions: Fit the bold words from the scripture below into the encircled squares. Words will read forward, backward, up, down, and diagonally and will normally cross other words. Start with the hints provided.

Mormon 8:5

Behold, my **father** hath **made** this **record**, and he hath **written** the **intent** thereof. And behold, I would write it also if I had **room** upon the **plates**, but I have not; and **ore** I have **none**, for I am **alone**. My father hath been **slain** in **battle**, and all my **kinsfolk**, and I have not **friends** nor **whither** to **go**; and how **long** the **Lord** will **suffer** that I may **live** I **know** **not**.

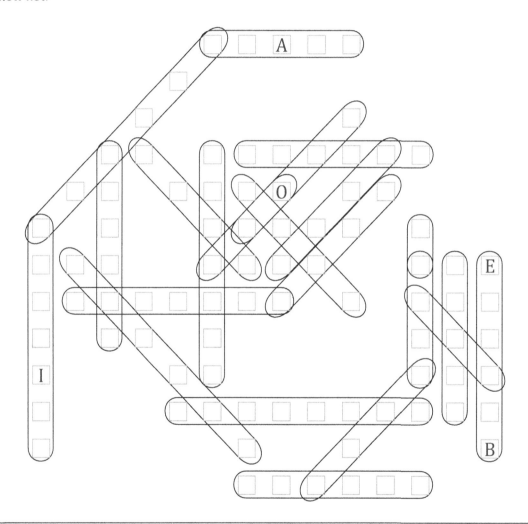

father	made	record	written	intent	room	plates
ore	none	alone	slain	battle	kinsfolk	friends
whither	go	long	Lord	suffer	live	know
not						

Keep The Commandments

You can keep the commandments even when you feel alone. Help these children reach the 10 commandments at the end of the maze.

Mormon 7–9

"I Speak unto You as If Ye Were Present"

Unscrambler

Instructions: Unscramble the words below; look at the bold words in the scripture for a hint.

Mormon 9:11, 17

But behold, I will **show** unto you a God of **miracles**, even the God of **Abraham**, and the God of **Isaac**, and the God of **Jacob**; and it is that same God who created the **heavens** and the **earth**, and all things that in them are…. Who shall say that it was not a miracle that by his **word** the heaven and the earth should be; and by the **power** of his word **man** was created of the **dust** of the earth; and by the power of his word have miracles been **wrought**?

sowh _____	wrod _____
hgrutwo _____	duts _____
caasi _____	acjbo _____
rewpo _____	avshnee _____
nam _____	aerth _____
mrelcias _____	rbhaama _____

Letter Sudoku

Instructions: Solve the letter sudoku puzzle the same way you'd solve a numeric sudoku. Check your puzzle against the answer key on ColorMeChristian.org. Every column, row, and group of nine must contain every letter in the worda **REASON WHY.** Letters are used only once;

Mormon 9:20–21

And the **reason why** he ceaseth to do miracles among the children of men is because that they dwindle in unbelief, and depart from the right way, and know not the God in whom they should trust.

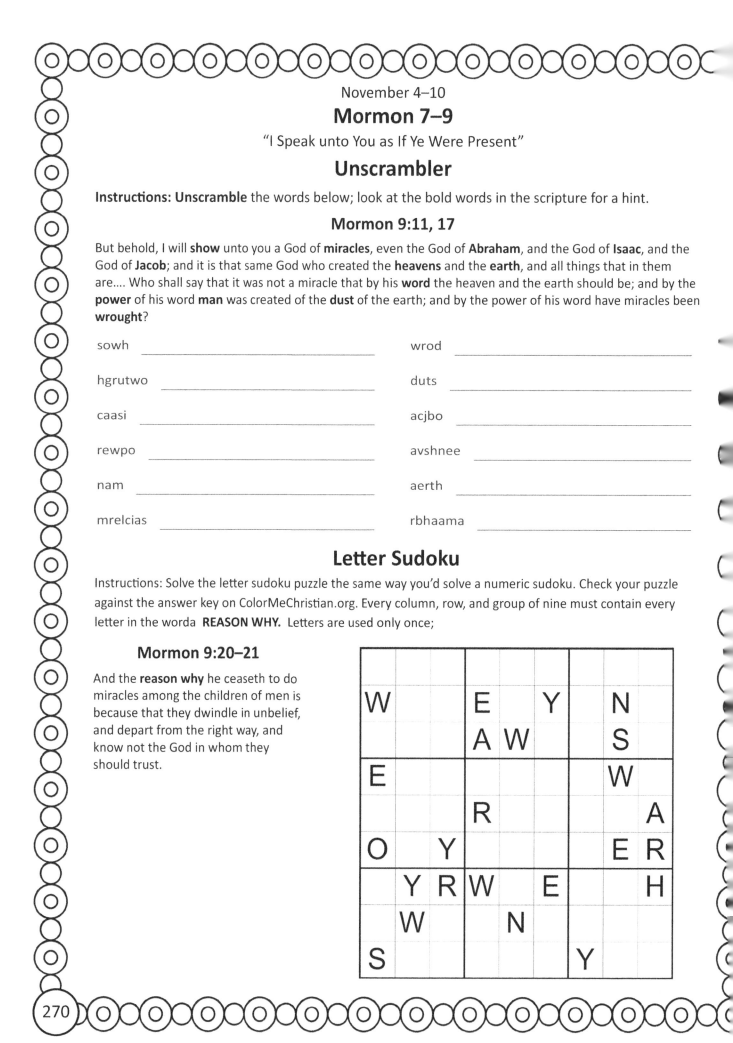

W		E		Y		N		
		A	W			S		
E							W	
		R						A
O		Y				E		R
	Y	R	W		E			H
	W			N				
S						Y		

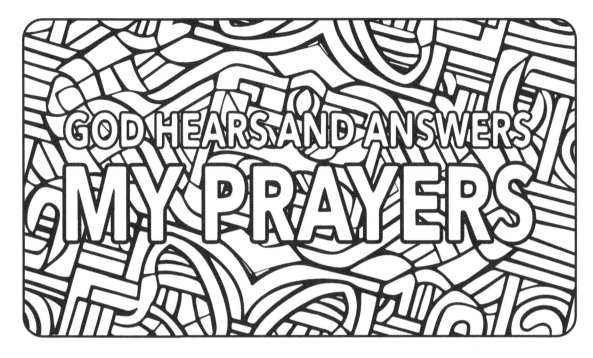

Cryptogram

Instructions: Each letter on the top stands for a letter in the alphabet. Solve the encrypted phrase by matching each letter on top to a letter in the alphabet on the bottom. Use the key to help you remember what the letters stand for so you can crack the code.

D	S	Q	Z	G	V	U	L	Y	A	E	O	W	N	P	M	B	C	K	J	H	X	T	F	R	I
A	B	C	D	E	F	G	H	I	J	K	L	M	N	O	P	Q	R	S	T	U	V	W	X	Y	Z

J N A   Z N   W U K   P L G W U   L X   W U Y K K

M Z W N K B B K B   B U J H H   W U K B K   W U Z N E B   Q K

K B W J Q H Z B U K A ;   J N A   W U K   W K B W Z P L N I

L X   W U Y K K ,   J N A   W U Z B   M L Y S ,   Z N   W U K

M U Z R U   B U J H H   Q K   B U L M N   X L Y W U   W U K

O L M K Y   L X   E L A   J N A   J H B L   U Z B   M L Y A ,   L X

M U Z R U   W U K   X J W U K Y ,   J N A   W U K   B L N ,

J N A   W U K   U L H I   E U L B W   Q K J Y   Y K R L Y A -

J N A   J H H   W U Z B   B U J H H   B W J N A   J B   J

W K B W Z P L N I   J E J Z N B W   W U K   M L Y H A   J W

W U K   H J B W   A J I .   K W U K Y   5 : 4

Ether 1–5

"Rend That Veil of Unbelief"

Missing Vowels Word Search

Instructions: Find the hidden words. The words have been placed horizontally, vertically, diagonally, forwards, or backwards, and the vowels have been removed. When you locate a word, draw an ellipse around it and fill the vowels in.

Ether 3:13, 15

And when he had said these words, behold, the **Lord showed himself** unto him, and said: **Because** thou **knowest** these things ye are **redeemed** from the **fall**; therefore ye are **brought back** into my **presence**; therefore I show myself unto you. And **never** have I showed myself unto man whom I have **created**, for never has man **believed** in **me** as thou hast. Seest thou that ye are created after **mine own image**? Yea, even all men were **created** in the **beginning after** mine own image.

```
R   V   N D D S K N   W   S T
    W N P   X R   D   M   D W
N S F W   B   T S C D R   L
    N   Y R   F   K   N W C F R
Y H B C C B W N   Y   M N X
S G W   S   B   C K S R   L X
D   W K G N P R   M C K S
D S L Z C   Q X   R N   T
    R V   Q N   G P V H R R
V F   L L N M R T   K G   F
B   F Z   S S   C   T Q   R
    G D B N F W D   F X   S
L N   N N G T B R   N R K H
    M   Q   T B X B T T   R
B M   V M H   M S   L F Y B H
```

I THINK WE NEED A BIGGER SIGN.

NO HABLO INGLÉS.

City of **Babel**
Welcome
Bienvenido
WILLKOMMEN
Dobro Došli
Ant Chukoa
Aloha
Sugeng Ruwah
Välkommen

mormoncartoonist.com

© Arie Van De Graaff

Hidden Picture: You were created in the image of God. You have a body like Jesus. Can you find 6 pictures of this girl in the hidden picture below? It will be tricky; the picture may be smaller, on its side, or even upside down! Then, see if you can find 1 image of the animals as well.

Ether 1–5

"Rend That Veil of Unbelief"

Instructions: Fill in the blank puzzle grid using the word bank with the bold words from the scripture below. Place the words in the correct place on the grid.

Ether 2:22-23

And he **cried** again unto the **Lord** saying: O Lord, behold I have **done** even as thou hast **commanded** me; and I have **prepared** the **vessels** for my **people**, and behold there is no **light** in them. Behold, O Lord, wilt thou **suffer** that we shall **cross** this great **water** in **darkness**? And the Lord said unto the brother of Jared: **What** will ye that I **should** do that ye may have light in your vessels? For behold, ye cannot have **windows**, for they will be **dashed** in **pieces**; neither shall ye **take fire** with you, for ye shall not go by the light of fire.

4 Letters	5 Letters	6 Letters	7 Letters	9 Letters
take	light	dashed	vessels	commanded
done	water	suffer	windows	
fire	cross	people		
Lord	cried	should	**8 Letters**	
What		pieces	darkness	
			prepared	

Ether 1–5

"Rend That Veil of Unbelief"

Instructions: Connect all of the letters in the phrase bolded below. Don't be tricked by letters that take you into a dead end! There is only one path through the maze.

_____ _____ ____ ___ _____ _____ _____ ____

_____ ___ _____ __ ___ ____ __ _____.

Come, Follow Me 2024

Finish

Start

Ether 1–5

"Rend That Veil of Unbelief"

Fill in the Blank

Ether 3:15

And _____ have I _____ myself unto _____ whom I have

_____, for never has man _____ in me as thou hast. _____

thou that ye are created _____ mine own _____? Yea, even all men were

created in the _____ after _____ own image.

image	beginning	believed	Seest	man	created
after	never	mine	showed		

Word Square

Instructions: Word squares are a liike Sudoku puzzles, but each letter can occur only once in each row and in each column. Check your puzzle against the answer key on ColorMeChristian.org. Every row and column must contain every letter in the word **FINGER.** This word can be written in the gray row.

Ether 3:6

And it came to pass that when the brother of Jared had said these words, behold, the Lord stretched forth his hand and touched the stones one by one with his **finger**. And the veil was taken from off the eyes of the brother of Jared, and he saw the finger of the Lord; and it was as the finger of a man, like unto flesh and blood; and the brother of Jared fell down before the Lord, for he was struck with fear.

		E	I	F	
		I	R		
N					I
	F	R			G
G		F		R	I

Ether 6–11

"That Evil May Be Done Away"

Word Search

Instructions: Find the bold words from the scripture in the word search puzzle. Each word could be hidden forwards, backwards, up, down, or diagonally.

Ether 6:6-7

And it came to pass that they were many times **buried** in the **depths** of the **sea**, because of the **mountain** **waves** which **broke** upon them, and also the **great** and **terrible** **tempests** which were caused by the **fierceness** of the **wind**. And it came to pass that when they were buried in the deep there was no water that could **hurt** them, their **vessels** being **tight** like unto a **dish**, and also they were tight like unto the **ark** of **Noah**; therefore when they were **encompassed** about by many **waters** they did **cry** unto the **Lord**, and he did **bring** them **forth** again upon the **top** of the waters.

```
A R K U H D S E L B I R R E T
T J I T I H L N I A T N U O M
D R R E T B R O K E A B C O M
P O U P B C I B E M F R M I R
F P E H R M J U F G Y E C M V
I D G N I R B R Q R H N T O P
E Y D R O L B I Q T S C M W A
R S T S E P M E T H I O N M R
C F E X V E E D Q G D M G X S
E V S S O T D N R I V P Z L G
N W B R O S T F X T U A E Q A
E M W H E A W I N D L S R Z R
S M K V E T U A E S S S R F A
S Q A R V O A A Y E C E F X C
U W G H A O N W V A B D G Q Q
```

Word Star

Instructions: Start with the capital letter in the puzzle. Then choose one of the two lines to the next letter. Only one route through the word star will make a word. Write the letters of the word you discover in the blanks below as you travel through the star:

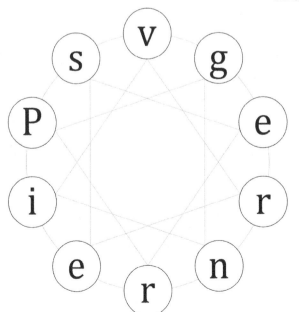

_ _ _ _ _ _ _ _ _ _

Now can you find this word in the following scripture?

Ether 9:34–35

Mystery Picture Graph

Instructions: Find the mystery picture below by plotting and connecting the points of each line on the coordinate graph. Connect all the points in Line 1, stop, pick up your pencil, and then connect all the points in Line 2, and so on for the rest of the lines. The dot for the first (X,Y) coordinate pair on Line 1 has been placed for you.

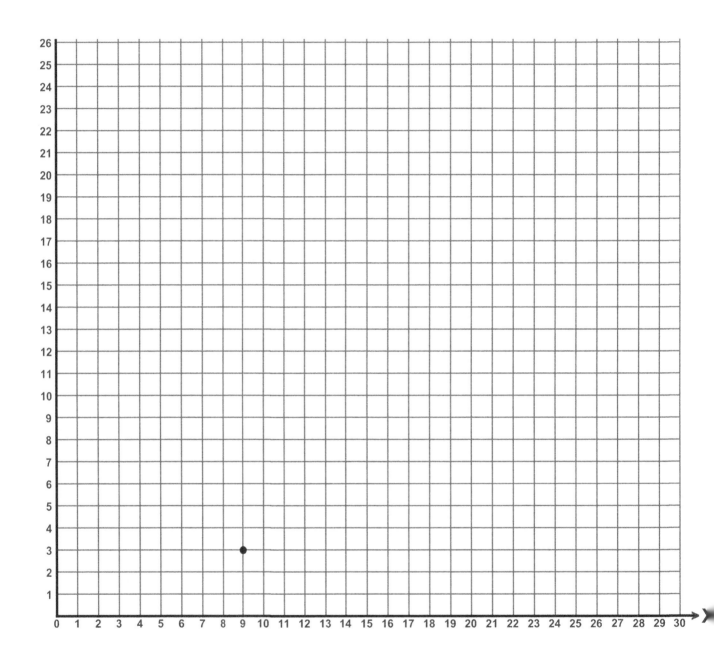

Line 1	(9, 3)	(19, 3)	(23, 9)	(24, 9)	(24, 13)	(23, 13)	(20, 19)	(8, 19)	(5, 13)	(4, 13)	(4, 9)	(5, 9)
(9, 3)	**Line 2**	(5, 13)	(23, 13)	**Line 3**	(5, 9)	(23, 9)	**Line 4**	(1, 6)	(3, 8)	(5, 6)	(7, 8)	(9, 6)
(11, 8)	(13, 6)	(15, 8)	(17, 6)	(19, 8)	(21, 6)	(23, 8)	(25, 6)	(27, 8)	(29, 6)			

Ether 6–11

"That Evil May Be Done Away"

Reverse Word Search

Instructions: Instead of looking for words in a grid, place the bold words in the scripture in the empty word search puzzle. The words may be forwards, backwards, up, down, or diagonally The start letter of the words have been placed in the grid to get you started.

Ether 7:25-26

And he did **execute** a **law throughout** all the land, which gave **power** unto the **prophets** that they should go **whithersoever** they **would**; and by this cause the **people** were brought unto **repentance**. And **because** the people did **repent** of their **iniquities** and **idolatries** the Lord did **spare** them, and they began to **prosper again** in the **land**. And it came to pass that Shule begat sons and daughters in his old age.

Ether 6–11

"That Evil May Be Done Away"

Instructions: Solve this word sudoku puzzle the same way that you'd solve a numeric sudoku. Each of the bold words in the scripture below is found once in every row, column and 3×3 box.

Ether 7:27

And there were no more wars in the days of **Shule**; and he **remembered** the great things that the **Lord** had **done** for his **fathers** in bringing them across the great **deep** into the **promised land**; wherefore he did execute judgment in **righteousness** all his days.

	land	remembered	righteousness		deep			fathers
promised	Shule			done	remembered		Lord	righteousness
		done		Shule		remembered	promised	land
	Lord				righteousness	done	deep	promised
fathers	promised	deep		Lord				Shule
		Shule	deep	land	promised	Lord		
Shule	fathers			deep		promised	remembered	
		Lord	promised		Shule		righteousness	done
done	remembered	promised					Shule	deep

November 18–24

Ether 6–11

"That Evil May Be Done Away"

I can be a **witness** of the Book of Mormon.

Come, Follow Me Manual, 2024

Translation Station

Instructions: Translate the sign language letters below into English to discover the hidden message. Write the alphabet letter beneath each hand sign. Use the key at the back of the book to help you.

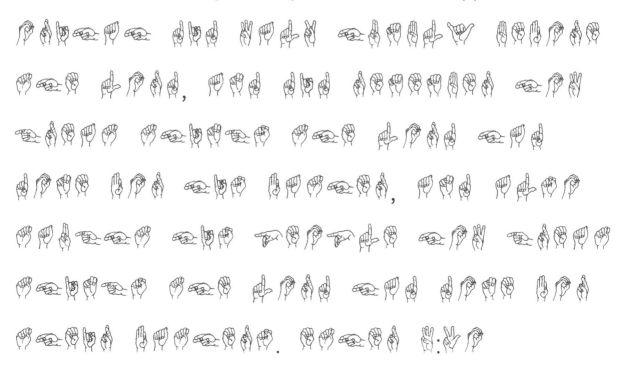

Ether 12–15

"By Faith All Things Are Fulfilled"

Wacky Word Trails

Instructions: Start with the circled letter, use the clues to find and mark the trail of letters of all the connected bolded words from the scripture through the maze to the last letter. The path can wander up, down, left, and right at any point, even in the middle of the word.

Ether 12:4

Wherefore, **whoso believeth** in **God** might with **surety hope** for a **better world**, yea, even a **place** at the **right hand** of God, which hope cometh of **faith**, maketh an **anchor** to the **souls** of **men**, which would **make** them **sure** and **steadfast**, **always abounding** in **good works**, being led to **glorify** God.

```
W  I  G  D  Q  L  H  O  E  N  G  O  O  D  S
Y  R  H  T  M  A  K  E  M  Y  Q  X  E  R  U
F  I  R  O  G  N  I  D  N  V  A  V  T  W  R
K  S  W  L  G  C  B  O  U  F  K  U  Y  S  U
R  X  H  O  S  O  A  L  X  F  V  J  B  Z  B
O  W  T  S  G  R  K  X  M  O  O  Q  E  T  Y
W  O  H  A  S  S  T  Y  N  P  P  L  A  T  F
E  P  A  F  H  Y  O  Q  W  B  A  W  R  E  F
T  E  A  D  N (A) W  L  G  L  Y  S  Q  Y  P
S  X  U  R  C  E  Q  X  J  C  E  B  N  O  L
H  C  A  B  H  O  Y  X  H  Q  L  I  E  V  P
T  I  S  C  H  R  Q  V  J  S  Q  D  I  E  T
I  A  F  O  G  P  L  A  C  I  U  C  W  S  H
D  F  E  D  D  W  E  R  E  L  Z  I  R  O  U
L  R  O  W  N  A  H  U  S  E  K  Z  E  S  L
```

Word Bricks

Instructions: A sentence is written on the wall. But brick layers built the wall in the wrong order. Your job is to put the bricks in the right order. Hint: **Moroni 7:41**

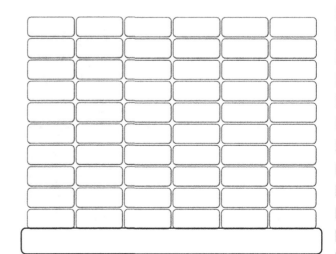

Ye	e	h	sha	hav	ope	l l
	h	t	thr	he	oug	
a t o			nem	ent		of
an	Chr	d	t h e			i s t
e r	his		p o w		o f	
r e s	e c t	,	t u r r	i o n	o	
r a i	s e d	u n	b e	t o		
e	e n a l	n d	t e r	l i f	,	a
t h i	e c a	u s e	s	b		o f
i m .	y o u	a i t	h	i n	h r	f

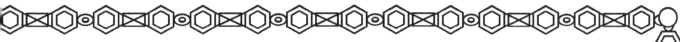

Ether 12–15

"By Faith All Things Are Fulfilled"

Instructions: Using the Across and Down clues, write the correct words in the numbered grid below. Hint: all of the words in the crossword come from the scripture below.

Moroni 7:40–42

ACROSS

4. gain with effort
6. a verbal commitment agreeing to do something in the future
7. Immanuel
9. dearly loved
10. Immanuel
13. use language
14. to raise up from the dead; restore to life
15. the act of making amends for sin or wrongdoing
17. continuing forever or indefinitely
18. person

DOWN

1. move upwards
2. "hoping for things which are not seen, which are true" (Alma 32:21)
3. the confident expectation of and longing for the promised blessings of righteousness; anticipation of eternal life through faith in Jesus Christ
5. brothers
8. the opposite of dead
9. brothers
11. gain with effort
12. the confident expectation of and longing for the promised blessings of righteousness; anticipation of eternal life through faith in Jesus Christ
13. use language
16. person

Ether 12–15

"By Faith All Things Are Fulfilled"

Translation Station

Instructions: Translate the Morse code below into English to discover the hidden message. Write the alphabet letter beneath each Morse Code letter. Each letter, number, and punctuation is separated by a slash: /. Use the key at the back of the book to help you.

−···/·/····/−−−/·−··/−···/−−·−− ··/−/ ·−−/·−/···/

−/····/·/ ··−·/·−/··/−/···/ −−−/··−·/

−·/·/·−−/····/··/ ·−/−·/−··/ ·−··/·/····/··/

−/····/·−/−/ ·−−/··/−−−/··−/−−·/····/−/

−/····/·/ −·−·/····/·−/−·/−··/·/ ··−/−−·/−−·/−·/ −/····/·/

·−·/··−/−−/·−/−·/··/−/·/·−−··· −/····/·−/−/

−/····/·/·/−·−·/ ·−−/·/·−·/·/ −···/·−/·−−/·−/−··/−−−/··/−··/

·−−/··/−/····/ ··−·/··/−·−/·/ ·−/−·/−··/ ·−−/··/−/····/

−/····/·/ ····/−−−/·−··/·/−−−/ −−·/····/−−−/·−/−·−·−−

·/−/····/·/·−· ·−−−−/··−−−/−−−···/·−−−−/····−

Ether 12–15

"By Faith All Things Are Fulfilled"

Instructions: Connect all of the letters in the phrase bolded below. Don't be tricked by letters that take you into a dead end! There is only one path through the maze.

___ ____ _____ ____ __, _____: _____ ____, ___ ____ _____ ____; ___ __ ____ __ _____ ___ ___ ___, ____ ____ _____ ____ __ _____ __ ____ _____.

Ether 12:26

Start

Finish

H	E	L	O	R	D	S	P	N	R	U	O	U	R	N	A	N	D	M	Y	G	O	F	Y	O	U	R
T	L	O	R	D	S	P	A	K	E	R	M	N	E	I	C	I	F	F	U	R	E	N	K	A	E	W
H	O	N	U	E	P	A	K	E	O	M	L	T	N	E	N	C	I	U	S	A	G	E	N	E	S	S
D	R	U	E	K	A	K	E	O	M	L	L	L	T	N	O	I	C	S	S	C	A	T	N	A	V	D
S	T	N	T	O	K	E	U	U	L	L	A	L	F	T	F	E	M	S	I	E	I	S	O	N	O	A
S	O	T	O	M	E	U	N	L	L	A	H	L	O	F	T	H	E	M	S	I	S	F	A	E	A	D
E	M	O	M	A	Y	I	T	C	K	B	S	T	R	O	R	T	M	E	S	S	U	D	K	E	V
S	E	M	E	S	A	Y	I	O	C	K	Y	H	T	R	T	E	E	E	U	S	U	F	K	A	K	E
A	Y	E	S	A	O	L	O	M	O	C	E	Y	H	T	H	E	M	K	F	U	E	K	A	T	A	K
Y	I	S	G	F	O	O	L	S	M	K	H	E	E	H	E	E	Y	S	F	I	C	A	T	L	T	A
I	Y	A	N	G	F	O	O	L	S	B	T	H	M	E	M	E	E	H	E	Y	S	T	L	L	A	K
N	I	Y	I	S	L	O	L	S	T	U	T	E	E	M	Y	E	H	T	H	E	Y	L	L	A	L	L
G	N	I	N	M	O	L	S	M	T	T	T	K	E	E	E	H	T	T	T	H	E	Y	S	H	A	L
F	G	N	G	O	C	K	M	S	Y	E	H	A	H	E	K	T	H	A	H	E	Y	S	H	A	T	L
L	O	O	F	C	K	B	U	T	A	H	E	H	T	K	T	H	A	T	E	Y	S	H	A	L	L	T
S	L	O	O	O	L	U	T	T	L	S	Y	A	H	T	H	A	T	T	H	S	H	A	L	L	T	A
M	S	L	O	L	S	T	T	L	A	H	S	T	T	H	A	T	T	Y	E	H	A	T	L	T	A	K
O	M	S	M	O	M	T	H	L	L	A	L	T	T	A	T	T	H	S	Y	A	L	E	K	A	K	E
C	K	M	O	C	O	H	E	M	L	L	E	H	T	H	T	H	E	H	A	L	L	N	E	K	E	N
K	B	U	C	K	B	S	Y	O	H	S	Y	E	H	E	Y	E	Y	A	L	A	T	O	N	E	N	O
B	U	T	U	B	U	H	S	U	A	H	S	Y	E	Y	S	Y	S	L	L	K	A	A	O	N	O	A
U	T	T	T	U	T	A	N	R	L	A	H	S	H	S	H	S	H	L	T	A	K	D	A	O	A	D
T	T	H	E	T	T	N	A	N	L	L	A	H	A	L	A	H	A	T	A	N	E	V	D	V	D	V
T	H	E	Y	S	H	D	N	A	N	L	L	A	L	L	T	A	K	A	K	E	N	O	N	A	V	A
Y	E	H	S	H	E	M	D	N	D	T	L	L	A	T	A	K	E	K	E	N	O	A	T	N	T	N
S	Y	S	H	A	L	Y	M	Y	M	A	T	L	T	A	K	O	N	E	N	O	V	D	A	T	A	T

Ether 12–15

"By Faith All Things Are Fulfilled"

Handwriting Practice

Practice your handwriting by tracing the sentence below. Then use the blank lines to write the sentence on your own.

Faith is believing in things I cannot see.

Letter Sudoku

Instructions: Solve the letter sudoku puzzle the same way you'd solve a numeric sudoku. Check your puzzle against the answer key on ColorMeChristian.org. Every column, row, and group of nine must contain every letter in the worda **SHOW GRACE.** Letters are used only once;

Ether 12:27

And if men come unto me I will **show** unto them their weakness. I give unto men weakness that they may be humble; and my **grace** is sufficient for all men that humble themselves before me; for if they humble themselves before me, and have faith in me, then will I make weak things become strong unto them.

A		G	C		O			
R	C	W			A	H		
H		R		W				C
	A			R		G	W	H
	G		H		C	R		
	R	H	G		S	W		A
G	O		A			C		
E				C	H			S

Moroni 1–6

"To Keep Them in the Right Way"

Fill in the Blank

Moroni 4:3

O God, the _____ Father, we ask thee in the name of thy _____, Jesus

Christ, to _____ and _____ this _____ to the souls of all those

who _____ of it; that they may eat in _____ of the body of thy Son, and

witness unto thee, O _____, the Eternal Father, that they are willing to take upon

them the _____ of thy Son, and always remember him, and keep his

_____ which he hath given them, that they may always have his _____

to be with them. _____.

bless	God	Amen	Eternal	sanctify	commandments
name	Spirit	bread	partake	Son	remembrance

Secret Code

Instructions: The secret message is written in symbols. In the code key you can find what each symbol means. Write the letter above the symbol and you can read the secret message.

a	b	c	d	e	f	g	h	i	j	k	l	m
□	◇	△	◹	◯	▷	◺	✕	◸	♡	▽	▷	◿

n	o	p	q	r	s	t	u	v	w	x	y	z
◁	▱	▽	▱	◯	▱	▢	⋈	⋈	◣	◁	△	Σ

6 : 5 – 6

Hidden Picture: You can prepare to be baptized, just like Jesus did. Can you find 4 pictures of Jesus being baptized in the hidden picture below? It will be tricky; the picture may be smaller, on its side, or even upside down! Then, see if you can find 1 image of the animals as well.

December 2–8

Moroni 1–6

"To Keep Them in the Right Way"

Word Angles

Instructions: Find the bold words from the scripture. Each word path may run north, east, south, or west, may make one right-angled turn, and may cross another word path. A few words may make no right angle turn at all.

Moroni 6:4

And after they had been **received** unto **baptism**, and were **wrought** upon and **cleansed** by the **power** of the **Holy Ghost**, they were **numbered among** the **people** of the **church** of **Christ**; and their **names** were **taken**, that they might be **remembered** and **nourished** by the good **word** of God, to **keep** them in the **right way**, to keep them continually **watchful** unto **prayer**, **relying** alone upon the **merits** of Christ, who was the author and the finisher of their faith.

```
H A Y U R E M E M B D E R E B M
H O L R O W T T S E I G N I Y U
N Y O D U A A Z I R P E O P L N
M E R I N E K Q R E X D J L E A
O M A T C N N H H D P B I E R O
N U O S V T U Z C N A E L C S R
G O V M W H P Z C S J A R P E R
P Z P J N G O G J E Q Y S S M J
C E R A D I W E R D T E T I A O
E C X N F R Y L A T S R S T N D
I O C L E L U F H C O D B P D G
V R I R U O N L C H H Y W A Y N
E S S F O C F E T U G V L B U V
D Y H A S P I U A R C H D X E K
Q V E H L U T K W U E M Q F E T
M H D Q P F H G U O R W I R P W
```

Moroni 1–6

"To Keep Them in the Right Way"

Handwriting Practice

Practice your handwriting by tracing the sentence below. Then use the blank lines to write the sentence on your own.

The Holy Ghost is a sacred gift.

ON THE BRIGHT SIDE, ELDER, YOU'RE HALF WAY TO A BROKEN HEART AND A CONTRITE SPIRIT.

Always Remember Him

We take the sacrament to show that we will always remember Jesus Christ. Can you help these children through the maze so they can go to church and partake of the sacrament?

Moroni 1–6

"To Keep Them in the Right Way"

Fallen Phrase

Instructions: The letters in each column have fallen from the grid. Put them back correctly to rebuild the phrase. Cross out each letter in the jumble below once you place it in the grid. Pay attention because the letters in each column are scrambled. Start with simple 1 or 2 letter words and use the process of elimination. To check your answer, read **Moroni 6:2**.

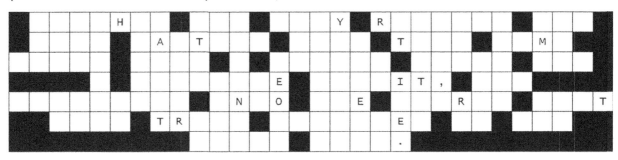

Word Square

Instructions: Word squares are a liike Sudoku puzzles, but each letter can occur only once in each row and in each column. Check your puzzle against the answer key on ColorMeChristian.org. Every row and column must contain every letter in the word **SANCTIFY**. This word can be written in the gray row.

Moroni 5:2

O God, the Eternal Father, we ask thee, in the name of thy Son, Jesus Christ, to bless and **sanctify** this wine to the souls of all those who drink of it, that they may do it in remembrance of the blood of thy Son, which was shed for them; that they may witness unto thee, O God, the Eternal Father, that they do always remember him, that they may have his Spirit to be with them. Amen.

F	A		C	Y			
T	I	C	A	N			S
I	T	Y	S	F			
					S	T	N
	C			S			F
F			T	Y	C		
	S			I	T	N	C

Moroni 7–9

"May Christ Lift Thee Up"

Missing Vowels Word Search

Instructions: Find the hidden words. The words have been placed horizontally, vertically, diagonally, forwards, or backwards, and the vowels have been removed. When you locate a word, draw an ellipse around it and fill the vowels in.

Moroni 9:25–26

My son, be **faithful** in Christ; and may not the things which I have written grieve thee, to weigh thee down unto death; but may **Christ lift thee** up, and may his **sufferings** and **death**, and the **showing** his **body** unto our **fathers**, and his mercy and long-suffering, and the **hope** of his **glory** and of **eternal life**, **rest** in your **mind forever**. And may the **grace** of God the **Father**, whose **throne** is high in the **heavens**, and our **Lord** Jesus Christ, who sitteth on the **right hand** of his **power**, until all things shall become subject unto him, be, and abide with you forever. Amen.

```
Y  H     N  D  K  C     T  S  B     D  Y  Y
S     M     T  S  G  F  N  R     H  T     F
H  N     L  S        W  C  N  F  S  V  G
   D     D     C  Z  L     F  H        K  V
R  S  R  V  R  T  S     R  H  C  R  F  Z  F
T     C        G  G  D  H     P     F  J
H  H  W  C  L     J        L  F  V     M
G     W     M     H  L  D           R  T  T
         K  P  K  T  R  Q  L  T  R           H
R  Y  G  L     R  Y  R  S     H  H  N  K  F
   T     R  N     L  Z     F        G  F
M     N  D        W  C     T  R     S     L
Y        G     T     S  M  H  S  K  T  T  H
P  F  D  H  B  R  N  P  T  G  H     J     Q
K  Q  T  J  G  Z  S  H     W     N  G     R
```

Knight Moves - Find a Word

Instructions: Start with the capital letter in the puzzle. To get to the next letter, jump two squares in any direction except diagonally, and then one square in a different direction. Your path will look like a capital L. To show you how it works, Only one route through the puzzle will make a word. Write the letters of the word you discover in the blanks below as you jump through the squares:

$$\underline{}\ \underline{}\ \underline{}\ \underline{}\ \underline{}\ \underline{}\ \underline{}\ \underline{}$$
$$\quad\ 2\quad 3\quad 4\quad 5\quad 6\quad 7\quad 8$$

Now can you find this word in the following scripture?

Ether 12:33

s	M	o
n		n
a	i	s

Moroni 7–9

"May Christ Lift Thee Up"

Instructions: Fit the bold words from the scripture below into the encircled squares. Words will read forward, backward, up, down, and diagonally and will normally cross other words. Start with the hints provided.

Ether 12:33–34

And again, I **remember** that thou hast said that thou hast **loved** the **world**, even unto the **laying down** of thy **life** for the world, that thou mightest **take** it **again** to **prepare** a **place** for the **children** of men. And now I **know** that this love which thou hast had for the children of men is **charity**; wherefore, **except** men shall have charity they cannot **inherit** that place which thou hast prepared in the **mansions** of thy **Father**.

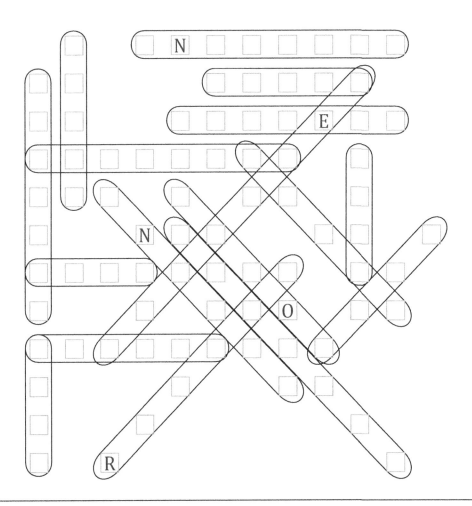

remember	loved	world	laying	down	life
take	again	prepare	place	children	know
charity	except	inherit	mansions	Father	

Mystery Picture Graph

Instructions: Find the mystery picture below by plotting and connecting the points of each line on the coordinate graph. Connect all the points in Line 1, stop, pick up your pencil, and then connect all the points in Line 2, and so on for the rest of the lines. The dot for the first (X,Y) coordinate pair on Line 1 has been placed for you.

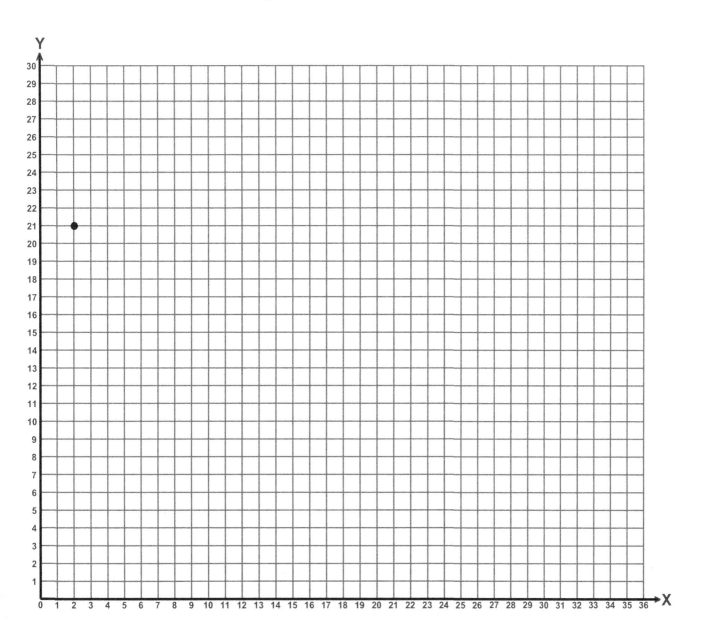

Line 1	(2, 21)	(10, 24)	(18, 21)	(18, 13)	(16, 6)	(10, 2)	(4, 6)	(2, 13)	(2, 21)	Line 2	(9, 17)	(9, 21)
(4, 20)	(4, 17)	(9, 17)	Line 3	(11, 21)	(16, 20)	(16, 17)	(11, 17)	(11, 21)	Line 4	(4, 15)	(9, 15)	(9, 5)
(5, 9)	(4, 12)	(4, 15)	Line 5	(11, 15)	(16, 15)	(16, 12)	(15, 9)	(11, 5)	(11, 15)			

Moroni 7–9

"May Christ Lift Thee Up"

Instructions: Solve this word sudoku puzzle the same way that you'd solve a numeric sudoku. Each of the bold words in the scripture below is found once in every row, column and 3×3 box.

Moroni 7:41

And what is it that ye shall **hope** for? Behold I say unto you that ye shall have hope through the **atonement** of Christ and the **power** of his **resurrection**, to be **raised** unto **life eternal**, and this because of your **faith** in **him** according to the promise.

	raised	resurrection			atonement			power
eternal	power		hope			raised		
		atonement		power	him			eternal
				life		resurrection	raised	hope
resurrection	hope			him			faith	
life		raised			resurrection		eternal	
power				raised		life	him	
raised			him	faith				resurrection
him	resurrection	hope		atonement				

December 9–15
Moroni 7–9
"May Christ Lift Thee Up"

Charity is the pure love of Christ.

Come, Follow Me Manual, 2024

Start

End

Moroni 7–9

"May Christ Lift Thee Up"

Cryptogram

Instructions: Each letter on the top stands for a letter in the alphabet. Solve the encrypted phrase by matching each letter on top to a letter in the alphabet on the bottom. Use the key to help you remember what the letters stand for so you can crack the code.

Y	Q	T	E	S	J	D	U	W	V	R	L	C	X	H	B	G	A	F	P	Z	N	O	I	K	M
A	B	C	D	E	F	G	H	I	J	K	L	M	N	O	P	Q	R	S	T	U	V	W	X	Y	Z

R V G   M O K X E C   O R C O   E R X G :   X S   A D   I X L L

O R J D   S R X C O   X V   Z D   A D   E O R L L   O R J D

T W I D K   C W   G W   I O R C E W D J D K   C O X V Q   X E

D N T D G X D V C   X V   Z D .   Z W K W V X   7 : 3 3

Moroni 10

"Come unto Christ, and Be Perfected in Him"

Word Search

Instructions: Find the bold words from the scripture in the word search puzzle. Each word could be hidden forwards, backwards, up, down, or diagonally.

Moroni 10:9–16

For behold, to one is **given** by the **Spirit** of **God**, that he may **teach** the **word** of **wisdom**; And to another, that he may teach the word of **knowledge** by the same Spirit; And to another, exceedingly **great faith**; and to another, the gifts of **healing** by the same **Spirit**; And again, to another, that he may **work** mighty **miracles**; And again, to another, that he may **prophesy** concerning all things; And again, to another, the **beholding** of **angels** and **ministering spirits**; And again, to another, all kinds of **tongues**; And again, to another, the **interpretation** of **languages** and of divers kinds of tongues.

```
Q Y S E U G N O T K M T T I E
M S G E D G U X K I Z I M N L
Z E N H V R X E N V R D X T Q
O H I F C T O I Y I T O E E M
A P L S N A S W P G I G P R B
T O A P E T E S W P R V A P L
D R E I E N L T C A I E A R A
X P H R K M C D R I P U A E N
E A I I R O A B W I S L R T G
U N Z T A D R F A I T H S A U
G F V S G N I D L O H E B T A
A N G E L S M O D S I W R I G
V Q V E V G I V E N O U Q O E
K N O W L E D G E R S X P N S
Q V G V N E G I K O K E C A G
```

OH, SURE, WHEN MORONI DOES IT WE PUT HIM ON TOP OF THE TEMPLE; BUT WHEN I DO IT, I'M SENT TO TIME OUT.

mormoncartoonist.com

© Arie Van De Graaff

Moroni 10

"Come unto Christ, and Be Perfected in Him"

Reverse Word Search

Instructions: Instead of looking for words in a grid, place the bold words in the scripture in the empty word search puzzle. The words may be forwards, backwards, up, down, or diagonally The start letter of the words have been placed in the grid to get you started.

Moroni 10:8

And again, I **exhort** you, my brethren, that ye **deny not** the **gifts** of God, for they are **many**; and they **come from** the **same God**. And there are **different ways** that these gifts are **administered**; but it is the same God who **worketh all** in all; and **they** are **given** by the **manifestations** of the **Spirit** of God unto men, to **profit them**.

Translation Station

Instructions: Translate the sign language letters below into English to discover the hidden message. Write the alphabet letter beneath each hand sign. Use the key at the back of the book to help you.

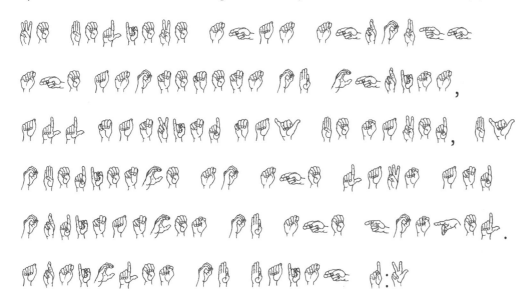

December 16–22

Moroni 10

"Come unto Christ, and Be Perfected in Him"

Instructions: Using the Across and Down clues, write the correct words in the numbered grid below. Hint: all of the words in the crossword come from the scripture below.

Moroni 10:3–5

ACROSS

3. make a request or demand for something to somebody
5. showing or giving forgiveness
9. accumulated knowledge or erudition or enlightenment
12. an anticipated outcome that guides your planned actions
13. "hoping for things which are not seen, which are true" (Alma 32:21)
14. spur on or encourage
15. showing or giving forgiveness
16. recall knowledge; have a recollection
17. possession of the qualities required to do something
18. The Holy Ghost is the third member of the Godhead. He is a personage of spirit, without a body of flesh and bones.

DOWN

1. the original bringing into existence of the world by God.
2. look at and say out loud something written or printed
3. the name of the first man: husband of Eve
4. a factual statement
6. an anticipated outcome that guides your planned actions
7. recall knowledge; have a recollection
8. reflect deeply on a subject
10. open and genuine; not deceitful
11. possession of the qualities required to do something
13. "hoping for things which are not seen, which are true" (Alma 32:21)

Moroni 10

"Come unto Christ, and Be Perfected in Him"

Instructions: Connect all of the letters in the phrase bolded below. Don't be tricked by letters that take you into a dead end! There is only one path through the maze.

___ ___ _____ _____ ____ __ ___ _____ __ _____; ___

____ ____ ____ _____ ___ _____, _____ __ __ ____.

Moroni 10:17

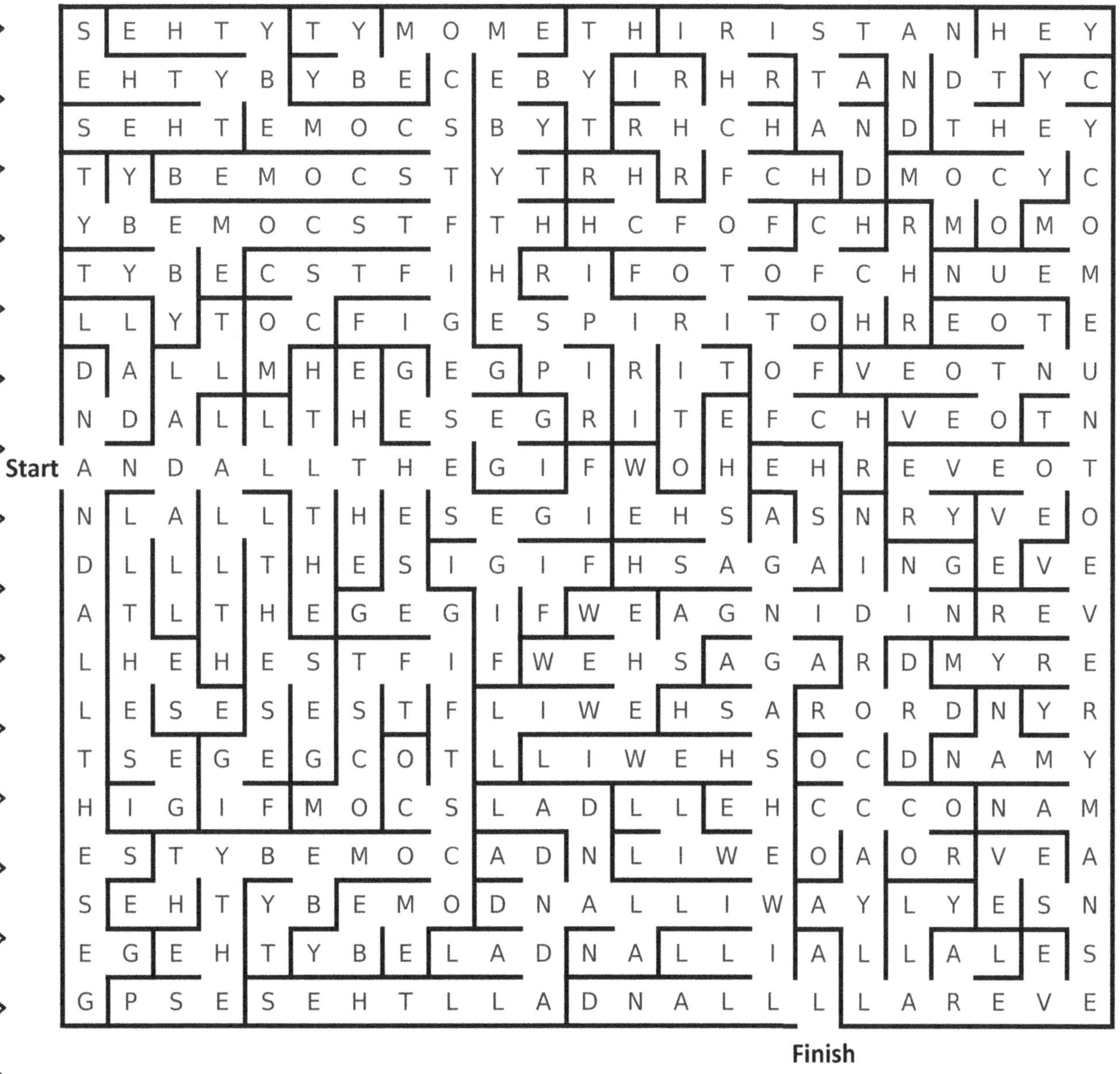

Start

Finish

Moroni 10

"Come unto Christ, and Be Perfected in Him"

Unscrambler

Instructions: Unscramble the words below; look at the bold words in the scripture for a hint.

Moroni 10:32

Yea, **come** unto **Christ**, and be **perfected** in him, and **deny** yourselves of all **ungodliness**; and if ye shall deny yourselves of all ungodliness, and **love** God with all your **might**, **mind** and **strength**, then is his **grace sufficient** for you, that by his grace ye may be **perfect** in Christ; and if by the grace of God ye are perfect in Christ, ye can in nowise deny the power of God.

tfeeprc _____   feeceprtd _____

crgea _____   ovle _____

ictshr _____   ssoedlgunin _____

endy _____   ocme _____

dnmi _____   ifcfentisu _____

hgtmi _____   hrtgtnse _____

Letter Sudoku

Instructions: Solve the letter sudoku puzzle the same way you'd solve a numeric sudoku. Check your puzzle against the answer key on ColorMeChristian.org. Every column, row, and group of nine must contain every letter in the worda **GRACE HOLY.** Letters are used only once;

Moroni 10:33

And again, if ye by the grace of God are perfect in Christ, and deny not his power, then are ye sanctified in Christ by the **grace** of God, through the shedding of the blood of Christ, which is in the covenant of the Father unto the remission of your sins, that ye become **holy**, without spot.

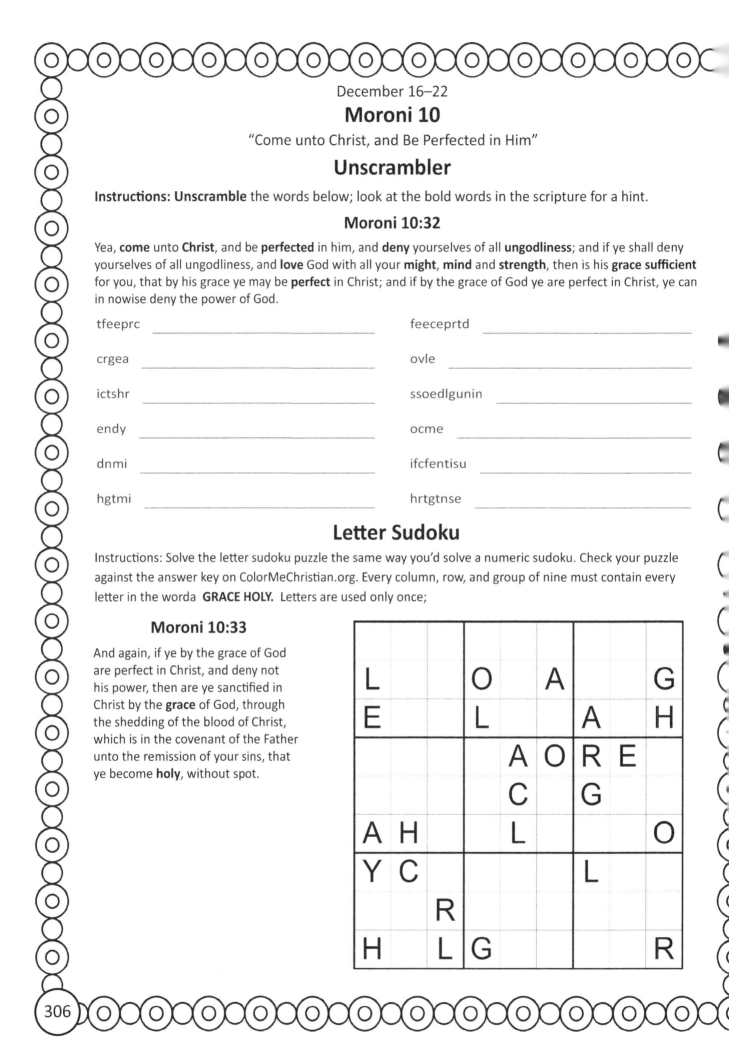

December 23–29

Christmas

"He Shall Come into the World to Redeem His People"

Wacky Word Trails

Instructions: Start with the circled letter, use the clues to find and mark the trail of letters of all the connected bolded words from the scripture through the maze to the last letter. The path can wander up, down, left, and right at any point, even in the middle of the word.

1 Nephi 11:18-20

And he said unto me: Behold, the **virgin** whom thou seest is the **mother** of the **Son** of **God**, after the **manner** of the **flesh**. And it came to pass that I beheld that she was **carried** away in the **Spirit**; and after she had been carried away in the Spirit for the **space** of a **time** the **angel** spake unto me, saying: **Look**! And I looked and beheld the virgin again, **bearing** a **child** in her arms.

```
E  F  V  B  X  S  K  D  Q  O  S  V  T  X  W
S  A  T  E  P  D  E  P  G  K  Y  Y  N  P  Z
P  V  R  O  X  R  I  R  C  M  F  B  X  C  T
V  G  Y  Y  Q  E  D  R  A  C  L  E  G  N  A
R  F  L  H  S  P  I  S  W  U  X  B  Q  E  R
E  H  E  S  T  I  R  W  Y  U  W  D  K  N  N
C  T  K  N  S  O  V  W  E  X  I  M  E  M  A
(M) O  C  I  V  N  U  K  M  Y  T  W  C  W  T
A  M  G  R  A  I  I  M  H  T  E  A  U  M  H
U  E  I  I  L  D  L  R  I  Y  C  A  M  Z  I
E  B  N  H  C  I  O  O  O  D  S  P  K  B  T
A  R  I  N  G  S  C  K  G  J  I  K  V  B  Z
U  C  X  I  W  U  B  Q  D  T  U  C  R  Q  H
P  S  D  A  J  C  N  L  P  K  G  Q  G  D  Z
J  F  T  N  M  R  G  J  M  E  K  I  F  O  Q
```

December 23–29

Christmas

"He Shall Come into the World to Redeem His People"

Handwriting Practice

Practice your handwriting by tracing the sentence below. Then use the blank lines to write the sentence on your own.

Jesus Christ was born to be my Savior.

EBENEZER, TONIGHT YOU WILL BE VISITED BY THREE GHOSTS...AND THEN TOMORROW BY TWO REPRESENTATIVES FROM THE CHURCH OF JESUS CHRIST OF LATTER-DAY SAINTS.

mormoncartoonist.com

© Arie Van De Graaff

Hidden Picture: JJesus Christ is Heavenly Father's gift to you. Can you find 5 pictures of Baby Jesus in the hidden picture below? It will be tricky; the picture may be smaller, on its side, or even upside down! Then, see if you can find 1 image of the animals as well.

Christmas

"He Shall Come into the World to Redeem His People"

Instructions: Fill in the blank puzzle grid using the word bank with the bold words from the scripture below. Place the words in the correct place on the grid.

3 Nephi 1:13-14

Lift up your **head** and be of **good cheer**; for behold, the **time** is at **hand**, and on this **night** shall the **sign** be **given**, and on the **morrow** come I into the **world**, to **show** unto the world that I will **fulfil** all that which I have **caused** to be **spoken** by the mouth of my holy **prophets**. Behold, I come unto my own, to fulfil all things which I have made known unto the children of men from the **foundation** of the **world**, and to do the **will**, both of the **Father** and of the **Son**—of the Father because of me, and of the Son because of my flesh. And behold, the **time** is at hand, and this night shall the sign be given.

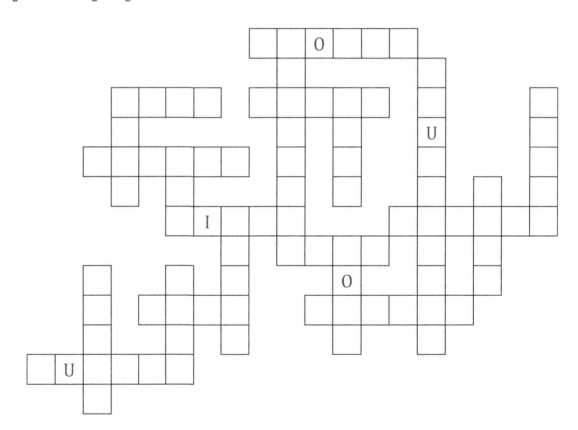

3 Letters	sign	5 Letters	6 Letters	8 Letters
Son	good	night	spoken	prophets
	head	given	fulfil	
4 Letters	hand	world	morrow	10 Letters
time	show	world	caused	foundation
will		cheer	Father	
Lift				

Finding The Manger

The shepherds want to worship Jesus. Can you guide the shepherds through the maze to the manger?

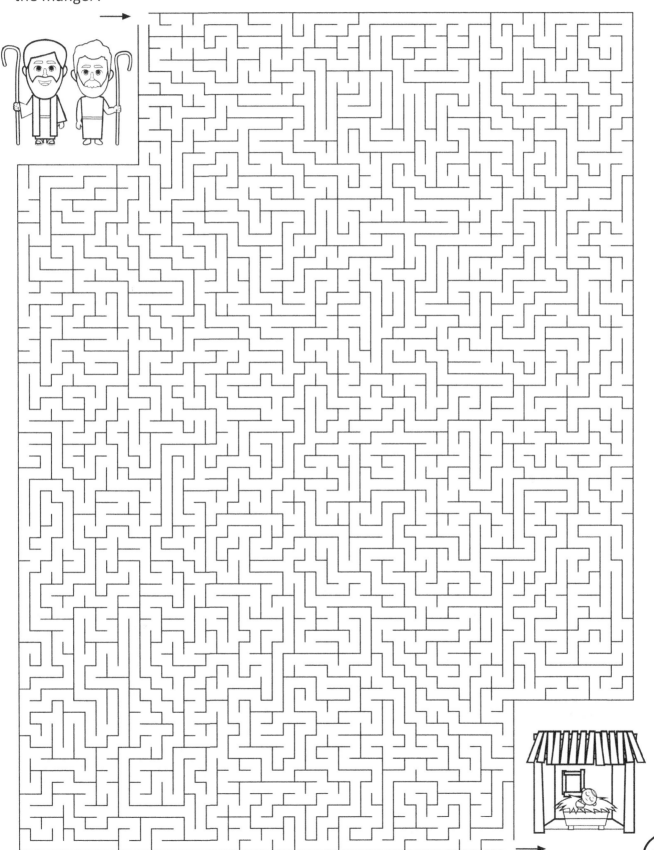

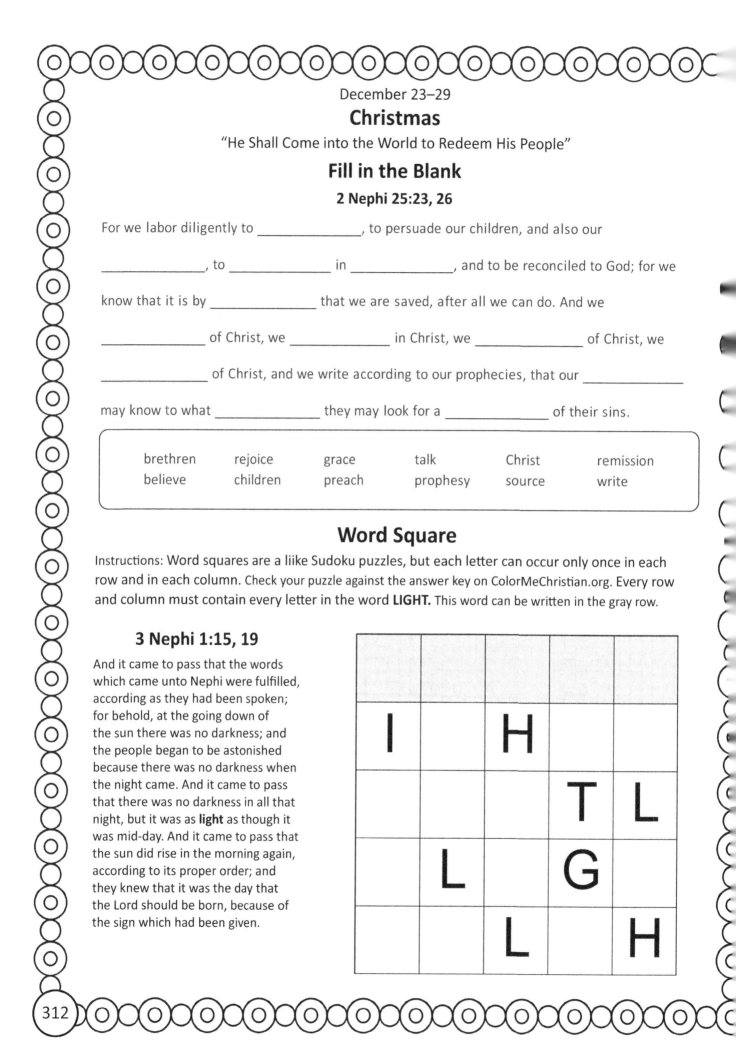

Christmas

"He Shall Come into the World to Redeem His People"

Fill in the Blank

2 Nephi 25:23, 26

For we labor diligently to _____, to persuade our children, and also our

_____, to _____ in _____, and to be reconciled to God; for we

know that it is by _____ that we are saved, after all we can do. And we

_____ of Christ, we _____ in Christ, we _____ of Christ, we

_____ of Christ, and we write according to our prophecies, that our _____

may know to what _____ they may look for a _____ of their sins.

brethren	rejoice	grace	talk	Christ	remission
believe	children	preach	prophesy	source	write

Word Square

Instructions: Word squares are a liike Sudoku puzzles, but each letter can occur only once in each row and in each column. Check your puzzle against the answer key on ColorMeChristian.org. Every row and column must contain every letter in the word **LIGHT.** This word can be written in the gray row.

3 Nephi 1:15, 19

And it came to pass that the words which came unto Nephi were fulfilled, according as they had been spoken; for behold, at the going down of the sun there was no darkness; and the people began to be astonished because there was no darkness when the night came. And it came to pass that there was no darkness in all that night, but it was as **light** as though it was mid-day. And it came to pass that the sun did rise in the morning again, according to its proper order; and they knew that it was the day that the Lord should be born, because of the sign which had been given.

I		H		
		T		L
	L		G	
			L	H

Translation Station: Morse Code Key

A
− ·

B
− · · ·

C
− · − ·

D
− · ·

E
·

F
· · − ·

G
− − ·

H
· · · ·

I
· ·

J
· − − −

K
− · −

L
· − · ·

M
− −

N
− ·

O
− − −

P
· − − ·

Q
− − · −

R
· − ·

S
· · ·

T
−

U
· · −

V
· · · −

W
· − −

X
− · · −

Y
− · − −

Z
− − · ·

comma

,

− − · · − −

period

.

· − · − · −

semi-colon

;

− · − · − ·

colon

:

− − − · · ·

The slash mark / is used to indicate the end of a letter or punctuation mark. The apostro-phe ' is not in morse code and is written like usual.

Translation Station: American Sign Language Key

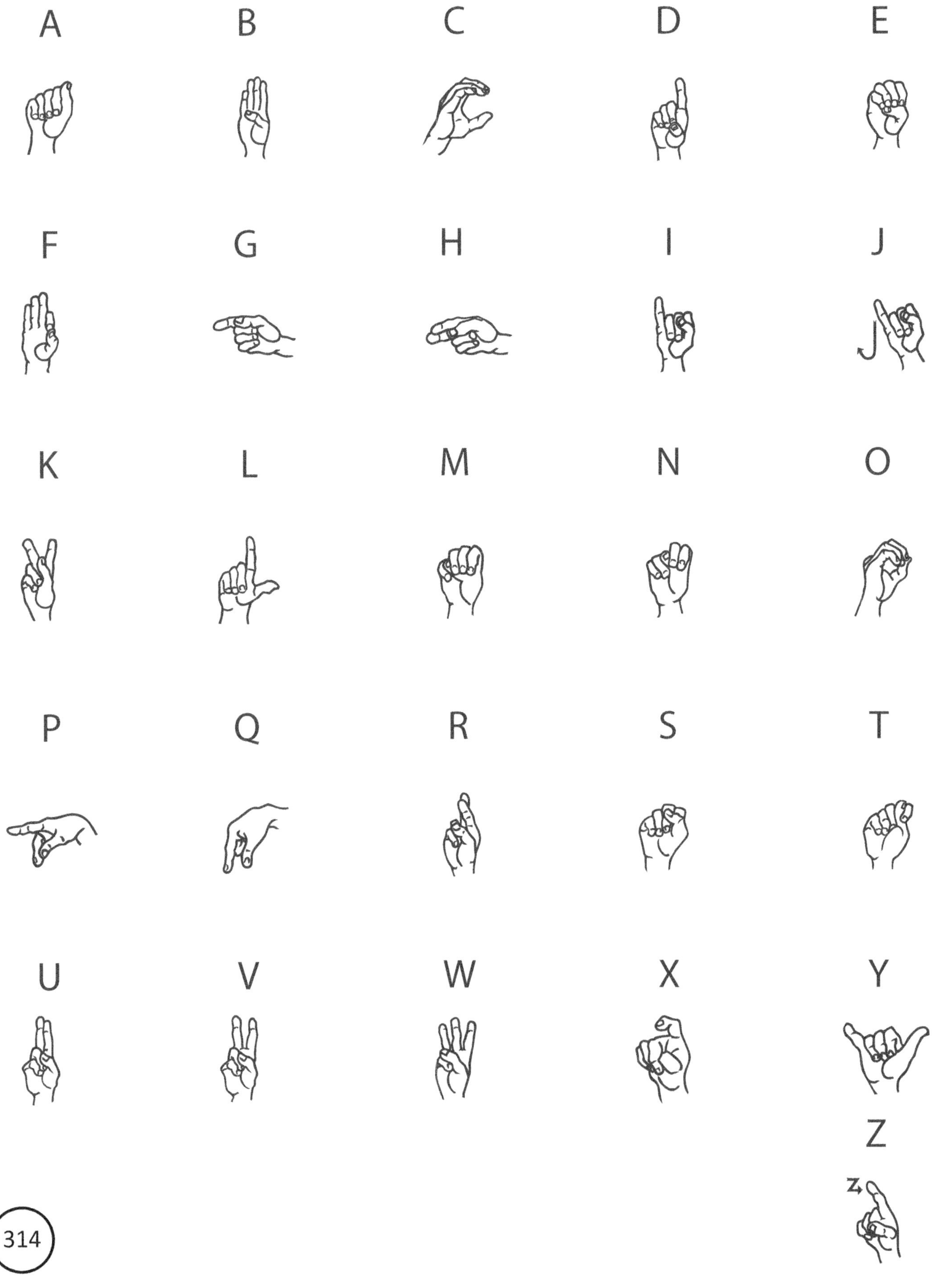

A

B

C

D

E

F

G

H

I

J

K

L

M

N

O

P

Q

R

S

T

U

V

W

X

Y

Z

Made in the USA
Las Vegas, NV
17 February 2024

85932980R00175